By Great Waters

A Newfoundland and Labrador Anthology

This anthology presents a splendid portrait of Newfoundland past and present. The sixty-five items begin with an extract from the Vinland sagas and end with contemporary writings, to provide a broad survey of the province's historical and cultural development. The editors have selected first-hand accounts of life in Newfoundland and also imaginative writing with Newfoundland as the setting. These have been arranged chronologically in four sections: Discovery and Exploration; Transatlantic Outpost; Colonial Era; and Breakers Ahead. This is the first time that such an anthology has been compiled; it is especially timely as Newfoundlanders celebrate the twenty-fifth anniversary of their confederation with Canada. It brings to popular view the rich and diverse body of writing that exists about the area and its people. A special feature is the biographical information on the authors represented in the anthology. Many of them have not been included in Canadian reference works. Peter Neary and Patrick O'Flaherty have also compiled the first select bibliography of Newfoundland, which will be of value to scholars in many disciplines.

PETER NEARY, a Newfoundlander, is a member of the Department of History at the University of Western Ontario. He is author of *The Political Economy of Newfoundland 1929-1972.*

PATRICK O'FLAHERTY, also a Newfoundlander, is a member of the Department of English at Memorial University.

The social history of Canada

MICHAEL BLISS, GENERAL EDITOR

A NEWFOUNDLAND AND LABRADOR ANTHOLOGY

By great waters

EDITED AND INTRODUCED BY
PETER NEARY & PATRICK O'FLAHERTY

UNIVERSITY OF TORONTO PRESS

Toronto and Buffalo

Reprinted in paperback 2014

ISBN 978-0-8020-2125-0 (cloth)
ISBN 978-0-8020-6233-8 (paper)
LC 73-91561
CN ISSN 0085-6207
Social History of Canada 21

This book has been published with the assistance of a grant from the Canada Council.
The maps on pp xii-xiii were prepared by Geoffrey Matthews of the Department of Geography, University of Toronto.

Contents

To our parents, Newfoundlanders who belong to Conception Bay

PREFACE

OUR INTENTION in preparing this anthology was to offer readers a selection of Newfoundland writing which would illuminate the unfolding of the province's history and culture, and at the same time merit attention as literature. We have in general confined our attention to first-hand accounts of life in Newfoundland and to imaginative writing with Newfoundland as a setting. Readers who wish to locate evaluative and other pertinent commentary on aspects of Newfoundland writing may find the appended bibliography of selected secondary material of use.

The selections are arranged chronologically according to the dates of the events they describe or the dates of first publication. Certain of the early texts have been slightly modernized.

While we have benefited from the work of Newfoundland scholars in general, we wish to acknowledge specific indebtedness to the following: David Alexander, Joyce Coldwell, David Davis, John Feltham, Burnham Gill, John Greene, J.K. Hiller, Elizabeth Lebans, Ken Kerr, Ian McDonald, D.G. Pitt, G.O. Roberts, Neil Rosenberg, E.R. Seary, the Honourable Joseph R. Smallwood, G.M. Story, and W.H. Whiteley.

We would like to thank as well the following librarians and researchers at the Newfoundland Studies Centre of Memorial University's Henrietta Harvey Library and at the Hunter Library in the Arts and Culture Centre, St John's: Agnes O'Dea, who has given us particular encouragement and assistance, Margaret Chang, Madeline Gosse, Coleen Shea, Grace Butt, Mona Cramm, Stephanie Edwards, Helen Porter, Catherine Power, and C.I.G. Stobie.

Margaret Williams, Acting Librarian of the Henrietta Harvey Library, Joan Halley, Research Assistant in the Folklore and Language Archive of Memorial University, Margaret Rose, Paulette Bradbury, and Gerald Reid helped us in important ways. Mary Neary and Frankie O'Flaherty helped and encouraged us throughout the enterprise.

PN
PO'F

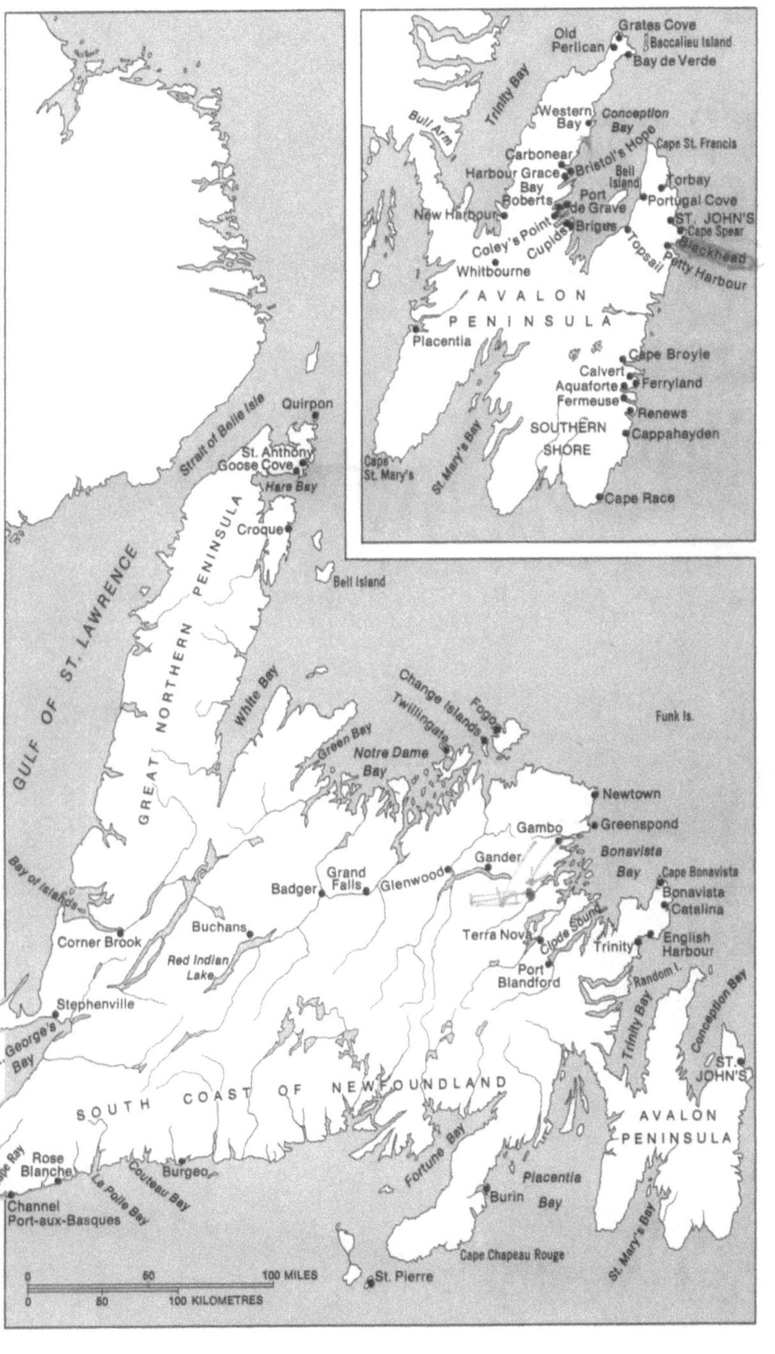

Grates Cove
Old Perlican
Baccalieu Island
Bay de Verde
Trinity Bay
Bull Arm
Western Bay
Conception Bay
Cape St. Francis
Carbonear
Bristol's Hope
Harbour Grace
Bell Island
Bay Roberts
Torbay
Port de Grave
Portugal Cove
New Harbour
ST. JOHN'S
Cape Spear
Coley's Point
Cupids
Brigus
Topsail
Blackhead
Whitbourne
Petty Harbour
AVALON PENINSULA
Placentia
Cape Broyle
Calvert
Aquaforte
Ferryland
Fermeuse
Renews
SOUTHERN SHORE
Cappahayden
St. Mary's Bay
Cape St. Mary's
Cape Race
Quirpon
Strait of Belle Isle
St. Anthony
Goose Cove
Hare Bay
Croque
Bell Island
GULF OF ST. LAWRENCE
GREAT NORTHERN PENINSULA
White Bay
Change Islands
Fogo
Twillingate
Funk Is.
Green Bay
Notre Dame Bay
Newtown
Gambo
Greenspond
Bonavista Bay
Gander
Cape Bonavista
Bonavista
Grand Falls
Badger
Glenwood
Catalina
Bay of Islands
Buchans
Terra Nova
Clode Sound
English Harbour
Trinity
Corner Brook
Red Indian Lake
Port Blandford
Random I.
Conception Bay
Stephenville
Trinity Bay
St. George's Bay
ST. JOHN'S
SOUTH COAST OF NEWFOUNDLAND
AVALON PENINSULA
Cape Ray
Rose Blanche
Burgeo
Fortune Bay
Placentia Bay
Le Poile Bay
Couteau Bay
Burin
Channel Port-aux-Basques
Cape Chapeau Rouge
St. Mary's Bay
St. Pierre
0 50 100 MILES
0 50 100 KILOMETRES

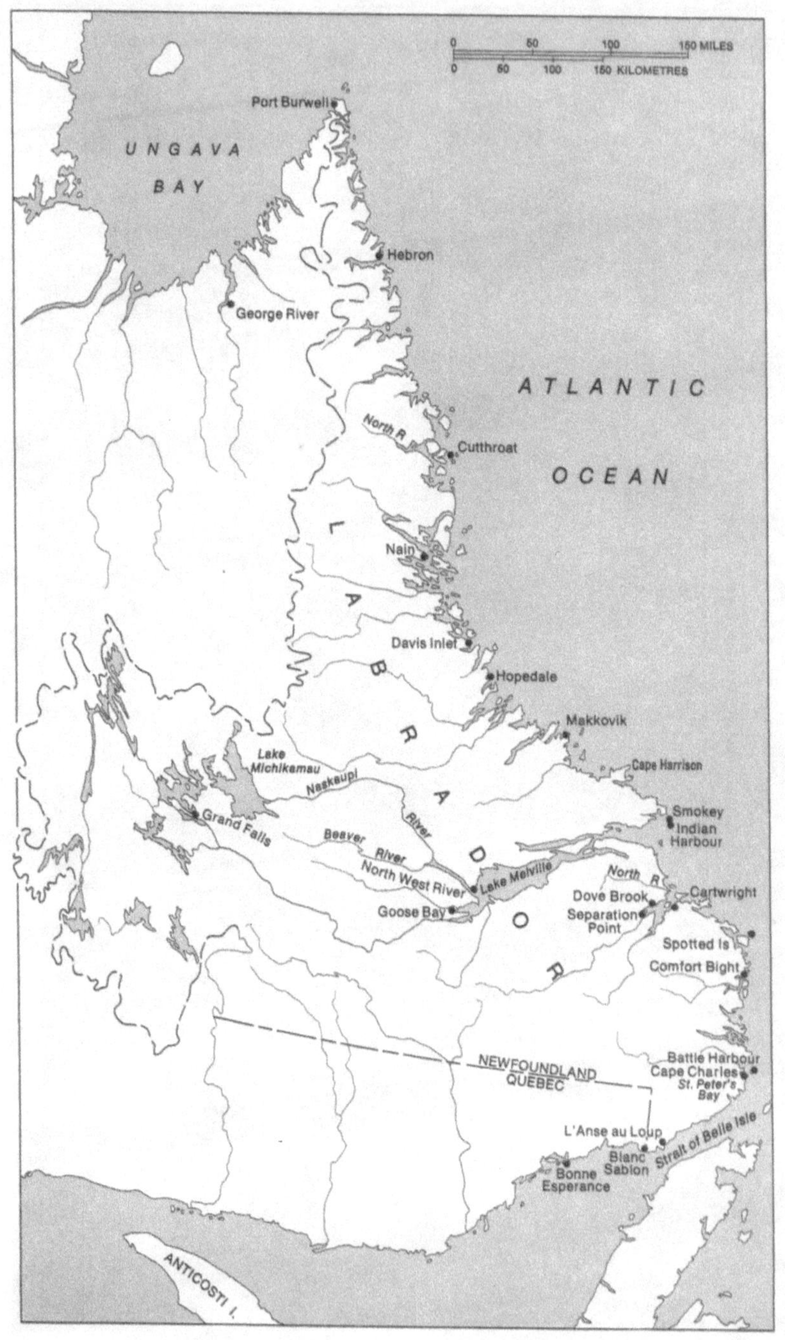
0 50 100 150 MILES
0 50 100 150 KILOMETRES
UNGAVA BAY
Port Burwell
Hebron
George River
ATLANTIC OCEAN
North R
Cutthroat
LABRADOR
Nain
Davis Inlet
Hopedale
Makkovik
Cape Harrison
Lake Michikamau
Naskaupi River
Grand Falls
Beaver River
North West River
Lake Melville
Goose Bay
Smokey
Indian Harbour
North R
Cartwright
Dove Brook
Separation Point
Spotted Is
Comfort Bight
Battle Harbour
Cape Charles
St. Peter's Bay
NEWFOUNDLAND
QUEBEC
L'Anse au Loup
Blanc Sablon
Strait of Belle Isle
Bonne Esperance
ANTICOSTI I.

1 DISCOVERY AND EARLY EXPLORATION

VINLAND*

The Sagas assumed a new interest for Canadians with the discovery at L'Anse aux Meadows in 1960 of the remains of what appears to have been a Viking settlement. Helge Ingstad, the Norwegian archeologist who uncovered the L'Anse aux Meadows site, has argued that the wine mentioned in the Sagas may have been made 'from wild gooseberries, from the squash-berries that grow in clusters on bushes, from currants, or from other kinds of wild berries.' All these berries are found in northern Newfoundland. For these and other reasons Ingstad has identified Vinland as the island of Newfoundland.

The translation from the original Old Icelandic which follows is by M. Magnusson and H. Palsson.

THERE WAS NOW great talk of discovering new countries. Leif the son of Eirik the Red of Brattahlid, went to see Bjarni Herjolfsson and bought his ship from him, and engaged a crew of thirty-five.[1]

Leif asked his father Eirik to lead this expedition too, but Eirik was rather reluctant: he said he was getting old, and could endure hardships less easily than he used to. Leif replied that Eirik would still command more luck than any of his kinsmen. And in the end, Eirik let Leif have his way.

As soon as they were ready, Eirik rode off to the ship which was only a short distance away. But the horse he was riding stumbled and he was thrown, injuring his leg.

'I am not meant to discover more countries than this one we now live in,' said Eirik. 'This is as far as we go together.'

Eirik returned to Brattahlid, but Leif went aboard the ship with his crew of thirty-five. Among them was a Southerner called Tyrkir.[2]

They made their ship ready and put out to sea. The first landfall they made was the country that Bjarni had sighted last. They sailed right up to the shore and cast anchor, then lowered a boat and landed. There was no grass to be seen, and the hinterland was covered with great glaciers, and between glaciers and shore the land was like one great slab of rock. It seemed to them a worthless country.

* *The Vinland Sagas: The Norse Discovery of America* trans. Magnus Magnusson & Hermann Palsson (London: Penguin Books 1965) 54-8.

Then Leif said, 'Now we have done better than Bjarni where this country is concerned – we at least have set foot on it. I shall give this country a name and call it *Helluland.*'[3]

They returned to their ship and put to sea, and sighted a second land. Once again they sailed right up to it and cast anchor, lowered a boat and went ashore. This country was flat and wooded, with white sandy beaches wherever they went; and the land sloped gently down to the sea.

Leif said, 'This country shall be named after its natural resources: it shall be called *Markland.*'[4]

They hurried back to their ship as quickly as possible and sailed away to sea in a north-east wind for two days until they sighted land again. They sailed towards it and came to an island which lay to the north of it.

They went ashore and looked about them. The weather was fine. There was dew on the grass, and the first thing they did was to get some of it on their hands and put it to their lips, and to them it seemed the sweetest thing they had ever tasted. Then they went back to their ship and sailed into the sound that lay between the island and the headland jutting out to the north.

They steered a westerly course round the headland. There were extensive shallows there and at low tide their ship was left high and dry, with the sea almost out of sight. But they were so impatient to land that they could not bear to wait for the rising tide to float the ship; they ran ashore to a place where a river flowed out of a lake. As soon as the tide had refloated the ship they took a boat and rowed out to it and brought it up the river into the lake, where they anchored it. They carried their hammocks ashore and put up booths. Then they decided to winter there, and built some large houses.

There was no lack of salmon in the river or the lake, bigger salmon than they had ever seen. The country seemed to them so kind that no winter fodder would be needed for livestock: there was never any frost all winter and the grass hardly withered at all.

In this country, night and day were of more even length than in either Greenland or Iceland: on the shortest day of the year, the sun was already up by 9 AM, and did not set until after 3 PM.

When they had finished building their houses, Leif said to his companions, 'Now I want to divide our company into two parties and have the country explored; half of the company are to remain here at the houses while the other half go exploring – but they must not go so far that they cannot return the same evening, and they are not to become separated.'

They carried out these instructions for a time. Leif himself took turns at going out with the exploring party and staying behind at the base.

Leif was tall and strong and very impressive in appearance. He was a shrewd man and always moderate in his behaviour.

One evening news came that someone was missing: it was Tyrkir the Southerner. Leif was very displeased at this, for Tyrkir had been with the family for a long time, and when Leif was a child had been devoted to him. Leif rebuked his men severely, and got ready to make a search with twelve men.

They had gone only a short distance from the houses when Tyrkir came walking towards them, and they gave him a warm welcome. Leif quickly realized that Tyrkir was in excellent humour.

Tyrkir had a prominent forehead and shifty eyes, and not much more of a face besides; he was short and puny-looking but very clever with his hands.

Leif said to him, 'Why are you so late, foster-father? How did you get separated from your companions?'

At first Tyrkir spoke for a long time in German, rolling his eyes in all directions and pulling faces, and no one could understand what he was saying. After a while he spoke in Icelandic.

'I did not go much farther than you,' he said. 'I have some news. I found vines and grapes.'

'Is that true, foster-father?' asked Leif.

'Of course it is true,' he replied. 'Where I was born there were plenty of vines and grapes.'

They slept for the rest of the night, and next morning Leif said to his men, 'Now we have two tasks on our hands. On alternate days we must gather grapes and cut vines, and then fell trees, to make a cargo for my ship.'

This was done. It is said that the tow-boat was filled with grapes. They took on a full cargo of timber; and in the spring they made ready to leave and sailed away. Leif named the country after its natural qualities and called it *Vinland.*

NOTES

1 Brattahlid was a Viking settlement in southeast Greenland. Bjarni

Herjolfsson, on a journey from Iceland to Greenland, was blown off course and sighted land far to the southwest of his destination.

2 He was from southern Europe.

3 i.e., 'slab-land'; possibly Baffin Island

4 i.e., 'forest-land'; possibly Labrador

JOHAN DAY'S LETTER (1497)*

In 1955 an important addition was made to the existing body of information about the Cabot voyages with the discovery of 'Johan Day's Letter' in the Archivo de Simancas in Spain. The letter is addressed to the 'Almirante Mayor,' thought by its discoverer, the American scholar L.A. Vigneras, to be either Fadrique Enriquez, hereditary Grand Admiral of Castile, or Christopher Columbus. Day, an English merchant, wrote the letter while on a business trip to Spain. The letter is undated but was probably written during the last four months of 1497. Though not a first-hand account, it is in all likelihood based on authentic reports of the voyages.

Day's letter was written in Spanish, and the translation which follows was made by L.A. Vigneras.

YOUR LORDSHIP WILL know that [Cabot] landed at only one spot of the mainland, near the place where land was first sighted, and they disembarked there with a crucifix and raised banners with the arms of the Holy Father and those of the King of England, my master; and they found tall trees of the kind masts are made, and other smaller trees and the country is very rich in grass. In that particular spot, as I told your Lordship, they found a trail that went inland; they saw a site where a fire had been made, they saw manure of animals which they thought to be farm animals, and they saw a stick half a yard long pierced at both ends, carved and painted with brazil, and by such signs they believe the land to be inhabited. Since he was with just a few people, he did not dare advance inland beyond the shooting distance of a cross-bow, and after taking in fresh water he returned to his ship. All along the coast they found many fish like those which in Iceland are dried in the open and sold in England and

* L.A. Vigneras 'The Cape Breton Landfall: 1494 or 1497' *Canadian Historical Review* XXXVIII (1957)

other countries, and these fish are called in English 'stockfish'; and thus following the shore they saw two forms running on land one after the other, but they could not tell if they were human beings or animals; and it seemed to them that there were fields where they thought might also be villages, and they saw a forest whose foliage looked beautiful. They left England toward the end of May, and must have been on the way 35 days before sighting land; the wind was east north-east and the sea was calm going and coming back, except for one day when he ran into a storm two or three days before finding land; and going so far out, his compass needle failed to point north and marked two rhumbs below.[1] They spent about one month discovering the coast and from the above mentioned cape of the mainland which is nearest to Ireland, they returned to the coast of Europe in fifteen days. They had the wind behind them, and he reached Brittany because the sailors confused him, saying that he was heading too far north. From there he came to Bristol, and he went to see the King to report to him all the above mentioned; and the King granted him an annual pension of twenty pounds sterling to sustain himself until the time comes when more will be known of this business, since with God's help it is hoped to push through plans for exploring the said land more thoroughly next year with ten or twelve vessels – because in his voyage he had only one ship of fifty tons and twenty men and food for seven or eight months – and they want to carry out this new project. It is considered certain that the cape of the said land was found and discovered in the past by the men from Bristol who found Brasil,[2] as your Lordship well knows. It was called the Island of Brasil, and it is assumed and believed to be the mainland that the men from Bristol found.

Since your Lordship wants information relating to the first voyage, here is what happened: he went with one ship, his crew confused him, he was short of supplies and ran into bad weather, and he decided to turn back.

NOTES

1 Compasses were divided into 32 points or *rhumbs*, each rhumb being the equivalent of $11^\circ\ 15'$.

2 A legendary island appearing on some early maps

JACQUES CARTIER VISITS THE FUNKS (1534)*

Jacques Cartier was born in Saint-Malo, Brittany, probably in 1491. His career to 1532 is obscure, but in that year he was mentioned by the bishop of Saint-Malo in connection with a proposed expedition to the New World. Cartier was ordered by the King of France in March 1534, 'to discover certain islands and lands where it is said that a great quantity of gold, and other precious things, are to be found.' At least one historian has concluded from the course Cartier charted across the Atlantic to Catalina in 1534 that he had been in Newfoundland previously. Cartier died at Saint-Malo in 1557 and is remembered as one of the principal European explorers of North America. It was he who described Labrador as 'the land God gave to Cain.'

The text which follows was translated from the original French by H.P. Biggar.

WHEN SIR CHARLES de Mouy, Knight, Lord of La Meilleraye and Vice-Admiral of France, had received the oaths of the captains, masters and sailors of the vessels, and had made them swear to conduct themselves well and loyally in the King's service, under the command of the said Cartier, we set forth from the harbour and port of St Malo with two ships of about sixty tons' burden each, manned in all with sixty-one men, on [Monday] April 20 in the said year 1534; and sailing on with fair weather we reached Newfoundland on [Sunday] May 10, sighting land at cape Bonavista in latitude 48° 30′ ... And on account of the large number of blocks of ice along that coast, we deemed it advisable to go into a harbour called St Catherine's harbour [Catalina] lying about five leagues south-south-west of this cape [Bonavista], where we remained the space of ten days [May 11-21], biding favourable weather and rigging and fitting up our long-boats.

And on [Thursday] the twenty-first of the said month of May we set forth from this harbour with a west wind, and sailed north, one quarter north-east of cape Bonavista as far as the isle of Birds, which island was completely surrounded and encompassed by a cordon of

* H.P. Biggar, ed. *The Voyages of Jacques Cartier* Publications of the Public Archives of Canada II (Ottawa: King's Printer 1924) 3-9. Reprinted by permission of the Public Archives of Canada

loose ice, split up into cakes. In spite of this belt [of ice] our two long-boats were sent off to the island to procure some of the birds, whose numbers are so great as to be incredible, unless one has seen them; for although the island is about a league in circumference, it is so exceeding full of birds that one would think they had been stowed there. In the air and round about are an hundred times as many more as on the island itself. Some of these birds are as large as geese, being black and white with a beak like a crow's. They are always in the water, not being able to fly in the air, inasmuch as they have only small wings about the size of half one's hand, with which however they move as quickly along the water as the other birds fly through the air. And these birds are so fat that it is marvellous. We call them apponats [the great auk]; and our two long-boats were laden with them as with stones, in less than half an hour. Of these, each of our ships salted four or five casks, not counting those we were able to eat fresh.

Furthermore there is another smaller kind of bird that flies in the air and swims in the sea, which is called a tinker [the razor-billed auk]. These stow and place themselves on this island underneath the larger ones. There were other white ones larger still that keep apart from the rest in a portion of the island, and are very ugly to attack; for they bite like dogs. These are called gannets. Notwithstanding that the island lies fourteen leagues from shore, bears swim out to it from the mainland in order to feed on these birds; and our men found one as big as a calf and as white as a swan that sprang into the sea in front of them. And the next day, which was Whitsuntide, on continuing our voyage in the direction of the mainland, we caught sight of this bear about half way, swimming towards land as fast as we were sailing; and on coming up with him we gave chase with our long-boats and captured him by main force. His flesh was as good to eat as that of a two-year-old heifer.

THE LETTER OF STEPHEN PARMENIUS (6 AUGUST 1583)*

The poet and scholar Stephen Parmenius was born around 1541 in Hungary. In 1581 he arrived in England and subsequently attended

* *The New Found Land of Stephen Parmenius* ed. D.B. Quinn & N.M. Cheshire (Toronto: University of Toronto Press 1972)

Oxford University, where he knew Richard Hakluyt. Hakluyt introduced him to Sir Humphrey Gilbert, with whom he sailed to Newfoundland in 1583. The ship on which he left Newfoundland, the *Delight*, was lost at sea and Parmenius was drowned, probably near Sable Island.

His surviving letter to Richard Hakluyt from St John's was written in Latin; the translation which follows was made by D.B. Quinn and N.M. Cheshire.

WE PUT IN to this place [St John's] on August 3, and on the 5th the admiral [Gilbert] took these regions into the possession and authority of himself and of the realm of England, having passed certain laws about religion and obedience to the Queen of England. At the moment we are regaling ourselves rather more cheerfully and sumptuously. For you will surely have gathered, from considering the length of time we took, what sort of winds we have used and how exhausted we were able to become. From now on we shall not go short of anything, because apart from the English we have come across some twenty Portuguese and Spanish ships in this place, and they, being no match for us, will not allow us to go hungry. The English group, although strong enough themselves and unthreatened by us, attend us with all deference and kindness, respecting the authority of our letters patent from the Queen.

Now I ought to tell you about the customs, territories and inhabitants: and yet what am I to say, my dear Hakluyt, when I see nothing but desolation? There are inexhaustible supplies of fish, so that those who travel here do good business. Scarcely has the hook touched the bottom before it is loaded with some magnificent catch. The whole terrain is hilly and forested: the trees are for the most part pine. Some of these are growing old and others are just coming to maturity, but the majority have fallen with age, thus obstructing a good view of the land and the passage of travellers, so that no advance can be made anywhere. All the grass is tall, but scarcely any different from ours. Nature seems even to want to struggle towards producing corn; for I found some blades and ears that resembled rye and they seem capable of being adapted easily to cultivation and sowing in the service of man. There are blackberries in the woods, or rather very sweet strawberries growing on bushes. Bears sometimes appear round the shelters and are killed: but they are white, so far as I have been able to make out from their skins, and smaller than ours.

I am not clear whether there are any inhabitants in this area, nor have I met anyone who was in a position to say (and who could be, I ask you, since it is impossible to travel any distance?). Nor do we know any better whether there is any metal in the mountains; and for the same reason, even though their appearance may indicate underlying minerals.

We made representations to the admiral to burn the forests down, so as to clear an open space for surveying the area; nor was he averse to the idea, if it had not seemed likely to bring a considerable disadvantage. For some reliable people asserted that, when this had occurred by accident at some other settlement post, no fish had been seen for seven whole years, because the sea-water had been turned bitter by the turpentine that flowed down from the trees burning along the rivers.

At this time of the year the weather is so hot that if the fish which are put to dry in the sun were not regularly turned over they could not be prevented from scorching. But the huge masses of ice out to sea have taught us how cold it is in winter. Some of our company have reported that in the month of May they were stuck for sixteen whole days on end in so much ice that some of the icebergs were sixty fathoms thick; and when their sides facing the sun melted, the entire mass was turned over, as it were on a sort of pivot, in such a way that what had previously been facing upwards was then facing down, to the great danger of any people at hand, as you can well imagine. The atmosphere on land is moderately clear, but there is continuous fog over the sea toward the east. And on the sea itself around the Bank (which is what they call the place about forty miles off shore where the bottom can be reached and they start catching fish) there is scarcely a day without rain.

When we have provided for all our requirements in this place we shall advance southwards, with God's help; and the more that is reported about the regions we are making for, the greater will our expectations be from day to day.

JOHN GUY'S ENCOUNTER WITH THE SAVAGES (1612)*

What we know about John Guy dates from the first decade of the seventeenth century when he was active in the commercial life of Bristol. His interest in western exploration and settlement led to his appointment in 1610 as governor of a colony being planned in Newfoundland by the London and Bristol Company. He arrived in Newfoundland with a group of colonists in August 1610, and settled at Cuper's Cove (Cupids, Conception Bay). His encounter with the Indians described below occurred in October 1612, at Bull Arm, Trinity Bay.

IN OCTOBER, John Guy, with thirteen others, in the *Indeavour*, and five in the *Shallop*, went upon discovery. At Mount Eagle Bay, they found store of scurvey-grasse, on an island. In the south bottom of Trinitie Bay – which they called 'Savage Harbor,' they found savages' houses, no people in them; in one they found a copper kettle, very bright, a furre goune of Elke-skin, some seale skins, an old saile, and a fishing reele. Order was taken that nothing should be diminished, and, because the Savages should know that some had been there, every thing was removed out of his place, and brought into one of the cabins, and laid orderly one upon the other, and the kettle hanged over them, wherein there was put some bisket, and three or four amber beads. This was done to begin to win them by faire meanes...

November the sixth, two canoes appeared, and one man alone, coming towards us with a flag in his hand, of a wolfe skin, shaking it, and making a loud noise, which we took to be for a parley; whereupon a white flag was put out, and the barke and shallop rowed towards them, which the savages did not like of, and so took them to their canoes againe, and were going away: where upon the barke wheazed unto them, and then they staied: presently after the shallop landed Master Whittington with the flag of truce went towards them. Then they rowed into the shoare with one canoe, the other standing aloofe off, and landed two men, one of them having the white skin in his hand, and coming towards Master Whittington, the savage

* J.P. Howley *The Beothucks or Red Indians* (Cambridge: University Press 1915)

made a loud speech, and shaked the skin, which was answered by Master Whittington in like manner, and as the savage drew neare, he threw downe the white skin on the ground; the like was done by Master Whittington; whereupon both the savages passed over a little water streame towards Master Whittington, dancing, leaping, and singing; and coming together, the foremost of them presented unto him a chaine of leather full of small periwinkles shels, a splitting knife, and a feather that stake in his eare; the other gave him an arrow without a head; and the former was requited with a linnen cap, and a hand towell, who put presently the linnen cap upon his head: and to the other he gave a knife: and after, hand in hand, they all three did sing and dance: upon this, one of our company, called Francis Tipton, went ashore, unto whom one of the savages came running and gave him a chaine, such as is before spoken of, who was gratified by Francis Tipton with a knife and a small peece of brasse. Then all four together danced, laughing and making signs of joy and gladnesse, sometimes striking the breasts of our company, and sometimes their owne. When signs were made that they should be willing to suffer two of our company more to come on shore for two of theirs more to be landed, and that bread and drink should be brought ashore, they made likewise signs that they had in their canoes meate also to eate. Upon this the shallop rowed aboard and brought John Guy and Master Teage ashoare, who presented them with a shirt, two table napkins, and a hand towell, giving them bread, butter, and reasons of the sunne to eate, and beere, and aqua-vitae to drinke: and one of them, blowing in the aqua-vitae bottle, made a sound, which they fell all into laughing at. After, Master Croote and John Crouther came ashore, whom they went to salute giving them shell chains, who bestowed gloves upon them. One of the savages who came last ashore, came walking with his oare in his hand, and, seemed to have some command over the rest, and behaved himself civilly: For when meate was offered him, he drew off his mitten from his hand before he would receive it, and gave an arrow for a present without a head: who was requited with a dozen of points. After they had all eaten and drunke, one of them went to their canoe, and brought us deeres flesh, dried in the smoke or winde, and drawing his knife from out of his necke, he cut every man a peece, and that savoured very well. At the first meeting, when signs were made of meate to eate, one of the savages presently ran to the bank side, and pulled up a roote, and gave it to Master Whittington, which the other savage perceiving to be durtie, took it out of his hand, and went to the water to wash it, and after dividing it among the foure, it tasted very well: hee that came ashore with the oare in his hand, went and tooke the white skin that they hailed us with, and gave it to Master Whittington; and presently after they did take our white flagge with them in the canoe, and made signs unto us that we should repaire to our barke, and so they put off, for it was almost night.

In the two canoes there were eight men, if none were women, (for commonly in every canoe there is one woman). They are of a reasonable stature, of an ordinary middle size, they goe bare-headed, wearing their hair somewhat long but round: they have no beards; behind they have a great locke of haire platted with feathers, like a hawke's lure, with a feather in it standing upright by the crowne of the head and a small lock platted before, a short gown made of stags' skins, the furre innermost, that raune down to the middle of their legges, with sleeves to the middle of their arme, and a bever skin about their necke, was all their apparell, save that one of them had shooes and mittens, so that all went bare-legged and most bare-foote. They are full-eyed, of a blacke colour; the colour of their hair was divers, some blacke, some browne, and some yellow, and their faces something flat and broad, red with oker, as all their apparell is, and the rest of their body: they are broad brested, and bould, and stand very upright.

JOHN MASON'S ACCOUNT OF NEWFOUNDLAND (1620)*

John Mason (1586-1635) succeeded John Guy as governor at Cupids around 1615. He probably lived in Newfoundland from 1616 to 1619, when he returned to England to advance the cause of Newfoundland settlement.

THE AIR subtle & wholesome, the summer season pleasant, conform to the like latitude in Europe, saving that the woodie places in

* John Mason *A Briefe Discourse of the Newfoundland* (Edinburgh, 1620)

June & July are somewhat pestered with small flies bred of the rottenness of ruined wood & moisture as in Russia. The winter degenerating therefrom, being as cold & snowy as 60 degrees in Europe, & of the like temperature in December, Jan. Febr. March as the northermost parts in Scotland; viz. the Hebrides and the Orcades wherein I have twice wintered, or the coast betwixt Hamburg & the mouth of the Sound or Nose of Norway: yet more comfortable for the length of the day in winter, which exceedeth theirs three hours at the least. And albeit it be thus cold in the winter season by accidental means, contrarie to the natural position thereof in the sphere, yet it is tolerable, as by experience, so that there needs no stoves as in Germany; likewise fruitful enough both of summer and winter corn, an example for our confirmation thereof we have in Poland one of the greatest corn countries of Europe & yet as cold and subject to freezing as Newfoundland, as also our own experience both in wheat, rye, barley, oats, and peas, which have grown and ripened there as well and as timely as in Yorkshire in England. And for growth of garden herbs of divers sorts as hyssop, thyme, parsley, clary, nepe, French mallows, bugloss, columbines, wormwood, &c. There is at this present of 3 years old of my sowing likewise rosemary, fennel, sweet marjoram, basil, purslane, lettuce, and all other herbs & roots: as turnips, parsnips, carrots, and radishes we have found to grow well there in the summer season. The common wild herbs of the country are angelica, violets, mints, scabious, yarrow, fern, salsilla, with divers other sorts whereof I am ignorant, but suppose would for variety and rarity compose another herbal. Of these kinds we have only made use of certain great green leaves plentifully growing in the woods and a great root growing in fresh water ponds, both good against the scurvy, and another pretty root with a blue stalk and leaves of the nature of a skirret growing in a dry beachy ground: good meat boiled. The country wild fruits are cherries small, whole groves of them, filberts good, a small pleasant fruit called a pear, damask roses single very sweet, excellent strawberries and hartleberries, with abundance of raspberries and gooseberries somewhat better than ours in England, all which replanted would be much enlarged. There is also a kind of wild currants, wild peas or vetches, which we have both found good meat and medicine for the scurvy. The land of the north parts most mountainy and woody, very thick of fir trees, spruce, pine ... asp, hazel, a kind of stinking wood, the three foremost goodly timber and most convenient for building. No oaks, ash, beech or elms have we seen or heard of. The greatest parts of the plains are marsh and bogs, yet apt to be drawn dry by means of many fresh lakes intermixt which pay tribute to the sea; and on the brinks of these lakes, through which the water drains away from the roots of the grass, it flourisheth. In the other parts of the plains where the water standeth and killeth the growth of the grass with his coldness, it is rushy and sedgy; in some parts is barren & mossie ground; but that that is firm and dry beareth good grass. The spring beginneth in the end of April, & harvest continueth [until] November. I have seen September and October much more pleasant than in England. The south part is not so mountainous nor so woodie ... having pretty groves and many fresh lakes replenished with eels and salmon-trouts great and in great plenty. The beasts are ellans, follow deer, hares, bears harmless, wolves, foxes, beavers, catnaghenes excellent, otters, and a small beast like a ferret whose excrement is musk. And the plantations have prettie store of swine and goats. The fowls are eagles, falcons, tassills, marlins, a great owl much deformed, a lesser owl, bustards, gripes, ospreys which dive for fishes into the water, ravens, crows, wild geese, snipes, teals, twillockes, excellent wild ducks of divers sorts and abundance, some whereof rare and not to be found in Europe, their particulars too tedious to relate; all good meat. Partridges white in winter and gray in summer, greater than ours; butters, black birds with red breasts, phillidas, wrens, swallows, jays, with other small birds, and 2 or 3 excellent kinds of beach birds very fat and sweet, & at the plantations English pigeons. The sea fowls are gulls white and gray, penguins, sea pigeons, ice birds, bottle noses, with other sorts strange in shape, yet all bountiful to us with their eggs as good as our turkey or hens, wherewith the islands are well replenished. But of all, the most admirable is the sea, so diversified with several sorts of fishes abounding therein, the consideration whereof is readie to swallow up and drowne my senses, not being able to comprehend or express the riches thereof. For could one acre thereof be enclosed with the creatures therein in the months of June, July, and August, it would exceed one thousand acres of the best pasture with the stock thereon which we have in England. May hath herrings one equal to 2 of ours, lants and cods in good quantity; June hath caplin, a fish much resembling smelts in form and eating, and such abundance dry on shore as to load carts; in some parts pretty store of salmon, and cods so thick by the shore that we hardlie have been able to row a boat through them. I have killed of them with a pike. Of these, three men to sea in a boat with some on shore to dress and dry them in 30 days will kill commonlie betwixt 25 and 30 thousand worth, with the oil arising from them 100 or 120 pounds. And the fish and train in one harbour called Saint Johns is yearly in the summer worth 17 or 18 thousand pounds. July, and so till November, hath mackerel in abundance, one thereof as great as two of ours; August hath great large cods, but not in such abundance as the smaller, which continueth with some little decreasing till December. What should I speak of a kind of whales called gibberts, dogfish, porpoises, herringhogs, squids (a rare kind of fish, at his mouth squirting matter forth like ink), flounders, crabs, conners, catfish, millers, thunnes, &c., of all which there are innumerable in the summer season. Likewise of lobsters plentie, and this last year store of smelts not having been known there before. I have also seen tonnie fish in Newland; now of shell fish there is scallops, mussels, ursenas, hens, periwinkles &c. Here we see the chief fishing with his great commoditie expressed, which falleth so fitly in the summer season betwixt seed-time and harvest that it cannot be any hindrance to either.

A LETTER FROM FERRYLAND (18 AUGUST 1622)*

In 1621 George Calvert, 1st Baron Baltimore, sent Captain Edward Wynne with a small group of colonists to establish a settlement at Ferryland. The letter that follows was written the following year by one 'N.H.' to a friend in England. Two of Wynne's colonists were Nicholas Hoskins and Nicholas Hinckson, the latter a carpenter.

MY HUMBLE SERVICE remembered; accounting myself bound unto you in a double bond, namely, love and duty, I could not be unmindful to shew the same unto you in these rude lines, thereby to acquaint you with our health, the temperature of our country, and

* Richard Whitbourne *A Discourse and Discovery of Newfoundland* (London 1623)

the commodities and blessings therein. And first, for the first: concerning our health, there is not any man amongst our company that hath been sick scarcely one day since he came but hath been able to follow his work. The climate differs but little from England, and I myself felt less cold here this winter than I did in England the winter before, by much. The air is sweeter; for I never smelt any evil savour in the country, nor saw any venomous creature. God's blessings upon this land are manifold. As for wood and water, it passeth England: the one most sweet in growing and burning, the other most pleasant to taste and good to drink. For in the Whitsun holydays I (taking with me Master Stoning) did coast some ten miles into the country westward from our plantation. to make some discovery of the country and to kill a deer; and being some five miles into the land, where we lodged that night, we found much champion ground and good levels of one, two, three or four hundred acres together. And at the foot of each mountain and small hill we always met with a fair fresh river or a sweet brook of running water whereof we freely drank, and it did quench my thirst as well as any beer and much refresht us both and never offended our stomachs at all. We travelled three days but found no deer, save their footings; which came to pass by means of a great fire that had burned the woods a little before, ten miles compass. It began between Fermeuse and Aquaforte: it burned a week and then was quenched by a great rain.

I know not who or what he was that gave fire to it, but I think he was a servant hired by the devil to do that wicked deed, who (I do not doubt) will pay him for his work. In the night, the wolves being near, did something affright us with their howlings but did not hurt us; for we had dogs, fire and sword to welcome them. As for bears, although there be many, they bear us no ill will, I think, for I have eaten my part of two or three and take no hurt by them. Foxes are here many, and as subtle as a fox, yet we cozened many of them for their rich coats, which our worthy Governor keeps carefully ... as fitting presents for greater persons...

All our corn and seeds have prospered well and are already grown almost to perfect maturity. What shall I say? To say that I know not, I dare not. Thus much I know, as an eye witness, & much more good the country doth promise to shew me: the which, when I see you, my heart shall command and my tongue to certify you. Our Governor's letters (I doubt not) will bring you news at large; I wrote but this in haste to satisfy myself and shew my duty, desiring you to look through it, as through a prospective glass, wherein you may discern afar off what I have seen near hand, and see that your poor well-wishing friend is alive and in good health at Ferryland, who in the lowest step of duty takes his leave with prayers for your preservation.

SIR RICHARD WHITBOURNE'S DESCRIPTION OF HIS NEWFOUNDLAND ADVENTURES (1623)*

Sir Richard Whitbourne (fl. 1579-1628) was born at Exmouth in Devonshire and made his first voyage to Newfoundland in 1579. His subsequent involvement with Newfoundland was varied, but perhaps his most notable contribution to life on the island occurred in 1615 when he held vice-admiralty courts there to investigate reported atrocities committed by visiting fishermen. He was probably the most able of the early propagandists for settlement in Newfoundland.

MY FIRST VOYAGE thither was about 40 years since in a worthy ship of the burthen of 300 tunne, set forth by one Master Cotten of Southampton. We were bound to the grand Bay (which lyeth on the north side of that land) purposing there to trade then with the savage people (for whom we carried sundry commodities) and to kill whales, and to make traine oil,[1] as the Biscaines do there yearly in great abundance. But this our intended voyage was overthrown by the indiscretion of our Captain and faintheartedness of some gentlemen of our company, who loved soft feather beds better than hard cabins, and longed rather to sit by a tavern fire than to have the cold weather blast of those seas blow on their faces. Whereupon we set sail from thence and bare with Trinity Harbour in Newfoundland, where we killed great store of fish, deer, bears, beavers, seals, otters and such like, with abundance of sea fowl; and so returning to England, we arrived safe at Southampton...

* Richard Whitbourne *A Discourse and Discovery of Newfoundland* (London 1623)

In the year 1611 being in Newfoundland, at which time that famous arch-pirate Peter Easton came there and had with him ten sail of good ships, well furnished and very rich, I was kept eleven weeks under his command, and had from him many golden promises and much wealth offered to be put into my hands, as is well known. I did persuade him much to desist from his evil course; his entreaties then to me being that I would come for England to some friends of his and solicit them to become humble petitioners to your Majesty for his pardon. But having no warrant to touch such goods, I gave him thanks for his offer; only I requested him to release a ship that he had taken upon the coast of Guinea, belonging to one Captain Rashly of Foy in Cornwall, a man whom I knew but only by report; which he accordingly released. Whereupon I provided men, victuals, and a fraught for the said ship, and so sent her home to Dartmouth in Devon, though I never had so much as thanks for my kindness therein. And so leaving Easton, I came for England and gave notice of his intention, letting pass my voyage that I intended for Naples, and lost both my labour and charges; for before my arrival there was a pardon granted and sent him from Ireland...

In the year 1615 I returned again to Newfoundland, carrying with me a Commission out of the High Court of Admiralty authorizing me to impanel juries, and to make inquiry upon oath of sundry abuses and disorders committed amongst fishermen yearly upon that coast, and of the fittest means to redress the same, with some other points having a more particular relation to the office of the Lord Admiral...

In the year 1616 I had a ship at Newfoundland of 100 tun which returning laden from thence, being bound for Lisbon, was met with by a French pirate of Rochelle, one Daniel Tibolo, who rifled her to the overthrow & loss of my voyage in more than the sum of 860 pounds, and cruelly handled the master and company that were in her; and although I made good proof thereof at Lisbon and represented the same also to this kingdom, as appertained, after my return from thence, yet for all this great loss I could never have any recompense.

Shortly after my return from Lisbon I was sent for by Doctor Vaughan, who about a year before, by a grant from the patentees, had undertaken to settle people in Newfoundland. He acquainted me with his designs, and after some conference touching the same, he gave me a conveyance under his hand and seal for the term of my life with full power to govern within his circuit upon that coast; whereupon (being desirous to advance that work) in Anno 1618 I sailed thither in a ship of my own, which was victualled by that gentleman, myself, and some others. We likewise then did set forth another ship for a fishing voyage, which also carried some victuals for those people which had been formerly sent to inhabit there; but this ship was intercepted by an English erring Captain, one Captain Whitney (who went forth with Sir Walter Raleigh). He took the master of her, the boatswain, and two other of the best men, with much of her victuals (the rest of the company for fear running into the woods) and so left the ship as a prize, whereby our intended fishing voyages of both ships were overthrown and the plantation hindered...

Although I have often suffered great losses by sea rovers and other casualties of the sea, yet in this point I have tasted of God's exceeding great mercy, that never any ship wherein I myself was present miscarried or came then to any mischance or any casualty of the sea, whereunto all ships are subject. ... My life hath been a mixture of crosses and comforts, wherein nevertheless they have not been so equally balanced but that the one hath overweighed the other; for now after more than 40 years spent in the foresaid courses, there remains little other fruit unto me, saving the peace of a good conscience, which gives me this testimony, that I have ever been a loyal subject to my Prince and a true lover of my country, and was never as yet in all my time beholding to any doctor's counsel or apothecary's drugs for the preservation of my health. And it will be to me a contentment, if I may be so happy, as to become the instrument of any public good herein and in whatsoever for the good of my Prince and country...

Now also I will not omit to relate something of a strange creature which I saw there in the year 1610 in a morning early, as I was standing by the river side in the harbor of Saint Johns; which very swiftly came swimming towards me, looking cheerfully on my face as it had been a woman – by the face, eyes, nose, mouth, chin, ears, neck, and forehead, it seemed to be so beautiful & in those parts so well proportioned, having round about the head many blue streaks resembling hair. But certainly it was no hair, for I beheld it long and another of my company also yet living, that saw the same coming so swiftly towards me, whereat I stepped back (for it was come within the length of a long pike) supposing it would have sprung aland to me, because I had often seen huge whales to spring a great height above the water, and divers other great fishes the like; and so might this strange creature [have] done to me if I had stood still where I was (as I verily believe it had such a purpose). But when it saw that I went from it, it did thereon dive a little under water & swam towards the place where a little before I landed, and it did often look back towards me; whereby I beheld the shoulders & back down to the middle to be square, white & smooth as the back of a man. And from the middle to the hinder part it was pointing in proportion something like a broad hooked arrow. How it was in the forepart from the neck and shoulders I could not discern, but it came shortly after to a boat in the same harbour (wherein one William Haukrige, then my servant, was that hath been since a captain in a ship to the East Indies and is lately there so employed again) and the same creature did put both its hands upon the side of the boat and did strive much to come into him and divers others then in the same boat, whereat they were afraid & one of them struck it a full blow on the head; whereby it fell off from them, and afterwards it came to two other boats in the said harbour where they lay by the shore. The men in them for fear fled to land and beheld it. This (I suppose) was a maremaid or mareman. Now because divers have writ much of maremaids, I have presumed to relate what is most certain of such a strange creature that was thus there seen; whether it were a mareman or no I leave it for others to judge...

NOTE

1 whale oil

'COMPOSED AND DONE AT HARBOUR GRACE' (1628)*

Robert Hayman (1575-1629), Newfoundland's first poet, was a graduate of Exeter College, Oxford, and an acquaintance of such poets as Michael Drayton, Ben Jonson, and George Wither. He was

* Robert Hayman *Quodlibets, Lately Come Over from New Britaniola* (London 1628)

governor of a colony at Bristol's Hope, Conception Bay, where, as Wither noted, 'among unpeopled woods and hills' he wrote his modest verses.

A SKELTONICALL CONTINUED RYME,
IN PRAISE OF MY NEWFOUNDLAND

Although in cloaths, company, buildings faire,
With England, Newfoundland cannot compare;
Did some know what contentment I found there,
Alwayes enough, most times somewhat to spare,
With little paines, lesse toyle, and lesser care,
Exempt from taxings, ill newes, lawing, feare,
If cleane, and warme, no matter what you weare,
Healthy, and wealthy, if men carefull are,
With much, much more, then I will now declare,
(I say) if some wise men knew what this were,
(I doe believe) they'd live no other where.

TO THE FIRST PLANTERS OF NEWFOUNDLAND

What ayme you at in your Plantation?
Sought you the Honour of our Nation?
Or did you hope to raise your owne renowne?
Or else to adde a Kingdome to a Crowne?
Or Christ's true Doctrine for to propagate?
Or draw Salvages to a blessed state?
Or our o're peopled Kingdome to relieve?
Or shew poore men where they may richly live?
Or poore men's children godly to maintaine?
Or amy'd you at your own sweet private gaine?
All these you had atchiev'd before this day,
And all these you have balk't by your delay.

VAUGHAN'S 'GOLDEN ISLAND' RECONSIDERED (1630)*

In 1619, his own settlement at Renews having failed, Sir William Vaughan (1575-1641) gave some of his land grant on the Avalon

* Sir William Vaughan *The Newlander's Cure* (London 1630)

Peninsula to Sir George Calvert. The account which follows is an explanation of the subsequent failure of Calvert's settlement. It also marks a retreat by Vaughan from the enthusiasm which had earlier led him to call Newfoundland his 'Golden Island.'

THE DISASTERS WHICH happened to my Lord Baltimore and his colony the last winter at Ferryland in our New-land Plantation, by reason of the scurvy, have moved me to insert some more specific remedies against that disease which not only in those climates bears dominion, but likewise here in England, although hooded with other titles yet commonly sprung of the same causes.

For sometimes the scurvy is engendered of outward causes, and sometimes from within the body, or from both. And therefore they that dwell near the seaside, where the northeast winds rage, are most subject to this infirmity. Before the said Lord ever began his Plantation, he cannot deny but I advised him to erect his habitation in the botton of the bay at Aquaforte, two leagues distant from that place, which for ought I hear is not much to be discommended and more into the land where my people had wintered two years before and found no such inconvenience. Nay, his Lordship himself suspected the place; for in his letters he complained that unless he might be beholding to me for the assignment of both those places out of my grant, he was in a manner disheartened to plant on that coast by reason of the easterly winds, which with the mountains of ice floating from Estotiland and other northern countries towards Newfoundland render that easterly shore exceeding cold. Yet notwithstanding, his Lordship being persuaded by some which had more experience in the gainful trade of fishing than in the situation of a commodious seat for the wintering of his new inhabitants, bestowed all his charge of building at Ferryland, the coldest harbour of the land where those furious winds and icy mountains do play and beat the greatest part of the year. Whereas if he had built either at Aquaforte or in the westerly part in the Bay of Placentia, which hath above 50 miles overland betwixt it and that eastern shore, his entreprize had succeeded most luckily; and to this of Ferryland might have served well for his profit in the fishing and also for a pleasant summer dwelling.

Sir Francis Tanfield, under the right honourable the Lord Viscount Falkland, continued two years but three leagues more southward at Renews, and did well enough; in which place likewise my colony remained one winter without any such mortal accidents. But all winters, I confess, are not alike in that country, no more than they are here with us in Europe. Yea and here too in the same parallel the season differs. Who will imagine that we in Wales have less snow and frosts than London and Essex? And yet by experience we find it so, whereof the very cause proceeds from the eastern winds whose rigorous force before they arrive overland into our western parts cannot but be much broken and abated.

Besides these winds, snows, and frosts, the scurvy is engendered by eating of those meats which are of corrupted juice, raw, cold, salted, or of ill nourishment, which breed gross blood and melancholy. Among which I reckon bacon, fish, beans, peas, &c. And among drinks I rank all strong liquors whatsoever, specially if they be taken in frosty weather, when the stomach overabounds with heat and consequently at that time most subject to inflammations, which when the thaw comes will certainly break out into some dangerous disease.

2 TRANSATLANTIC OUTPOST

A PLYMOUTH SURGEON IN NEWFOUNDLAND (1663)*

James Yonge was born in Plymouth in 1647, the son of a medical doctor. At the age of ten he was apprenticed to a naval surgeon and beginning in 1662 served an apprenticeship of seven years with his father. He visited Newfoundland as a ship's surgeon for the first time in 1663. He was in Newfoundland in the same capacity in 1664, 1669, and 1670. He became mayor of Plymouth in 1694 and a fellow of the Royal Society in 1702. He died in July 1721, in Plymouth.

IN FEBRUARY [1663] my father shipped me to go Chyrurgeon of the *Reformation*, Mr Wm. Cock, commander, 70 men, 3 guns, 100 ton, bound for Newfoundland, to make a voyage. I were glad of the voyage, but so sorrowfully provided for it as is scarce credible. I had not the common necessaries that every sailor had. I had few and ill clothes, few and common medicines and utensils, 6 quarts of brandy, a small pot of butter, and books I had pickt up, a few. My comfort was I should be under no one ... and that Mr Cock was a kind man...

We came before Renoose, and the wind being north we entered the harbour and anchored, found no ship there, but divers possessors. We presently hired a sloop from a planter and sent the mate with divers men alongshore to get possessions, as they call it. The manner is thus: they put a man on shore at every harbour and at last, according to their turns, they take the best place they can of all their possessions. There were 4 at Renoose before us. Only one stuck there, which was Mr Thomas Waymouth of Dartmouth, who kept 18 boats, in the *Dorcas*, so our master resolved to be his vice-admiral.[1] Besides us, there fished Mr Thomas Hammett of Barnstaple, with 12 boats, Mr Francis Martin of Plymouth, 4 boats, and Mr Scott of Barnstaple, 6 boats. The planters were Mr John Kirk, 3 boats. Richard Pooly, 1 boat. Richard Codner, one boat, Mrs Gilder, 3 boats, and James Kelling, a two-man boat.

* *The Journal of James Yonge* ed. F.N.L. Poynter (London: Longmans 1963) 53-60. Reprinted by permission of Longman Group Ltd and Archon Books

Mr Waymouth, (who is Admiral and always wore a flagstaff, Sundays a flag, and is called my Lord, the vice-admiral my Lady) had a chyrurgeon. Now the manner of this country is, for those that have no chyrurgeon to agree with one, and give 18d, 20d, or 2s per man for the season to look after their men, which the masters pay in fish at the end of the summer. This surgeon of Mr Waymouth, named Edward Cutt, had been formerly in the country and knew the way better than I did. We two agreed to share profits and made a bargain with all the planters and the ships, and not only so, but went over to Firmoose, a harbour 4 little mile from that wherein we were. It happened there fished 7 Barnstaple men and no surgeon; with those we agreed at 2s per man, and to come over twice a week, Sundays and Wednesdays. If any great occasion, they were to send the men to us.

Every week I went over once, and my companion once. The walk was through the woods and two marshes. I used to leave a bottle of brandy hid behind a tree, which I would mark, and take a dram in my way. Sometimes I should get company, but usually had a dog and a gun, because of the wolves and bears (besides the foxes) wherewith this country abounds. I forbear to describe the harbours because the maps I shall draw of them will do that sufficient. The harbour we were in was very much esteemed for a good fishing place – the Barnstaple men prefer it above any – yet we had poor fishing and made not above 130 quintalls per boat, and £3 5s a share. At the head of this river are many salmon; we caught abundance and our master saved several hogsheads and dried abundance in the smoke. As soon as we resolve to fish here, the ship is all unrigged, and in the snow and cold all the men go into the woods to cut timber, fir, spruce, and birch, being here plentiful. With this they build stages, flakes, cookroom, and houses. The houses are made of a frythe of boughs, sealed inside with rinds, which look like planed deal,[2] and covered with the same, and turfs of earth upon, to keep the sun from raning them. The stages are begun on the edge of the shore, and built out into the sea, a floor of round timber, supported with posts, and shores of great timber. The boats lie at the head of them, as at a key, and throw up their fish, which is split, salted, &c. They throw away the heads and sound bones...

The complement of men to a boat are 5; that is 3 for to catch the fish, two to save it. Those 3 are the boat's master, midshipman, and foreshipman. The boat is 3 or 4 tons and will carry 1000 or 1200 cod, but these three men will row these great boats a long way. The boat's master rows at the stern, against the other two, who row one side; he belays against them, and so not only rows, but steers the boat. The boats' masters, generally, are able men, the midshipman next, and the foreshipmen are generally striplings. They bring the fish at the stage head, the foreshipman goes to boil their kettle, the other two throw up the fish on the stage-head by pears, that is, a staff with a prong of iron in him, which they stick in the fish and throw them up. Then a boy takes them and lays them on a table in the stage, on one side of which stands a header, who opens the belly, takes out the liver, and twines off the head and guts (which fall through the stage into the sea) with notable dexterity and suddenness. The liver runs through a hole in the table, into a coole or great tub, which is thrown into the train fatt. A train fatt is a great square chest the corners of which are frythed athwart; the liver is thrown into the middle, which melting, the train leaks through this fryth and is by tappe drawn out and put into cask. When the header has done his work, he thrusts the fish to the other side of the table, where sits a spilter, or splitter, who with a strong knife splits it abroad, and with a back stroke cuts off the bone, which falls through a hole into the sea. There are some that will split incredibly swift, 24 score in half an hour. When the fish is split, he falls into a drooge barrow, which, when full, is drawn to one side of the stage, where boys lay it one on top of another. The salter comes with salt on a wooden shovel and with a little brush strews the salt on it. When a pile is about 3 foot high they begin with another. A salter is a skilful officer, for too much salt burns the fish and makes it break, and wet, too little makes it redshanks, that is, look red when dried, and so is not merchantable.

The fish being salted, lies 3 or 4 days, sometimes (if bad weather) 8 or 10 days, and is then washed by the boys in salt or fresh water and laid in a pile skin upward on a platt of beach stones, which they call a horse. After a day or thereabout, it's laid abroad on flakes, that is, boughs thinly laid upon a frame, like that of a table, and here the fish dries. By night, or in wet weather, it's made up in faggots (as they call it), that is, 4 or 5 fishes with the skin upward, and a broad fish on top. When well dried, it's made up into prest pile, where it sweats; that is, the salt sweats out, and corning, makes the look white. After it's so done, it's dried one day on the ground and then put up in dry pile, as they call it, that is a pile bigger than the prest pile by 3 times. There it lies till shipt off, when it's dried part of a day, then weighed, carried on board, laid, and prest snug with great stones.

The men in these voyages have no wages but are paid after this manner: the owners have two thirds and the men one third; this one third is divided into so many shares as there are men in the ship. Now, tho some men have money above the share from the master, yet others have much less, so that I believe in our ship the master might have 9 shares clear, the mate 2 shares and 40d, spilters 1 share and 3 or 4 pounds, header 1 share 20d, salter 5 pounds, sometimes less, boat's master 1 share and 6 or 7 pounds, midshipman 1 share and twenty or 30 shillings, foreshipman 3 pounds, or half a share and ten shillings, boys, lurgens,[3] and such, 20d, 30d, or 40d.

The manner of paying the chyrurgeon is this: the owners give 5, 6, 7, or 9 pounds on the hand towards the chest, the master gives him a share, and every man half-a-crown, out of his share, besides which he has one hundred of poor Jack[4] from the whole. Mr Cock was very civil to me, and here I lived in the greatest content imaginable. I had much to do in my profession, yet leisure to study, to walk, to fish, and take pleasure. At the end of the season I went by boat to Cape Broyle, to Caplin bay,[5] to Feryland, and home. Here are beaver, otter, and deer plentiful; for fruits, strawberry, raspberries, whorts, and wild grapes incredible.

The diseases of this country are: breaking out of the arm wrests, colds and coughs, and the scurvy, of which they have two sorts, the one an acute scurvy, soon caught, soon cured, the other a cachexy, or dry scurvy, which makes the patient look thin, yellow, squalled, with pain and paresis of the limbs, and is often mortal. The other is an acute scurvy; their gums rot, thick-breathed, swollen, black, indurated hams and thighs, tumors of the legs, yielding to the touch, extravasation of the blood, a disease not curable by all the medicines which can be carried there, but easily by a few vegitives of the country. Viz. first purging with the roots of the Spatula foetida, or stinking gladwin, steept in water, which works violently both ways, then giving them the tops of spruce, wild vetches, agrimony, a sort of wild succory (called here scurvy leaves) steept in beer, and bathing them in decoctions of the same. Bleeding is found pernicious in that disease. The cause of this so common a malady is partly from the great mutation of the weather, which when we first come is very cold, and in July shall be intolerably hot, partly from the aqueous and crude nourishment, fish, and from sudden colds after the fatigues of labour, but mostly from the air, which is crude, foggy and scorbutick. The ground, being uncultivated, yields very ill vapors, being towards the sea most woody for 5 or 6 miles, but inward is ponds, marshes, rivers, mountains, and rocks. There will some mornings come down upon the rivers a foggy cloud, or vapor, which will burn and exulcerate like fire, and that mostly between Christmas and April...

In the midst of the season, men are apt to have vexatious hemorrhages of the nose, which they are sensible proceeds from eating much of the liver of the cods, which is here very delicious. ... Also, when the herrings come, (which is in June, the fairest, fattest, sweetest, and largest in the world) they surfeit on them, and then shall have vomitings and scouring, which I cured by a vomit, and at night a little diascordium and a drop of chymical oil of wormwood or mint.

In July, the muscetos (a little biting fly) and garnippers (a larger one) will much vex us. Sometimes the boys are so tired with labour they will steal off and hide under the flakes, or get into the woods and sleep 3 or 4 hours, so hearty that they feel not the muscetoes, who by the time he wakes shall have swoln him blind, and then he knows not to get out. I have seen them prodigiously swoln by them...

When the fishermen lade, or sometimes moor in the day, it's hard work for the shore men, so as they rest not above two hours in a night. Nor are the fishermen better to pass, who row hard and fish all day, and every second night take nets and drive to catch herrings for bait. They have divers kinds of bait. In the beginning of the year they use mussels, then come herrings and generally last all the year. The middle or end of June came the capling, a small sweet fish and the best bait, and when they come we have the best fishing, the cods pursuing them so eager that both have run ashore. I have seen capling so thick that one might dip them in maunds[6] on the shore. After the capling come the squids, a fish like soaked leather.

They catch them in nets or scaines, and sometimes by bobbing (as they call it), which is thus: they take a small cod and skin him, and hanging him a little under the water in the night, the squids will lug at it; then they pull it up softly and clap a cap-net under, and so secure them.

In the winter, the planters employ themselves in getting fish, sawing deal boards, making oars, catching beaver, and fowling. They have innumerable ducks, several geese, wild pigeons, partridge, hares, &c.

September the 14th, we left Renoose and sailed for England, where we arrived (without any memorable accident by the way) on Michaelmas day, at Plymouth.

NOTES

1 The first captain to establish himself in a harbour became admiral of that harbour for the season.

2 A 'firth' is a hedge, which the outside of these crude houses resembled. A 'deal' is a slice sawn from a log of timber.

3 the lowest type of helper

4 dried fish

5 Calvert, Southern Shore

6 a measure of capacity varying locally; around one gallon

THE 'WINTER WAR' OF 1696-7*

Jean Baudoin was born at Nantes, c 1662. He entered the priesthood in the Sulpician order in 1685, having abandoned the career of soldier. In 1687 he met in Paris the first two bishops of Quebec, Laval and Saint-Vallier, the former having just retired. The following year he arrived in Acadia. He went to France in 1694 but returned to North America in the spring of 1696 with Pierre Le Moyne d'Iberville. The Canadian-born d'Iberville (1661-c 1706), who has been called 'the most renowned son of New France,' had been charged by the government of France with attacking English settlements on the Atlantic seaboard of North America. In the case of Newfoundland, d'Iberville was to fulfil his mission admirably, despite his differences

* L'Abbé Jean Baudoin *Journal* trans. H. Bedford-Jones; in *The Daily News* St John's (March 1923). Reprinted by permission of *The Daily News*

with the governor of Placentia, Jacques-François de Mombeton de Brouillan. Abbé Baudoin accompanied d'Iberville on his mission of destruction and his journal affords an interesting insight into both his leader's military prowess and daring and the precarious state of settlement in Newfoundland.

The selection from that journal which follows is taken from a translation by H. Bedford-Jones.

NOVEMBER 10TH: We arrived at Ferryland, whither M. d'Iberville went ahead of us, taking ten men with him. This trip could easily be made in five days of good weather. It would have been as short for us to have gone straight to St John's. Provisions failing us through two days, we were glad to find a dozen horses which served us for food until that which we had on the *Profound* came up. The same evening came a longboat from Renews, where the *Profound* was anchored, awaiting some coureurs which M. du Brouillon had sent to St John's...

November 28th: In the morning Montigny[1] took the lead [from Bay Bulls] with 30 Canadians, marching five hundred paces ahead. M. du Brouillon and M. d'Iberville followed with the main body, which M. du Brouillon led, with orders to let the Canadians pass ahead of him in case of attack. After two and a half leagues of march, our vanguard discovered a pistol shot away, the enemy; they were well posted, 88 in number, in a burnt wood full of boulders, behind which they took cover. Our vanguard opened fire on the enemy, who believed this to be our full force. We were not far off, however, as the gentlemen soon discovered. After having received absolution, each man dropped his pack and attacked. M. du Brouillon attacked in the centre and d'Iberville threw himself on the left of the enemy as they hid behind the boulders and killed many of them. After half an hour's fighting they gave way. D'Iberville followed them sword in hand with a few of his men, fighting as far as St John's, about three-fourths of a league, where he arrived a good quarter of an hour ahead of the main body which M. du Brouillon led. D'Iberville entered St John's with the enemy. He seized the first two forts which the enemy abandoned, making 33 prisoners and some families. The others saved themselves in the large fort and in a ketch which was in the harbour. Terror was so great among them, brought by the eighty-eight, that if d'Iberville had had a hundred men with him he could have entered the large fort where, as he learned later from prisoners, there were 200 men poorly equipped. Du Brouillon came up with the main body. Demuid[2] camped with 60 men in the fort nearest that of the enemy. A cannon shot from that fort was a palisade. The main body camped in the houses. The wind being good the ketch made sail, laden with as much goods as possible, with eighty or a hundred men. The enemy lost 55 men; the trumpeter of M. du Brouillon was killed there and three others of his people wounded, and two of the Canadians. Du Brouillon did all that a brave man could. I was very near the fort, and know that those people certainly needed one or two campaigns to teach them how to take cover before an enemy.

The Canadians frightened them. These had heard for a long time of the terrible war with the Iroquois, in which, as in this one, it was better to be killed on the field than to be wounded or cut off from all aid. One could do little for the wounded unless it were possible to carry them away like the provisions, on one's back, in a country so rough as that of this island. We now sent a prisoner to summon the fort, which refused to yield.

November 30th, St Andrew's Day: A man left the fort with a white flag to parley. The commanders held an interview with the governor of the fort, who came with four of his chief settlers. He would not suffer any of us to enter the fort, being afraid to let us see the wretched state to which they were reduced. He insisted on deferring the surrender until the next day, hoping that two large ships which had been seen two days previously, standing two leagues to sea off the harbour, might have a favourable wind to enter; but we refused to give any delay. They concluded to surrender the fort the same day, on condition that we should give them two ships to take them to England, and that those who wished to go to Bonavista might do so; also that they should not be searched. This was granted...

St John's is a very fine harbour in which two hundred ships can shelter. The entry, the width of a scant musket shot, is between two very high hills with a battery of 8 guns on the right. The settlers, to the number of 58, were very well established along the north side of the harbour for the space of half a league. They had there 3 forts. That on the west side toward the forest, another in the midst, which also had a settler for governor who lived here with 16 men, and the third, which gave us the most trouble and later surrendered. This one defended the entrance of the harbour, which, though some way off, it commanded absolutely, as it also did a good share of the houses– the best in St John's being situated around the fort – which we unhappily burnt the night before the capitulation.

January 2nd: We burned about 80 sloops, holding out ten to take prisoners to Placentia. There are already nearly two hundred fishing sloops in this harbour. We have also quite demolished and burned St John's, so that there remain only some houses for our sick, whom it is impossible to carry away from here through the woods.

May 18th: This trip from Placentia to the enemy's shores by land seemed impossible to the men of Placentia, who before we came had so little troubled themselves that three English women, prisoners of M. de Brouillon, had all gone by land to Carbonear and Ferryland. If women could so save themselves, you may judge what could be done by men who were unguarded. In truth it would be difficult to do otherwise. I do not doubt that some might have perished in the woods, but without difficulty they could get through, and we were pretty sure that they would not find any boats, all the harbours being destroyed. In truth this journey did not appear difficult except to the French. I say to the shame of our nation that we were regarded as dead men when we started out in the autumn over the warnings of du Brouillon and Demuid, who assuredly did well to embark for Ferryland, not wishing to risk it with d'Iberville. I do not blame them in this, for they considered only rumours. The English did not regard it in the same manner. They knew perfectly the island by land, even that part which was French, for they guided us everywhere we went through the woods. Along the coast for more than 190 leagues they had broken trails going from one settlement to another by horseback, throughout their part of the land. Every autumn they go hunting to the deepest part of the forests, even to the gates of Placentia. It was within 8 or 10 leagues of here, along the bay, that the English came on a hunt last year; as they were dressed like French, they learned the news that 190 Canadians and Indians had come to make the winter war, which gave them alarm and made them go home instantly. We took some English who told us all this.

There are more than 200 English hunters who spend all winter in the woods, taking beaver, as well as deer and bear; in a word, all the wild beasts of the island. These hunters are excellent marksmen and trailers, according to the French settlers, who fear them, not being up to their standard. These could have done us much harm, had not God prevented them. They have no courage, except in hunting animals, for to tell the truth we had only to show ourselves to make them flee. I have never seen a better example of God's protection than in making one of us put a hundred to flight.

NOTES

1 one of d'Iberville's officers

2 another French officer

GOVERNMENT AND RELIGION (1762)*

Although the first attempt at systematic settlement was made in Newfoundland in the first decade of the seventeenth century, the representative institutions that were to typify the government of the other English-speaking North American colonies were not established there until 1832. Instead there evolved in Newfoundland a unique form of government by 'fishing admirals' and naval officers. It was a system of government that reflected the peculiar needs of a transatlantic industry.

THE FORM OF government in this island has never yet been established as in other colonies of the English. Here all differences among the fishermen in the several harbours are determined by the Admiral of the harbour, who is the commander of any ship that first arrives in these harbours; from his judgment an appeal lies to the Commodore of the King's ships stationed there, who determines in equity; and he is Governor in chief during his continuance there. Felonies are not triable in this island, but may be tried in any county in Great Britain. Subordinate to the commander in chief are the lieutenant-governors of Placentia and St John's, whose salaries are ten shillings per day; and in his and the Admiral of the harbour's absence, judgment in all cases, except felony, is given by the

* *Royal Magazine* VII (July 1762)

lieutenant-governor of Placentia and St John's, the one and the other being lord chancellors, and judge arbitrarily in all cases.

As no extraordinary care has been taken in establishing the civil government of this island, less has been of the ecclesiastical; seldom any clergymen settled, till the society for propagating the gospel in foreign parts, out of a tender regard to the deplorable state of the English inhabitants (many of whom had lost not only the name, but the notions of any religion) sent two missionaries to instruct them; those at present are the Rev. Mr Langman at St John's town, and the Rev. Mr Lindsay at Trinity Bay.

'HERE IS AN INNUIT' (1764)*

Jens Haven, the founder of the Moravian Church in Labrador, was born in Jutland in 1724. He came into contact with the Moravian Church when apprenticed to a carpenter of that faith in Copenhagen. In 1748 he went to Herrnhut in Saxony, the spiritual centre of the Moravian Church. In 1752 a Moravian attempt to make contact with the Labrador Eskimos ended in failure when several members of the expedition, including its leader, John Christian Ehrhardt, disappeared after having been invited ashore by an Eskimo party. Jens Haven was deeply stirred by these events. From 1758 to 1762 he worked in the Greenland missions of the Church and mastered the Eskimo language. In 1764 he realized an ambition to lead a new expedition to the Labrador Eskimos.

IN THE YEAR 1752, hearing, at Herrnhut, that Br Erhardt, a Missionary, sent to the coast of Labrador, had been murdered by the Esquimaux, I felt for the first time a strong impulse to go and preach the Gospel to this very nation, and became certain, in my own mind, that I should go to Labrador. I agreed with a Brother of the name of Jeppe Nielsen, that, as soon as there appeared the least probability of our going, we would offer ourselves for that purpose. Meanwhile, in the year 1758, I received a call to go to Greenland, which I cheerfully accepted, in reliance upon our Saviour. Before my departure, I had a confidential conversation with the late Count

* *Memoir of the Life of Br Jens Haven* (London [n.d.])

Zinzendorf,[1] in which I told him, that though I never felt a call to go to Greenland, but for these seven years past had earnestly desired to go to Labrador, yet I could consider this appointment as coming from the Lord, and would therefore go in His name, with a willing heart. I travelled in company of Br Matthew Stach, and my own brother, Peter Haven, by way of Copenhagen, and arrived safe at Lichtenfels. In the year following, I was remarkably happy in my situation, learnt the Greenland language, felt great love for the people, and began to believe that it was my destination to spend my days in this country. But I had scarcely formed the resolution to make myself easy and happy in this land, than I was alarmed by a remarkable dream: I thought I heard somebody say to me, 'This is not the place where you are to stay, for you shall preach the Gospel to a nation that has heard nothing of their Saviour.' I awoke, and being unwilling to quit this country, considered it as fancy and fell asleep again. But, to my surprise, I heard the same words repeated a second and a third time. On awaking, I wept exceedingly, and cried, 'Ah, Lord! what am I? I am unfit for Thy work; but if this be Thy will, Thou must Thyself prepare the way.' I was again assured of my call to Labrador, but felt quite resigned to the will of God as to time and circumstances. In the year 1762, I obtained leave to pay a visit in Europe, and arrived, in January 1763, in company of Br David Crantz, at Herrnhut, where I staid till 1764...

February 2nd, 1764, I was dismissed, with prayer and supplication, by the Bishops and Elders of the Church, and set out on foot for Holland, whence I arrived with much difficulty in London, not understanding the English language. After many fruitless attempts to attain the object proposed, I was at last recommended to the Governor of Newfoundland, Sir Hugh Palliser, who received me with great kindness, and even offered to carry me out on board his ship. This I declined, but begged for a recommendatory note to the Governor of St John's, which he willingly provided for me; and I now went with the first ship to St John's, where I lodged at the house of a merchant, who shewed me all possible civility. I worked here at my trade, and expected patiently the arrival of the Governor. Meanwhile many people, having heard of my intentions, came to see me, and several proposals were made to me, to establish myself and make my fortune in Newfoundland. As soon as the Governor arrived, he issued a proclamation concerning my voyage to the coast of Labrador, stating my views, and commanding that every assistance should be given me. In this proclamation it is said: 'Hitherto the Esquimaux have been considered in no other light than as thieves and murderers, but as Mr Haven had formed the laudable plan, not only of uniting these people with the English nation, but of instructing them in the Christian religion, I require, by virtue of the powers delegated to me, that all men, whomsoever it may concern, lend him all the assistance in their power,' &c. This proclamation was the foundation of all that liberty and protection which the Brethren have enjoyed ever since, under the British Government. Having soon found a ship bound to the north, I went on board, and proceeded with her to the north-coast, where, after many fruitless attempts to continue my voyage, I went on board an Irish fishing shallop, which was bound to the coast of Labrador. When we arrived on that coast, I saw the Esquimaux for the first time, rowing about in their kayaks, but none were permitted to approach us, being fired upon by our boat's crew. Having once landed, I found their huts, utensils, &c., made exactly in the Greenland fashion. But all my attempts to meet and converse with them were in vain; for it happened, that when I landed, not one Esquimaux appeared, and scarcely had I left the coast, when many arrived. The boat's crew, therefore, laughed at me, and the few who expressed sorrow at my disappointment advised me to return, refusing to lend me any further assistance: I was even told that a resolution was formed to kill all the Esquimaux. All this gave me the most pungent sorrow, and made me cry unto the Lord for help in this distressing situation, so heavy both for my mind and body. As I was once writing down my thoughts in my journal, the master entered my cabin, and seeing me in tears, asked me whether I was going to make a complaint to his owners. I answered 'No; but I mean to complain of you to God, that He may notice your wicked conduct on the present occasion, for you have taken His name in vain, and mocked His work,' &c. He was terrified, begged I would not do it, for he had offended God too much already, asked my pardon, and promised, that from henceforth he would do everything to promote my design. This he punctually performed, and brought me the next day to Quirpoint. Here some people had arrived, who intended to destroy the Esquimaux, and were holding a council for that purpose. I went boldly to them, shewed them the Governor's proclamation, found it difficult to divert them from their evil designs, but succeeded at last.

September 4th, 1764, was the joyful day when I saw an Esquimaux arrive in the harbour. I ran to meet him, and called to him in the most friendly manner, addressing him in the Greenland language, which, to my inexpressible joy, he understood. I desired he would return and bring four of the chiefs of his tribe, which he willingly complied with. Meanwhile I dressed in my Greenland habit, and met them on their arrival on the beach, inviting them to come on shore. They cried, 'Here is an *innuit*, (or countryman of ours).' I answered, 'I am your countryman and friend.' They were surprised at my address, behaved very quietly, and I continued my conversation with them for a long time. At last they desired me to accompany them to an island, about an hour's row from the shore, adding, that there I should find their wives and children, who would receive me as a friend. This seemed at first a most hazardous undertaking, but conceiving it to be of essential service to our Saviour's cause, that I should venture my life amongst them, and endeavour to become better acquainted with their nation, I turned simply to Him, and said, 'I will go with them in Thy name. If they kill me, my work on earth is done, and I shall live with Thee; but if they spare my life, I will firmly believe that it is Thy will that they should hear and believe Thy Gospel.' I went accordingly, and as soon as we arrived, there was a general shout, 'Our friend is come!' They carried me ashore, and I was immediately so closely beset on all sides, that I could neither stir nor turn about. I endeavoured to make them place themselves in rows before me, which being done, I told them my view in coming to visit them – to make them acquainted with their God and Saviour; and promised, that, if they were willing to be taught, I would return next year with more of my brethren, build a house on their land, and speak to them every day of the way of life and happiness. Having entered into much agreeable conversation with them, I returned in the same boat, and staid about a fortnight longer at Quirpont, where I had several opportunities of preaching to the boat's crew, being filled with joy and gratitude to God, who had thus mercifully heard my prayers and helped me.

After our return to St John's, which was attended with many hardships, I waited upon Sir Hugh Palliser, who received me with great kindness, and expressed his entire approbation of my proceedings. I returned to England in a frigate, and arrived, November 5th, with my Brethren in London. Here I entered into a negotiation with several gentlemen in office, relating to the proposed Mission on the coast of Labrador, and had several conferences with them, as also with Lord Hillsborough,[2] who made several advantageous offers for the promotion of that cause.

NOTES

1 Count Nikolaus Ludwig von Zinzendorf (1700-60), upon whose estate in Saxony Herrnhut was established

2 President of the Board of Trade and Foreign Plantations

AN ENGLISH VIEW OF IRISH SETTLERS (1765)*

Griffith Williams, a captain in the Royal Regiment of Artillery, spent fourteen years in Newfoundland as a lieutenant before becoming commander of his unit there. He was stationed in Newfoundland when he wrote this comment on the island.

AN IRISHMAN can't catch as much fish as a West Country or Newfoundland man, which is as true, as that a man who never had an oar in his hand, cannot row equal to a wherryman, who has been used to it all his life.

I have seen two boats along side of each other fishing, the one manned by People of West Country and Newfoundland, the other by Irish; the former has loaded in seven or eight hours, and the latter not able to load in the day; the former are people who were trained up in it from the time they were able to walk, the latter seldom or ever engage in it till they are above twenty years of age; therefore can never be able to arrive to the same degree of perfection as the other; for there is as much attention required in catching a cod, as there is in striking a salmon or trout with a fly.

Unfortunately for the government, as well as those concerned in the Newfoundland trade, soon after the Treaty of Aix la Chapelle,

* Griffith Williams *An Account of the Island of Newfoundland* (London 1765)

several of the forts were dismantled, and most part of the troops taken from the other garrisons, and sent to the continent of America. By this means the traders and inhabitants were left to shift for themselves without troops to support the magistrates in the execution of justice. At this time great numbers of Irish Roman Catholics were in the island as servants; but no sooner had the troops been sent away, than they became the most outrageous set of people that ever lived: robberies were committed almost every day in one place or other, the magistrates insulted in the execution of their office, and the Chief Justice murdered; many hundreds of the West of England people were afraid of going over, many of the Newfoundland men left the island, and the Roman Catholics transported themselves by hundreds from Ireland: so that at the time the French took the country, the Irish were above six times the number of the West Country and Newfoundlanders: in short, they were in possession of above three quarters of the fish rooms and harbours of the island, who consequently received the French with open arms. And during the time the French were in possession of the island, the merchants and inhabitants suffered more cruelties from the Irish Roman Catholics, than they did from the declared enemy.

The fisheries of Newfoundland were originally carried on by the ships only, and none allowed to fish but such as cleared out of some port in Great Britain: but, in time, those concerned in that trade found much greater advantage by fishing in boats along the shore; in consequence of which, they found it necessary for numbers to remain in the island during the winter, in order to build boats for the service of the ensuing season, as also to get materials out of the woods, for their fishing rooms, &c...

I am of opinion, that none but the inhabitants of Great Britian, Newfoundland, with Jersey and Guernsey (being Protestants), should have the privilege of being possessed of any fish rooms, or plantations in the island of Newfoundland. The Irish Roman Catholics are useful as servants, but very dangerous in that part of the world, when in power.

JOSEPH BANKS, SCIENTIST AND GENTLEMAN (1766)*

Joseph Banks was born in London on 13 February 1743. He was educated at Harrow, Eton, and Christ Church, Oxford, manifesting from an early age a keen interest in science. He was elected a fellow of the Royal Society in May 1766, the year of his visit to Newfoundland. One of the most distinguished travellers and scientists of his time, Banks became president of the Royal Society in 1778, a position he held until his death in 1820.

WE LANDED IN St Peter's Bay[1] where we found the wreck of a birch bark canoe, a sign probably that some of the inland Indians live not very far from thence though as yet we know nothing of them.

This subject leads me to say something (though I have as yet been able to learn very little about them) of the Indians that inhabit the interior parts of Newfoundland and are supposed to be the original inhabitants of that country. They are in general thought to be very few (as I have been told), not exceeding 500 in number; but why that should be imagined I cannot tell as we know nothing at all of the interior parts of the island nor ever had the least connection with them, though the French we are told had. The only part of the island that I have heard of their inhabiting is in the neighbourhood of Fogo, where they are said to be as near the coast as 4 miles. Our people who fish in those parts live in a continual state of warfare with them, firing at them whenever they meet with them; and if they chance to find their houses or wigwams (as they call them), plundering them immediately, though a bow and arrows and what they call their pudding is generally the whole of their furniture. They in return look upon us in exactly the same light as we do them, killing our people whenever they get the advantage of them and stealing or destroying their nets wheresoever they find them.

The pudding which I mentioned in the last paragraph is, our people say, always found in their huts; [it is] made of eggs and deer's hair to make it hang together (as we put hair into our mortar) and baked in the sun. Our people believe it to be part of their food – but

* A.M. Lysaght, ed. *Joseph Banks in Newfoundland and Labrador, 1766* (London: Faber 1971). Reprinted by permission of Faber & Faber Ltd

do not seem certain whether it is intended for that or any other use. They are said to fetch eggs for this composition as far as Funk or Penguin Island, ten leagues from the nearest land. They are extremely dextrous in the use of their bows and arrows and will, when pressed by an enemy, take four arrows (three between the fingers of their left hand with which they hold the bow and a fourth notched in the string) and discharge them as quick as they can draw the bow and with great certainty. Their canoes, by the gentleman's account from whom I have all this, are made like the Canadians', of birch bark sewed together with deer's sinews or some other material, but differ from the Canadians' essentially in that they are made to shut up by the sides, closing together for the convenient carriage of them through the woods, which they are obliged to do on account of the many lakes that abound all over the island.

Their method of scalping too is very different from the Canadian, they not being content with the hair but skinning the whole face at least as far as the upper lip. I have a scalp of this kind which was taken from one Sam Frye, a fisherman, whom they shot in the water as he attempted to swim off to his ship from them. They kept this scalp a year, but the features were so well preserved that ... upon a party of them being pursued the next summer they dropped it. It was immediately known to be the scalp of the identical Sam Frye who was killed the year before.

So much for the Indians. If half of what I have wrote about them is true, it is more than I expect; though I have not the least reason to think but that the man who told it to me believed it and had heard it all from his own people and those of the neighbouring planters and fishermen.

After this short stay at Croque, intended only for filling water and getting on board the produce of the gardens and poultry, we sailed for St John's on the 10th [of October] and arrived there on the 13th without any particular transaction during our passage. Here we found the greater part of the squadron under the command of Mr Palliser in the *Guernsey*, whose civilities we ought to acknowledge as he showed us all we could expect. We all felt great pleasure in returning to society which we had so long been deprived of. St John's, though the most disagreeable town I ever met with, was for some time perfectly agreeable to us. I should not omit to mention the ceremonies with which we celebrated the Coronation, which happened whilst we were there. The *Guernsey* was dressed upon the occasion, and if I may compare great things with small, looked like a pedlar's basket at a horse race where ribbons of divers colours fly in the wind fastened to yard wands stuck around it. After this we were all invited to a ball given by Mr Governor, where the want of ladies was so great that my washerwoman and her sister were there by formal invitation; but what surprised me the most was that after dancing we were conducted to a really elegant supper, set out with all kinds of wines and Italian liqueurs, to the great emolument of the ladies who ate and drank to some purpose. Dancing, it seems, agreed with them by its getting them such excellent stomachs.

It is very difficult to compare one town with another, though that probably is the best way of conveying the idea. St John's, however, cannot be compared to any I have seen. It is built upon the side of a hill facing the harbour, containing two or three hundred houses and near as many fish flakes interspersed, which in summer time must cause a stench scarce to be supported. Thank heaven we were only there spring and fall, before the fish were come to the ground and after they were gone off. For dirt and filth of all kinds St John's may, in my opinion, reign unrivalled, as it far exceeds any fishing town I ever saw in England. Here is no regular street, the houses being built in rows immediately adjoining to the flakes; consequently no pavement. Offals of fish of all kinds are strewn about, the remains of the Irish men's chowder whom you see making it, skinning and gutting fish in every corner.

The dish ... called chowder, which I believe is peculiar to this country ... is the chief food of the poorer and, when well made, a luxury that the rich even in England, at least in my opinion, might be fond of. It is a soup made with a small quantity of salt pork cut into small slices, a good deal of fish, and biscuit, boiled for about an hour. Unlikely as this mixture appears to be palatable, I have scarce met with anybody in this country who is not fond of it. Whatever it may be in England, here it is certainly the best method of dressing the cod, which is not near so firm here as in London. Whether or not that is owing to the art of the fishmongers, I cannot pretend to say.

As everything here smells of fish, so you cannot get anything that does not taste of it. Hogs can scarce be kept from it by any care, and when they have got it are by far the filthiest meat I ever met with. Poultry of all kinds, ducks, geese, fowls, and turkeys [are] infinitely more fishy than the worst tame duck that ever was sold for a wild one in Lincolnshire. The very cows eat the fish offal, and thus milk is fishy. This last particular indeed I have not met with myself but have been assured it is often the case.

On a little hill just at the entrance of the town, a fort is situated, defended by a ditch and pallisades. It seems to be as indefensible a building as ever was called by that name, being commanded by heights immediately above it. It was taken last war by the French, who strengthened [it] as much as they could by outworks of picketing: but not withstanding all they could do was retaken in a very small time by Colonel Amherst. While we were there I went up on the hills on purpose to see the progress of his attack, which was extremely spirited, the French heaving possession not only of the heights, which there was an absolute necessity of his gaining, but of a situation which greatly molested the landing of his cannon. From the first he immediately dislodged them, fording the river; soon after he attacked them in their heights and drove them from thence also, without any material loss. Tis difficult for any but those who are acquainted with the country to conceive the advantages of their situation, which was on the tops of hills almost perpendicular, the ascent of which was thick grown with shrubs. Here they kept their fire till our people were within a few yards of them, but immediately on our people's returning it, quitted their ground. Scarce any of our wounded recovered, being torn not only with the shot but by the explosion of the piece fired almost at their breasts. This advantage being gained, they retired to the fort, where they capitulated as soon as our cannon were brought up.

It is remarkable that during the whole attack our people did not receive the least intelligence from the people of St John's nor countenance, not even seeing one of them till they were marching down to take possession of the fort; that and the behaviour of the Irish and fishermen, who almost one and all joined the French as soon as ever they saw them, give a pretty good idea of the loyalty of the inhabitants.

NOTE

1 On the east coast of Labrador

'TOO MANY HOUSES, TOO MUCH SMOKE, TOO MANY PEOPLE' (1772-3)*

George Cartwright (1740-1819) was born in Nottinghamshire. Between 1770 and 1786, having abandoned a military career, he made six voyages to Labrador. There he lived the life of hunter, trapper, and fisherman. In 1772, at the end of his first voyage, Cartwright took a group of five Eskimos (referred to sometimes by him as 'Indians') back with him to London. They were: a man named Attuiock, his youngest wife Ickcongoque, Ickcongoque's four-year-old daughter Ickeuma, Attuiock's youngest brother Tooklavinia, and Tooklavinia's wife Caubvick. The following extract describes their encounter with European civilization.

ON LANDING AT Westminster Bridge, we were immediately surrounded by a great concourse of people; attracted not only by the uncommon appearance of the Indians who were in their seal-skin dresses, but also by a beautiful eagle, and an Esquimau dog; which had much the resemblance of a wolf, and a remarkable wildness of look. I put them all into coaches with as much expedition as possible, and drove off to the lodgings which I had prepared in Leicester Street.

In a few days time, I had so many applications for admittance to see the new visitors, that my time was wholly taken up in gratifying the curiosity of my friends and their acquaintance; and the numbers who came made my lodgings very inconvenient to the landlord as well as to myself. I therefore resolved to look out for a house. I soon hired a small one, ready furnished, for ten guineas a month, in Little Castle Street, Oxford Market, and removed thither...

I once took the men to the opera when their Majesties were there, and we chanced to sit near Mr Coleman, the manager of Covent Garden Theatre, who politely invited all the Indians and myself to a play at his house. He fixed on *Cymbeline,* and they were greatly delighted with the representation. But their pride was most highly gratified, at being received with a thundering applause by the audience, on entering the box. The men soon observed to their wives, that they were placed in the King's box, and received in the same

* George Cartwright *Journal* 3 vols (Newark 1792)

manner as their Majesties were at the opera; which added considerably to the pleasure which they felt from the *tout ensemble.* Never did I observe so young a child pay such unremitting attention to the whole representation, as little Ickeuna: no sooner did the swords begin to clash, in the fighting scene between Posthumus and Iachimo, but she set up a most feeling scream.

About a fortnight after our arrival in town, having provided great-coats, boots, and hats for the men, in order that they might pass through the streets unobserved, I took Attuiock with me and walked beyond the Tower. We there took boat, rowed up the river, and landed at Westminster Bridge; from whence we walked to Hyde Park Corner, and then home again. I was in great expectation, that he would begin to relate the wonders which he had seen, the instant he entered the room; but I found myself greatly disappointed. He immediately sat down by the fire side, placed both his hands on his knees, leaned his head forward, fixed his eyes on the ground in a stupid stare; and continued in that posture for a considerable time. At length, tossing up his head, and fixing his eyes on the ceiling, he broke out in the following soliloquy: 'Oh! I am tired; here are too many houses; too much smoke; too many people; Labrador is very good; seals are plentiful there; I wish I was back again.' By which I could plainly perceive, that the multiplicity, and variety of objects had confounded his ideas; which were too much confined to comprehend any thing but the inconveniencies that he had met with. And indeed, the longer they continued in England, the more was I convinced of the truth of that opinion; for their admiration increased in proportion, as their ideas expanded; till at length they began more clearly to comprehend the use, beauty, and mechanism of what they saw; though the greater part of these were as totally lost upon them, as they would have been upon one of the brute creation.

Although they had often passed St Paul's without betraying any great astonishment, or at least not so much as all Europeans do at the first sight of one of those stupendous islands of ice, which are daily to be seen near the east coast of their own country, yet when I took them to the top of it, and convinced them that it was built by the hands of men (a circumstance which had not entered their heads before, for they had supposed it a natural production) they were quite lost in amazement. The people below, they compared to mice;

and insisted, that it must at least be as high as Cape Charles, which is a mountain of considerable altitude. Upon my asking them how they should describe it to their countrymen on their return, they replied, with a look of the utmost expression, they should neither mention it, nor many other things which they had seen, lest they should be called liars, from the seeming impossibility of such astonishing facts.

I continued in London till the month of February; at which time I took the Indians with me to my father's house at Marnham in Nottinghamshire, where we stayed six weeks. ... I soon found the country agreed much better with their inclinations, as well as their health, than London. Here they could enjoy fresh air and exercise, without being distressed by crowds of people gathering round them whenever they stirred out; which was always the case in town. The women, according to the universal disposition of the fair sex, enjoyed visiting and dancing; and I must say, that Caubvick attained to great perfection in that graceful accomplishment, during her short stay. ... The face of the country did not pass unobserved by them, and their expression was 'The land is all made'; for they supposed that we had cut down the woods, and levelled the hills. In the former supposition they were certainly right: and I do not wonder at the latter, since they would naturally suppose that all the world was like the small part of it which they had formerly seen; and which is almost an entire collection of hills covered with thick woods. As they had never before seen any cultivated land (except a few small gardens, which they observed were dug with a spade) they formed an idea of our immense numbers, by being able to till so much land and consume the produce of it in a year; exclusive of the animal food with which they saw our tables and markets abounded. How the inhabitants of London were supplied with food, I could never make them fully comprehend, any more than I could the number of people by which the metropolis was inhabited. Their arithmetic goes no higher than the number twenty-one; therefore, the best I could do, was to tell them, that a certain number of large whales would serve them for one meal only. Nothing surprized them more, than to meet with a man who assured them he could not shoot, had never killed an animal, nor seen the sea in his life.

After my return to town, by his Majesty's permission, I took them to Court; where their dresses and behaviour made them greatly taken notice of. They were also at the houses of several of the nobility and people of fashion; and I omitted nothing, which came within the compass of my pocket, to make their stay in England agreeable, or to impress them with ideas of our riches and strength. The latter I thought highly necessary, as they had often, when in Labrador, spoken of our numbers with great contempt, and told me they were so numerous, that they could cut off all the English with great ease, if they thought proper to collect themselves together; an opinion which could not fail to produce in me very unpleasant reflections. But they had not been long in London before they confessed to me, that the Esquimaux were but as one, compared to that of the English...

Having now [8 May 1773] completed all my business in town, and the wind being fair, at two o'clock this afternoon we made sail down the river; the Esquimaux well pleased in the expectation of soon seeing their native country, their relations and friends again; and I very happy in the prospect of carrying them back, apparently in perfect health.

We passed through the Downs this evening [11 May], when I discharged the pilot, and went to sea.

The pleasing prospects which I so lately had before me were of very short duration; for this evening as Caubvick was going to bed, she complained of great sickness at her stomach, had a very bad night, and daily grew worse. On my arrival at Lymmington on the thirteenth, and consulting a surgeon there, (for my own, I found, was utterly ignorant of her complaint) he declared her malady to be the small-pox: which had nearly the same effect on me, as if he had pronounced my sentence of death. As it was in vain to expect that the rest should escape the infection, medicines were immediately given to prepare them for it; and I thought it a fortunate circumstance, that an opportunity offered for doing it...

On the twenty-second Caubvick turned the height, and did not appear to be in the least danger. At the same time Ickcongoque began to complain. We sailed for Ireland on the twenty-eighth, but the wind taking us ahead when we got off the Bill of Portland, we put back and anchored in Portland Road. Tooklavinia now was taken ill.

At two o'clock in the morning of the twenty-ninth we weighed again, and proceeded down the Channel with a fair wind and pleasant weather; still in hopes of arriving in sufficient time for my business; but at ten o'clock, so dreadful a stench pervaded the whole vessel, all the Indians being now ill, that three of the ship's crew now were seized with a fever, and we had reason to expect, that a pestilential disorder would soon attack us all. I therefore ordered captain Monday to carry the vessel into Plymouth, although I foresaw that measure would prove an immense loss to me, by the ruin of my voyage, and we came to an anchor in Catwater the next afternoon at two o'clock. I went on shore immediately, and made a personal application to Earl Cornwallis, Admiral Spry, and the Mayor of Plymouth, for a house to put the Indians in, but could not succeed.

Ickeuna died this morning [31 May], Caubvick had a violent fever on her, and the rest were extremely ill. In the evening I bargained for a house at Stonehouse, for two guineas and a half per week. At four o'clock the next morning we weighed and removed the vessel to Stonehouse Pool, I got the Indians on shore immediately, and Ickcongoque died that night.

On the second I engaged Dr Farr, the physician to the Naval Hospital, and Mr Monier, an apothecary of Plymouth, to attend the Indians; and, by the doctor's directions, I removed the two men into separate tents, which I had pitched in an adjoining close. In the evening I went to Plymouth, in order to set off for London, which I did the next morning at six o'clock, and arrived there at two in the afternoon of the fifth...

I left London on my return to Plymouth at six o'clock this morning [10 June], and arrived at Stonehouse on Saturday evening. I was now informed that both the men died in the night of the third Instant, and that Caubvick had been given over, but was at length in a fair way of recovery, though reduced to a skeleton, and troubled with a great many large boils. She recovered so very slowly, that it was not until the fourth of July that I durst venture to remove her, when I once more embarked with her and all the rest of my family (except my maid whom I had discharged for bad behaviour) to proceed on my intended voyage.

We sailed from Plymouth early in the morning of the fifth, but meeting with contrary winds we had a tedious passage to Waterford, for we did not arrive there till the afternoon of the tenth. It was some consolation, however, to be favoured with fine weather, and to catch great plenty of mackarel every day.

My time was taken up till the sixteenth, in purchasing and getting on board such provisions as I had occasion for; I also hired another woman-servant, and on that day I sailed for Labrador...

Caubvick's hair falling off, and being matted with the small-pox, I had much difficulty to prevail on her to permit me to cut it off, and shave her head. Notwithstanding I assured her that the smell of the hair would communicate the infection to the rest of her country folks on her return, yet I was not able to prevail on her to consent to its being thrown overboard. She angrily snatched it from me, locked it up in one of her trunks, and never would permit me to get sight of it afterwards; flying into a violent passion of anger and grief whenever I mentioned the subject, which I did almost every day, in hopes of succeeding at last.

This evening [27 August] at sun-set we got sight of the land, and judged ourselves to be nine or ten leagues from it; the next morning at day-light we found ourselves about three leagues from Cape St Francis, and at eight o'clock at night came to an anchor in Charles Harbour...

About noon [31 August] almost the whole of the three southernmost tribes of Esquimaux, amounting to five hundred souls or thereabouts, arrived from Chateau in twenty-two old English and French boats (having heard of my arrival from some boats belonging to that port, which returned from this neighbourhood in the night of Saturday last) but the wind did not suit them to come hither till this morning.

I placed myself upon a rock near the water-side, and Caubvick sat down a few paces behind me. We waited for the landing of the Indians with feelings very different from their's; who were hurrying along with tumultuous joy at the thoughts of immediately meeting their relations and friends again. As the shore would not permit them to land out of their boats, they brought them to their anchors at a distance off, and the men came in their kayacks, each bringing two other persons, lying flat on their faces; one behind the other before, on the top of the skin covering. On drawing near the shore, and perceiving only Caubvick and myself, their joy abated, and their countenances assumed a different aspect. Being landed, they fixed their eyes on Caubvick and me, in profound, gloomy silence. At length, with great perturbation and in faltering accents, they enquired, separately, what was become of the rest; and were no sooner given to understand, by a silent, sorrowful shake of my head, that they were no more, than they instantly set up such a yell, as I had never before heard. Many of them, but particularly the women, snatched up stones, and beat themselves on the head and face till they became shocking spectacles; one pretty young girl (a sister to the late two men) gave herself so severe a blow upon the cheek-bone, that she bruised and cut the flesh shockingly, and almost beat an eye out. In short, the violent frantic expressions of grief were such, as far exceeded my imagination; and I could not help participating with them so far, as to shed tears most plentifully. They no sooner observed my emotion, than mistaking it for the apprehensions which I was under for fear of their resentment, they instantly seemed to forget their own feelings, to relieve those of mine. They pressed round me, clasped my hands, and said and did all in their power to convince me, that they did not entertain any suspicion of my conduct towards their departed friends. As soon as the first violent transports of grief began to subside, I related the melancholy tale, and explained to them, as well as I could, the disorder by which they were carried off; and pointed to Caubvick, who bore very strong, as well as recent, marks of it. They often looked very attentively at her, but, during the whole time, they never spoke one word to her, nor she to them. As soon as I had brought the afflicting story to a conclusion, they assured me of their belief of every particular, and renewed their declarations of friendship. Their stay afterwards was but short; they presently reimbarked, weighted their anchors, and ran across the harbour to Raft Tickle, where they landed and encamped: the rest of the afternoon and the whole of the night was spent in horrid yellings, which were considerably augmented by the variety of echoes, produced from the multiplicity of hills surrounding the harbour, till the whole rang again with sounds that almost petrified the blood of the brig's crew and my new servants.

'A PRECIOUS PEOPLE' (1776)*

In 1755 the Irishman Lawrence Coughlan, having converted to Methodism, became an itinerant preacher, first among the Irish and later in England. He is mentioned favourably in Wesley's *Journal* on 29 December 1758. He broke with Wesley before coming to Newfoundland in 1765 but neither the reason for their disagreement nor the motive for Coughlan's departure for the New World are fully understood. In 1766 Coughlan presented a petition from the residents of Harbour Grace, Conception Bay, to the general meeting of the Society for the Propagation of the Gospel in London, asking that he be made the Society's minister in Harbour Grace and given a stipend. This request was granted. After a stormy Newfoundland career, he returned to England in 1773.

AS RELIGION IS an offence the world will never forgive, a report soon spread over the bay, and great part of the land, that the people at Harbour-Grace and Carbonear were going mad; this was taken for granted; but out of this seeming evil, God brought forth good; *All Things work together for God, to them that love God, to them that are the Called according to his Purpose.* The report of the madness brought many from various quarters to hear for themselves; and when they heard, many of them were like the *Bereans, they searched the Scriptures,* and found what they heard to be agreeable thereto. Some came fifteen, some twenty miles, to hear the Word: I have known some come, with their dear infants in their arms, over mountains of snow, at the hazard of their lives; *so mightily did the Word of God prevail.*

I now had invitations from various quarters, which I attended to, when the weather permitted, as a great part of our travelling was by water, in little skiffs, not much larger than the small boats upon the River Thames, in London. The power of God attended the Word wherever I came: I could clearly see, it was *the Day of God's Power.*

But as my consolations now abounded, so did also my sufferings; I had such dreadful apprehensions of the sea, when going in such very small boats, that my life was one continued martyrdom; I had

* Lawrence Coughlan *An Account of the Work of God in Newfoundland* (London 1776)

little rest day or night. The work spread more and more; where Sabbath-breaking, playing, and many other vices had before abounded, the employment was now prayer, and singing of hymns. At this time, my health was greatly impaired, hard labour, and in general salt provisions, were what flesh and blood could not put up with; yet God gave strength proportionable to my day.

The winters in Newfoundland are very severe, there being great falls of snow, and hard frost; the houses there are mostly very disagreeable to those who are not used to them; in general, they are all wood; the walls, so called, are studs put into the ground close together, and between each, they stop moss, as they call it, to keep out the snow; this they cover with bark of trees, and put great clods over that; some are covered with boards: in such houses I have been, and in the morning my bedside has had a beautiful white covering of snow; my shoes have been so hard frozen, that I could not well put them on, till brought to the fire: but under all this, I was supported, feeling a glorious work going on.

Now, as *God opened the blind Eyes,* the people in remote parts, where I came, saw the need of forming themselves together, in order to read the Word of God, and to spend some time in singing and prayer, agreeable to the Scriptures: *They that feared the Lord spake often one to another.*

The Bay being very extensive, one church would not do; so that we soon had three churches. A proof of the great zeal, which filled those dear souls in one part of the Bay, called Black-Head, upon the North Shore, was this: they proposed to me, to point out a place where I would choose to build a church, which was agreed upon; accordingly all hands went into the wood, and cut down as much of it as they wanted, which they hauled out upon what they call slides. When they had the timber upon the place, they sent for me, and I went, thinking there was not one stick hewn; however they had made great progress in the work; the people there in general are very good hatchet men (there are very few carpenters in Europe, who are able to hew a piece of timber with those in Newfoundland, this they take up naturally) they are people of a very bright genius: I have known a man, who could not read a letter in a book, go into the wood, and cut down timber, bring the same out with the help of a servant, and build a boat, rig it, and afterwards go to sea with the same boat. But to return; the said church was framed, and covered in, in less than fourteen days, which contained about four hundred people. God raised up here a precious people; some, I doubt not, are from this place gone to Glory; and I trust there are a few to this day, that continue stedfast, and will be my crown of rejoicing in the Great Day.

Having preached in the new church at Black-Head sometimes, as I could come here but seldom, it being a very wild shore, I appointed them to meet together, and read the church service; and afterwards to read a sermon, which I furnished them with: this they continued to do, and when the weather permitted them, they would come to Harbour-Grace, and Carbonear, notwithstanding it was near eighteen miles by water. I have known them often come over the mighty waters at the hazard of their lives, with their little babes in their arms; but what will not precious souls, who have the love of God shed abroad in their hearts, go through for a dear Redeemer: God did great things, in a short time, in these parts.

A METHODIST MISSIONARY IN TRINITY BAY (1774-84)*

John Hoskins and his fifteen-year-old son arrived in Newfoundland in 1774. His missionary career there illustrates the conflict and conviction that characterized the early history of Methodism on the island. The account which follows is drawn from two letters by Hoskins, one written in 1781 to John Wesley, the other in 1784 to another correspondent in England.

IN 1746, I first heard the Methodists at Bristol. The word fell on my soul as dew on the tender herb. I received it with joy, and soon joined the Society. In about three weeks I received a clear sense of forgiveness; but soon fell into reasoning and doubting. Sometimes I was in heaviness through manifold temptations; and it was near ten years before I had the abiding Witness. Oh, how slow of heart to believe! and how unwilling to give up all to God!

After a passage of five weeks I arrived at Trinity, in Newfoundland. I saw myself indeed a poor pilgrim on the earth, having no money; nor did I know one person in the place. As I was walking

* *Arminian Magazine* VIII (1785)

about on the shore, seeing a few low, mean houses, or rather huts, built with wood; and a rocky, desolate country: and meditating on the destruction which sin hath made in the world, I rejoiced exceedingly, that I was under the care and protection of an almighty and all-gracious God. Going by one of these houses, I heard a child cry; and thought, as there was a family, there might be some person with whom I might advise how to get into business: yet I was afraid, as I had been on board a ship with a crew of English, cursing, swearing, savages, lest I should meet with the like people in this barren and uncultivated country. However I knocked at the door; when a woman, the mother of the family came out, and asked me and my son (a lad about sixteen who was with me) to come in. She gave us some seal and bread to eat, and some coffee to drink, the best the house afforded. She then directed me to several places, where she thought I might get business. The minister of the place advised me to keep a school at Old Perlican, a place seven leagues from thence, across the Bay. Accordingly I went in a boat to Old Perlican. The people received me, and were glad of one to teach their children; there being about fifty families in the place. They likewise desired I would read prayers, and a sermon to them on Sundays: there being no manner of public worship before; neither Sundays nor week-days.

I accepted the call, as from God, knowing it was my duty to do all the good I could, to the souls as well as bodies of my fellow-creatures. Accordingly I read the church prayers, and some of your sermons, and sung your hymns, by myself alone, for many weeks. For my congregation did not know how to behave in divine service; no not even to kneel in prayer, or to sing at all: but would stand at a distance and look at me, as if I had been a monster: and yet they called themselves members of the Church of England...

About the middle of August 1780, I went over to Trinity with an intent to preach there. And though many were willing to hear, they were afraid to let me have a house to preach in. However, I went to several of their houses, and conversed about the ways of God, and gave them some books. After staying three or four days, I went to one of the merchants, to ask him to let me go in one of his boats that was going to Perlican. I was informed by his clerk that he was on board one of his ships in the harbour. I went on board in order to speak to him. Presently one of the sailors came to me and said, 'Will you preach us a sermon?' The next salutation was, a dab in my face with the tar-brush, full of tar. Then one or two of them held me behind, while two or three more daubed me, almost all over with tar: the rest looking on: the merchant and captain were below in the cabin at the same time. I heard afterwards that the merchant said, if they had asked him, he would have given them feathers to have feathered me all over.

When they loosed me, I got into the boat that carried me on board, in order to go on shore, when they threw a piece of wood after me: but did me no hurt, being guided by an unseen hand. They then cursed me, and said, 'You will preach that people will be damned, will you? When we see you on shore we will make an end of you.' All that I said to them, from first to last, was, 'What harm have I done to any one of you?' To which they made me no answer. The merchant and captain being asked about it, were ashamed; and said, if they had known, I should not have been used so.

The next day some of the sailors went about looking for me: one of them went with a knotted rope in his hand, to beat me, or any of the converts (as they call the people) that he could find. As I was walking about, looking for a boat, not knowing their design, I went by him with the knotted rope; but he was asleep on the ground. When he awoke, he went in quest of some of the converts; and coming where some men were standing, one pointed to a poor man, signifying he was one of them. On this the sailor took hold of him, and beat him in a terrible manner. The poor man prayed him not to beat him so: assuring him, he was no convert, neither came from Perlican; but from English Harbour, (a fishery about three leagues from Trinity.) As for me, all the boats in the harbour were forbid to take me in; however, one from Perlican came by stealth, and took me away...

God has cleared my way before me in a wonderful manner, since I have been in this land: particularly of late, by an awful judgment which he sent upon the three men who abused me on board a ship, in Trinity-Harbour, about five years ago. In a former account of this affair I observed that two of the sailors held me, while a third tarred me almost all over; and told me, if they saw me on shore the next day they would kill me.

In about a month one of them fell overboard, and was drowned in the harbour of St John. Another of them coming to England the same winter, was killed by a fall. And he that tarred me, going up the Streights, by an accident got his death's-wound, and died on board the ship in great agonies of soul, on account of his abusing me. The whole ship's company was greatly alarmed on the occasion. The captain said, he very clearly saw me stand by one of the sailors as he was furling the top gallant, while he who tarred me was below in the agonies of death, calling for mercy! This took such an affect on the captain, that, when he returned to Newfoundland, he declared to the merchants in Trinity, that he would not abuse such a man as Mr Hoskins, or any other preacher of the gospel, for all the world. He also said, he could live no longer amongst such wickedness as he was then a witness of. Accordingly he left the service immediately, and went home to England to live a retired life.

The report of the affair has well nigh spread all over this island: so that the merchants (the chief men of the island) that before threatened to send me out of the country, now will not hurt or molest me; but rather give me a passage in their boats to any harbour where I am going to preach. I have therefore now no excuse to decline labouring for God. Notwithstanding this, I find great backwardness. My flesh is ready to shrink from suffering. Lord help me to take up my cross, and follow thee!

DAVID BUCHAN'S EXPEDITION TO THE INTERIOR (1811)*

David Buchan (1780-1838) was a lieutenant in the Royal Navy when, in 1811, he was sent into the interior of Newfoundland to make friendly contact with the Beothuck Indians. His mission was one manifestation of a new humanitarian interest in the Beothucks.

WE SAW BEFORE us an immense lake[1] extending nearly in a NE and SW direction, its surface a smooth sheet of ice. We saw tracks but could not be certain whether of deer or men. ... On approaching the pond or lake we discovered on its NW side two bodies in motion, but were uncertain if men or quadrupeds, it being nearly three o'clock. I drew the party suddenly into the wood to prevent discovery, and directed them to prepare a place for the night, I went on to

* James P. Howley *The Beothucks or Red Indians* (Cambridge: University Press 1915)

reconnoitre. Having skirted along the woods for nearly two miles, we posted ourselves in a position to observe their motions; one gained ground considerably on the other: we continued in doubt of their being men until just before losing sight of them in the twilight, it was discernible that the hindermost dragged a sledge. Nothing more could be done until morning; as it would have been impossible to have found their track in the dark; observing, on our return, a shovel in a bank of snow, we found that venison had been dug out; we however, found a fine heart and liver; this made a good supper for the party, whom we did not rejoin till dark. One-third of the party were successively under arms during the night which proved excessively cold and restless to all.

Jan. 24th: Wind NE and intensely cold. Having refreshed ourselves with breakfast and a dram to each, at 4 AM commenced our march along the east shore with the utmost silence; beyond the point from whence I had the last view of the two natives, we fell in with a quantity of venison, in carcases and quarters, close to which was a path into the wood. Conjecturing that the Indians' habitations were here, we advanced in, but found it to be an old one; the party complained much of the cold, and occasionally sheltered themselves under the lee of the points. It at length became necessary to cross the pond in order to gain the track of their sledge; this exposed us entirely to the bitterness of the morning; all complained of excessive cold. With the first glimpse of morn, we reached the wished-for track; this led us along the western shore to the NE, up to a point, on which stood an old wigwam; then [we] struck athwart for the shore we had left. As the day opened it was requisite to push forth with celerity to prevent being seen, and to surprise the natives whilst asleep. Canoes were soon descried, and shortly wigwams two close to each other, and the third a hundred yards from the former. Having examined the arms, [I] charged my men to be prompt in executing such orders as might be given, at the same time strictly charging them to avoid every impropriety, and to be especially guarded in their behaviour towards women. The bank was now ascended with great alacrity and silence; the party being formed into three divisions, the wigwams were at once secured. On calling to the people within, and receiving no answer, the skins which covered the entrance were then removed, and we beheld groups of men, women and children lying in the utmost consternation; they remained absolutely for some minutes without motion or utterance. My first object was now to remove their fears, and inspire confidence in us, which was soon accomplished by our shaking hands, and showing every friendly disposition. The woman embraced me for my attentions to their children; from the utmost state of alarm they soon became curious, and examined our dress with great attention and surprise. They kindled a fire and presented us with venison steaks, and fat run into a solid cake, which they used with lean meat. Everything promised the utmost cordiality; knives, handkerchiefs, and other little articles were presented to them, and in return they offered us skins; I had to regret our utter ignorance of their language, and the presents at a distance of at least twelve miles occasioned me much embarrassment; I used every endeavour to make them understand my great desire that some of them should accompany us, to the place where our baggage was, and assist bringing up such things as we wore, which at last they seemed perfectly to comprehend. Three hours and a half having been employed in conciliatory endeavours, and every appearance of the greatest amity subsisting between us; and considering a longer tarry useless, without the means of convincing them farther of our friendship, giving them to understand that we were going, and indicating our intention to return, four of them signified that they would accompany us. James Butler, corporal, and Thomas Bouthland, private of marines, observing this, requested to be left behind in order to repair their snow shoes; and such was the confidence placed by my people in the natives that most of the party wished to be the individuals to remain among them. I was induced to comply with the first request from a motive of showing the natives a mutual confidence, and cautioning them to observe the utmost regularity of conduct, at 10 AM, having myself again shook hands with all the natives, and expressed, in the best way I could, my intentions to be with them in the morning, we set out. They expressed satisfaction by signs on seeing that two of us were going to remain with them, and we left accompanied by four of them.

On reaching the river head, two of the Indians struck into our last night's fire place. One of these I considered to be their chief; finding nothing there for him, he directed two of them to continue on with us; these went with cheerfulness, though at times they seemed to mistrust us. Parts of the river having no ice, it was difficult to get along the banks, occasioning at times a considerable distance between me and the hindermost Indian. Being under the necessity of going single, in turning a point one of the Indians having loitered behind, took the opportunity, and set off with great speed calling out to his comrade to follow. Previous precautions prevented his being fired at. This incident was truly unfortunate as we were nearly in sight of our fire place. It is not improbable but he might have seen the smoke, and this caused his flight, or [he was] actuated by his own fears, as no action of my people could have given rise to his conduct. He had, however, evidently some suspicions, as he had frequently come and looked eagerly in my face, as if to read my intentions. I had been most scrupulous in avoiding every action and gesture that might cause the least distrust. In order to try the disposition of the remaining Indian, he was made to understand that he was at liberty to go if he chose, but he showed no wish of this kind. At 3 PM we joined the rest of our party, when the Indian started at seeing so many more men; but this was of momentary duration, for he soon became pleased with all he saw. I made him a few presents and showed the articles which were to be taken up for his countrymen, consisting of blankets, woollen wrappers, and shirts, beads, hatchets, knives and tin pots, thread, needles and fish hooks, with which he appeared much satisfied, and regaled himself with tea and broiled venison, for we brought down two haunches with us in the evening. A pair of trousers and vamps, being made out of a blanket, and a flannel shirt being presented to him he put them on with sensible pleasure, carefully avoiding any indecency; being under no restraint, he occasionally went out, and he expressed a strong desire for canvass, pointing to a studding sail which covered us in on one side. He laid by me during the night; still my mind was somewhat disturbed for it occurred to me that the natives on the return of their comrade who deserted us might be induced from his misrepresentation dictated by fear to quit the wigwams, and observe our motions, but I was willing to suppress any fear for the safety of our men, judging that they would not commit any violence, until they should see if we returned and brought their companion. I was moreover satisfied that the conduct of our men would be such as not to give occasion to any animosity, and in the event of their being removed they would see the impossibility of safety in any attempt to escape.

Friday the 25th of Jan: Wind NNE and boisterous with sleet. At 7 PM set out leaving only eight of the party behind. On coming up to the river head, we observed the tracks of three men crossing the pond in a direction for the other side of the river. The violence of the wind with the sleet and drift snow rendered it laborious to get on, and so thick was it at times that all the party could not be discerned, although at no great distance from each other. When within half a mile of the wigwams, the Indian, who walked sometimes on before, at others by my side, pointed out an arrow sticking in the ice; we also perceived a recent track of a sledge. At 3 PM we arrived at the wigwams, when my apprehensions were unfortunately verified; they were left in confusion, nothing of consequence remaining in them but some deer skins. We found a quantity of venison packs conveyed a little way off, and deposited in the snow; a path extended into the wood, but to no distance. Perceiving no mark of violence to have been committed, I hoped that my former conjectures would be realized, and that all would yet be well. The actions of the Indian however, were indicative of extreme perplexity and are not describable. Having directed the fire to be removed from the wigwam, we were now in to one more commodious; one of the people taking up a brand for that purpose, he appeared terrified to the last degree, and used his utmost endeavour to prevent its being carried out. He either apprehended that we were going to destroy the wigwams and canoes, (of which latter there were six) or that a fire was going to be kindled for his destruction. For some time he anxiously peeped through the crevices to see what was doing, for he was not at liberty. Perplexed how to act, and evening drawing on, anxiety for the two marines, determined me to let the Indian go, trusting that his appearance and recital of our behaviour would not only be the means of our mens' liberation, but also that the natives would return, with a favourable impression. After giving him several things, I showed a wish that his party should return, and by signs intimated not to hurt our people. He smiled significantly, but he would not leave us. He put the wigwam in order, and several times looked to the west side of the pond and pointed. Each wigwam had a quantity of deer's leg bones ranged on poles (in all three hundred). Having used the marrow of some of these opposite that we occupied, the Indian replaced them with an equal number of others, signifying that these were his; he pointed out a staff and showed that it belonged to the person that wore the high cap, the same that I had taken to be the chief; the length of this badge was nearly six feet, and two inches at the head, tapering to the end, terminating in not more than three quarters of an inch. It presented four plain equal sides, except at the upper end, where it resembled three rims, one over the other, and the whole stained red. The day having closed in, it blew very hard, with hail, sleet and rain. It became necessary to prepare against any attack that might be made upon us. The following disposition was made for the night, the wigwam being of a circular form, and the party formed into two divisions, they were placed intermediately, and a space left on each side of the entrance so that those on guard could have a full command of it; the doorway was closed up with a skin, and orders given for no one to go out. The rustling of the trees, and the snow falling from them would have made it easy for an enemy to advance close to us without being heard. I had made an exchange with the Indian for his bow and arrows, and at 11 o'clock laid down to rest; but had not been asleep more than ten minutes, when I was aroused by a dreadful scream, and exclamation of of 'O Lord' uttered by Mathew Hughster. Starting at the instant in his sleep, the Indian gave a horrid yell, and a musket was instantly discharged. I could not at this moment but admire the promptness of the watch, with their arms presented, and swords drawn. This incident, which had like to prove fatal, was occasioned by John Guieme, a foreigner, going out. He had mentioned it to the watch. In coming in again, the skin covering of the doorway made a rustling noise. Thomas Taylor, roused by the shriek, fired direct for the entrance, and had not Hughster providentially fallen against him at the moment, which moved the piece from the intended direction, Guieme must inevitably have lost his life. The rest of the night was spent in making covers of deer skin for the locks of the arms.

Saturday 26th Jan.: Wind ENE, blowing strong, with sleet and freezing weather. As soon as it was light the crew were put in motion, and placing an equal number of blankets, shirts and tin pots in each of the wigwams, I gave the Indian to understand that those articles were for the individuals who resided in them. Some more presents were given to him, also some articles attached to the red staff, all of which he seemed to comprehend. At 7 AM we left the place, intending to return the Monday following. Seeing that the

Indian came on, I signified my wish for him to go back; he however continued with us, sometimes running on a little before in a zigzag direction, keeping his eyes to the ice as having a trace to guide him, and once pointed to the westward, and laughed. Being now about two-thirds of a mile from the wigwams, he edged in suddenly, and for an instant halted; then took to speed. We at this moment observed that he had stopped to look at a body lying on the ice; he was still within half a musket-shot, but as his destruction could answer no end, so it would have been equally vain to attempt pursuit; we soon lost sight of him in the haze. On coming up we recognised with horror the bodies of our two unfortunate companions lying about a hundred yards apart; that of the corporal being first, was pierced by one arrow in the back; three arrows had entered that of Bouthland. They were laid out straight with their feet towards the river, and backs upwards; their heads were off, and carried away, and no vestige of garments left.

NOTE

1 Red Indian Lake

A PLEA FOR REFORM
THE CASE OF JAMES LANDERGAN (1818)*

The two men who led the fight for representatives institutions in the colony of Newfoundland were William Carson (1770-1843) and Patrick Morris (1789-1849). Their struggle gained momentum and their cause a hero with the rough naval justice meted out to James Landergan at Port de Grave in Conception Bay. The following account of Landergan's treatment is taken from a petition to the king, probably drafted by Patrick Morris.

WE HUMBLY represent to your Majesty, that it is hardly possible for an officer in your Majesty's Navy, if he has been attentive to his own profession, to acquire so competent a knowledge of the abstruse and difficult science of the law, as to enable him to dispense justice among his fellow men; and that he can barely take the judge's oath

* *A Report of Certain Proceedings* (St John's 1821)

of office, with a correct sense of its seriousness and importance. We beg to be understood to speak with every sentiment of respect for the Navy, as a profession. We feel a pride in the gallantry of its heroes, and gratitude for the security they afford us; but we cannot but know, that the gentlemen of the Navy are educated from their youth in a system of their own, apart from all the civil institutions of the country, and necessarily less conversant with those institutions than any other class of your Majesty's subjects. We speak from experience, and we hope without offence, when we state, that they are the last to preside in civil Courts of Law. Yet to such men is the dispensation of justice intrusted in Newfoundland, and justice according to the law of England...

We humbly beg to be permitted to lay before your Majesty two cases which occurred in the present year, exactly as they were developed in the Supreme Court of the island; and in order to save your Majesty trouble, we will briefly state the outline of one of them. James Landergan, a native of this island, and a respectable planter at Cubit's, in the district of Conception Bay, happened in the fishing season of 1818 to fall in debt for supplies, to the inconsiderable amount of twelve pounds. It is not usual with the suppliers for the fisheries in this island to distress the planters who may chance to be in arrears to them at the fall of the year, and more especially when they are possessed of fishing rooms as a security for the debt. But the sum due from Landergan to his suppliers was immediately put in suit in the Surrogate Court at Harbor-Grace, and judgment passed against him by default. Shortly after which, his fishing room was sold, and the clerk of his suppliers became the purchaser for the amount of the debt. He had personal property at the time, fully equal to satisfy the judgment, and his room was estimated at one hundred and fifty pounds in value. When the Sheriff's officer went to deliver possession of the room, Landergan was absent, and some uncourteous language passed between his wife and the officer, which was interpreted into a resistance of his authority, and made the subject of complaint to the Court. Accordingly, when Captain Buchan, of your Majesty's Brig *Grasshopper,* and the Reverend John Leigh, the Episcopal Missionary at Harbor-Grace, held a Surrogate Court at Port de Grave, Landergan was summoned to appear before them, and being found in the act of hauling a little fish for the present use of his family, he apologized for not being in a situation just then to attend the Court, and said he would do so the following morning; on being told by the officer that a party of marines would be sent to bring him, he simply replied, 'I wish you and the marines a good time of it.' The officer reported what had passed to the Court, and for this offence, if offence it can be called, the unhappy man was seized in his bed at night, and conveyed on board the *Grasshopper,* where he was confined until the following morning; he was then brought before the Court – the Sheriff's officer went through the ceremony of deposing to the facts before related, and Landergan was adjudged to be guilty of a high contempt of Court, and sentenced to receive thirty-six lashes on his bare back. This infamous sentence was immediately carried into execution by the boatswain's mate of the *Grasshopper,* and Landergan was tied up and flogged until he fainted under the severity of his punishment. He was then taken down and removed to the Court-House, where, at the first symptom of returning life, he was required to yield up the possession of his room, as the condition upon which the remainder of his punishment should be remitted; and in a few hours after, the unfortunate man, together with his wife and four infant children, became outcasts upon the world. Such is the manner in which the surrogates hold plea of civil suits in Newfoundland; and it cannot be matter of surprise to your Majesty, accustomed as your Majesty is to observe justice administered in the form of a blessing to your people, to learn that the naval circuits are looked upon rather as the angry visitations of offended power, than as the dispensation of the mild and beneficent precepts of British law.

An opinion has gone abroad, and is not without its abetors in this island, that Newfoundland is regarded by the parent country merely as a nursery of seamen; and with this view, that it is the policy of government to discourage all settlement in the island. Supposing this to be the case, it may be sufficient to explain how it has happened that this island, the oldest of the British settlements in America, placed in the same latitude as England, and possessed of a great staple which is peculiarly its own, should remain in the same state as when it was originally discovered – without cultivation, and without roads – the first requisite of civilized society. But we humbly conceive that such is not the policy of Great Britain. Before the statute of King William the Third, a number of persons were settled in Newfoundland, and it was one of the professed objects of that statute to regulate the respective rights of the transient and sedentary fisheries. In the treaties between your Majesty and foreign powers, the right of settling those parts of the island where strangers are permitted to fish, is expressly reserved to your Majesty's subjects; and this right of settlement is the only check upon foreign competition in the fisheries. It is well known that Newfoundland contains about one hundred thousand inhabitants; that its exports have in prosperous years exceeded two millions sterling per annum, and its imports, chiefly consisting of British manufactures and productions, have been more than half that amount; its trade is entirely carried on in British shipping, and employs more seamen in navigation, than were ever employed in fishing during the best years of the transient fishery – upwards of four hundred and sixty foreign vessels having entered the port of St John's alone during the present year. We must therefore look to other causes for our neglected condition, than the intentional policy of the parent state; and we are induced to believe that it has been owing solely to the exigencies of the late war, and the more pressing demands of the empire upon the attention of your Majesty's government. But we humbly hope that the time is at length arrived when the state of this island will be taken into consideration, and some system adopted which may be more in unison with the altered condition of these extensive, populous, and valuable possessions of your Majesty's Crown.

Your Petitioners therefore most humbly pray your Majesty will take their case into your most gracious consideration, and endow Newfoundland with all the rights and privileges of your Majesty's other transatlantic possessions, and especially to cause the Courts of Justice to be reformed, so that the laws may be administered to them by competent judges.

WILLIAM CORMACK REACHES THE INTERIOR OF NEWFOUNDLAND (1822)*

William Epps Cormack was born in St John's in 1796 and attended the University of Edinburgh. In 1822, travelling with his Indian guide Joseph Sylvester, he became the first person of European descent to walk across the interior of Newfoundland. His journey from Trinity Bay to St George's Bay lasted nine weeks.

EARLY IN THE day, on September 10th, the ground descending, we came unexpectedly to a rivulet about seventy yards wide, running rapidly over a rocky bed to the north-east, which we forded. ... From the position and course of this stream, we inferred that it was a branch of the river which runs into Clode Sound, in Bonavista Bay; and my Indian supposed, from his recollections of the reports of the Indians concerning Clode Sound River, that canoes could be brought up from the sea-coast to near where we were.

Leaving this rivulet, the land has a considerable rise for several miles. The features of the country then assume an air of expanse and importance different from heretofore. The trees become larger and stand apart; and we entered upon spacious tracts of rocky ground entirely clear of wood. Everything indicated our approach to the verge of a country different from the past.

We soon found that we were on a great granitic ridge, covered, not as the lower grounds are with crowded pines and green moss, but with scattered trees; a variety of beautiful lichens or reindeer moss, partridge berries, cowberries, and whortleberries loading the ground. A pretty erect shrub, a species of honeysuckle, was in full fruit by the sides of the rocks; grouse, the indigenous game-birds of the country, rose in coveys in every direction, and snipe from every marsh. The birds of passage, ducks and geese, were flying over us to and fro from their breeding-places in the interior and on the sea-coast; tracks of deer, of wolves fearfully large, of bears, foxes, and martens, were seen everywhere.

* W.E. Cormack *Narrative of a Journey Across the Island of Newfoundland in 1882* ed. F.A. Bruton (London: Longmans 1928). Reprinted by permission of Longman Group Ltd

On looking back towards the sea-coast, the scene was magnificent. We discovered that under the cover of the forest we had been uniformly ascending ever since we left the salt water at Random Bar, and then soon arrived at the summit of what we saw to be a great mountain ridge, that seems to serve as a barrier between the sea and the interior. The black dense forest through which we had pilgrimaged presented a novel picture, appearing spotted with bright yellow marshes and a few glossy lakes on its bosom, some of which we had passed close by without seeing them.

In the west, to our inexpressible delight, the interior broke in sublimity before us. What a contrast did this present to the conjectures entertained of Newfoundland! The hitherto mysterious interior lay unfolded below us, a boundless scene, an emerald surface, a vast basin. The eye strides again and again over a succession of northerly and southerly ranges of green plains, marbled with woods and lakes of every form and extent, a picture of all the luxurious scenes of national cultivation, receding into invisibleness. The imagination hovers in the distance, and clings involuntarily to the undulating horizon of vapour, far into the west, until it is lost. A new world seemed to invite us onwards, or rather we claimed the dominion, and were impatient to proceed to take possession. Fancy carried us quickly across the Island. Obstacles of every kind were dispelled and despised. Primitiveness, omnipotence, and tranquillity were stamped upon everything so forcibly that the mind is hurled back thousands of years and the man left denuded of the mental fabric which a knowledge of ages of human experience and of time may have reared within him...

It was manifest on every hand that this was the season of the year when the earth here offers her stores of productions; land berries were ripening, game birds were fledging, and beasts were emerging to prey upon each other. Everything animate or inanimate seemed to be our own. We consumed unsparingly our remaining provisions, confident that henceforward, with our personal powers, which felt increased by the nature of the objects that presented themselves (aided by what now seemed by contrast the admirable power of our firearms), the distruction of one creature would afford us nourishment and vigour for the destruction of others. There was no will but ours. Thoughts of the aborigines did not alter our determination to meet them, as well as everything living, that might present itself in a country yet untrodden and before unseen by civilised man. I now adopted, as well for self-preservation as for the sake of accomplishing the object of my excursion, the self-dependent mode of life of the Indian, both in spirit and action...

On September 11th we descended into the bosom of the interior.

SHANANDITHIT, THE LAST OF THE BEOTHUCKS (1823)*

The following account of the capture of Shananditheit, the last Beothuck ever seen by a European, was written by William Wilson, a Methodist minister on the St John's circuit, in his journal on 23 June 1823.

ST JOHN'S, June 23, 1823: Last week there were brought to this town, three Red Indians, so called, who are the aboriginal inhabitants of this island. They are all females, and their capture was accomplished in the following manner.

In the month of March last, a party of men from the neighborhood of Twillingate were in the country hunting for fur. The party went two and two in different directions. After a while one of these small parties saw, on a distant hill, a man coming toward them. Supposing him, while at a distance, to be one of their own party, they fired a powder gun to let their friend know their whereabouts. The Red Indian generally runs at the report of a musket: not so in the present instance. This man quickened his pace toward them. They now, from his gait and dress, discovered that he was an Indian, but thought he was a Micmac, and therefore still felt no anxiety. Soon they found their mistake, and ascertained that the stranger was one of the Red Indians. He was approaching in a threatening attitude, with a large club in his hand. They now put themselves in a posture of defence, and beckoned the Indian to surrender. This was of no use; he came on with double fury, and when nearly at the muzzle of their guns, one of the men fired, and the Indian fell dead at his feet. As they had killed a man without any design or intention, they felt deeply concerned, and resolved at once to leave the

* William Wilson *Newfoundland and its Missionaries* (Cambridge, Mass. 1866)

hunting-ground and return home. In passing through a droke of woods, they came up with a wigwam, which they entered, and took three Indian females, which have since been found to be a mother and her two daughters. These women they brought to their own home, where they kept them until they could carry them to St John's, and receive the government reward for bringing a Red captive Indian. The parties were brought to trial for shooting a man, but as there was no evidence against them they were acquitted.

The women were first taken to government house, and, by order of his excellency the governor, a comfortable room in the court-house was assigned to them as a place of residence, where they were treated with every possible kindness. The mother is far advanced in life, but seems in good health. Beds were provided for them, but they did not understand their use, and they slept on their deer-skins in the corner of the room. One of the daughters was ill, yet she would take no medicine. The doctor recommended phlebotomy, and a gentleman allowed a vein to be opened in his arm, to show her that there was no intention to kill her; but this was to no purpose; for when she saw the lancet brought near her own arm, both she and her companions got into a state of fury, so that the doctor had to desist. Her sister was in good health. She seemed about twenty-two years of age. If she had ever used red ochre about her person, there was then so sign of it in her face. Her complexion was swarthy, not unlike the Micmacs; her features were handsome; she was a tall, fine figure, and stood nearly six feet high; and such a beautiful set of teeth I do not know that I ever saw in a human head. In her manners she was bland, affable, and affectionate. I showed her my watch: she put it to her ear, and was amused with its tick. A gentleman put a looking-glass before her, and her grimaces were most extraordinary; but when a black-lead pencil was put into her hand, and a piece of white paper laid upon the table, she was in raptures. She made a few marks on the paper, apparently to try the pencil; then in one flourish she drew a deer perfectly; and, what is most surprising, she began at the tip of the tail. One person pointed to his fingers and counted ten, which she repeated in good English; but when she had numbered all her fingers, her English was exhausted, and her numeration, if numeration it were was in the Beothuck tongue. This person, whose Indian name is Shanandithit, is thought to be the wife of the man who was shot. The old woman was morose, and had the look and action of a savage. She would sit all day on the floor with a deer-skin shawl on, and looked with dread or hatred upon every one that entered the court-house.

When we came away Shananditihit kissed all the company, shook hands with us, and distinctly repeated 'good-by.'

June 24: Saw the three Indian women in the street. The ladies had dressed them in English garb, but over their dress they all had on their, to them indispensable, deer-skin shawl; and Shananditihit, thinking the long front of her bonnet an unnecessary appendage, had torn it off, and in its place had decorated her forehead and her arms with tinsel and colored paper.

3 THE COLONIAL ERA

WRECKING (1835)*

Edward Wix (1802-66) was the second Archdeacon of the Anglican Church in Newfoundland and the first to reside at St John's, moving there from Bonavista in 1830. Between February and August 1835 Wix conducted a coastal tour of Newfoundland, including Conception Bay, Trinity Bay, the south coast, and part of the west coast. The account which follows is taken from a journal he kept on this trip. In his dedicatory note to this journal he makes the following comment: 'Had it not been for some boxes of paper, which had been dispersed along the Shore from different wrecks, I might have failed entirely in procuring this convenience in some places where my application was successful.'

SATURDAY [MAY] 2: Off before seven AM, and, to my great regret, passed the Burgeo Islands, with the respectable inhabitants of which place I had kept up a correspondence, and supplied them with books, since my visit to them in 1830. We anchored at eight PM at Duck Island, Cutteau Bay, fourteen leagues. There, by the blaze of a cheerful fire, made from the wreck wood, so common on this coast, I held full service in a neat planter's cabin, and baptized six children.

Sunday, 3: Off at half-past five AM; struck, for an instant, upon a rock in working out with our deck-boat. Got, by one PM to Burnt Islands. We passed La Poile. This part of the shore is so fatal to European vessels which are outward bound to Quebec in the spring, that it is much to be regreted that the legislatures or Chambers of Commerce of Nova Scotia, New Brunswick, and the Canadas, do not unite with the government and merchants of Newfoundland, for the erection of light-houses here and at Port-aux-Basques, and at Cape Ray. Many vessels and many lives might, each year, be saved from destruction by such a measure. Mr Anthonie, indeed, a humane Jersey merchant, resident at La Poile, has erected, upon a rock off La Poile Bay, a small observatory. This is of some service to a few who know its situation; but the shore in this neighbourhood is so very low, and the ledges of rock extend so far out to sea, that a vessel may be in danger before the little beacon is discovered.

* Edward Wix, *Six Months of a Newfoundland Missionary's Journal* (London 1836)

At the cabin in which I stayed at Burnt Islands, the play-things of the children were bunches of small patent desk and cabinet keys, which had been picked up from wrecks. Beautiful old China plates and pieces of a more modern elegant breakfast set of dragon china, which had been washed ashore in the same way, were ranged upon the shelves alongside the most common ware; and a fine huckabac towel, neatly marked with the initial letters L.C.D., was handed me on my expressing a desire to wash my hands. This had been supplied from the wreck of a vessel in which were several ladies. To some hearts those letters, doubtless, would renew a sad period of anxiety, which preceded the intelligence of the melancholy certainty of a sad bereavement. I could not look at this relic of a toilet, now no more required, without emotions of deep interest, although I had no clue by which I could attach recollections of brilliant prospects early blighted, or pious faith exemplified in death to these three letters. Indeed, the scenes and circumstances, the very people by whom I was surrounded, roused within me a train of deeply melancholy sensations. My host may have been a humane man; his conduct to me was that of genuine hospitality; but it had been his frequent employment at intervals, from his youth till now, to bury wrecked corpses, in all stages of decomposition. There had been washed on shore here, as many as three hundred, and a hundred and fifty on two occasions, and numerous in others. This sad employment appeared to have somewhat blunted his feelings. I would not do him injustice – the bare recital of such revolting narratives ... unvarnished as such tales would naturally be, in the simpler expression of a fisherman, might give an appearance of a want of feeling, which nature may have not denied to him, and of which the scenes and occupations of his life may not have wholly divested him. I remember well my expressing my reluctance to allow him to disinter a delicate female foot, the last human relic, which the waves, or the wild cats, or the fox, or his own domestic dog, had deposited in the neighbourhood of his cabin. He had recently picked it up close to his door, and had buried it in his garden, and was very anxious to be allowed to shovel away the lingering snow, that he might indulge me with a sight of it. I suppose my countenance may have betrayed some feeling of abhorrence, when he said, 'Dear me, Sir, do let me; it would not give me any concern at all: I have had so much to do with dead bodies, that I think no more of handling them, than I do of handling so many codfish!'

I have said, that I believe him humane; yet wrecks must form his chief inducement to settle in a place so barren and bleak, and to live through the winter out upon the shore as he does, contrary to the usual habit of the people, which is to retire into the woods until late in the spring. But humanity might prompt a man to live where his services may occasionally be exerted usefully for the preservation of human life. Yet, did I wrong him in the judgment of charity, when I saw his quick eye kindle with the gale, as he watched the stormy horizon? Was I wrong when, as he went in the early dawn and dusk each evening, while I was there, to a hill a little higher than the rest, with his spy-glass, I thought his feelings and my own – on discerning that a vessel had, during the night, struck some of the numerous rocks which abound hereabouts, or was on her way to do so – might be of a very different character? This man is only a sample of many whom I saw on this part of the coast.

'OVERBOARD WITH YOU! GAFFS AND POKERS!' (1840)*

Joseph Beete Jukes (1811-69) was born in Birmingham and graduated from Cambridge University. In 1839, at the start of a notable scientific career, he began a geological survey of Newfoundland. In the book from which the following extracts are taken, he gave an account of his experiences in Newfoundland while engaged in this work. He returned to England aboard HMS *Spitfire*, the first steamer ever to put into St John's. Jukes is remembered as one of the leading geologists of the nineteenth century.

[FEBRUARY 1840]: There was now but little time left to make arrangements for our[1] voyage to the ice. The generality of the vessels 'going to the ice' are schooners and brigs from 80 to 150 tons, manned by a stout crew of rough fishermen, with a skipper at their head of their own stamp. These ships are inconceivably filthy, being often saturated with oil; and crew and skipper all live and lie together in a narrow dark cabin of the smallest possible dimensions, and the fewest possible conveniences, everything being in common.

* J.B. Jukes, *Excursions in and about Newfoundland,* 2 vols. (London 1842)

In such a vessel as this it was evidently impossible for us to be accommodated, nor would either crew or skipper have consented to take us. There are, however, one or two masters of ships of a superior description who reserve the after-cabin to themselves, and keep the crew in the forecastle. Among these, one of the most respectable was Mr Furneaux, who having been at one time unsuccessful as a merchant, had retrieved his fortune by successful sealing enterprises; and he had just built a new vessel called the *Topaz*, a brigantine of 120 tons, in which he was going out for the first time. She had a comfortable little after-cabin, with small state-rooms, containing altogether five berths. This cabin he agreed to share with us...

March 5th: This morning was dark and foggy, with the wind at south-east. At seven o'clock, after making a tack or two about an open lake, and finding no channel, we dashed into the ice, with all sail set, in company with two other vessels, on a north north-west course. The ice soon got firmer, thicker, and heavier, and we shortly stuck fast. 'Overboard with you! gaffs and pokers!' sung out the captain; and over went, accordingly, the major part of the crew to the ice. The pokers were large poles of light wood, six or eight inches in circumference, and twelve or fifteen feet long: pounding with these, or hewing the ice with axes, the men would split the pans near the bows of the vessel, and then, inserting the ends of the pokers, use them as large levers, lifting up one side of the broken piece and depressing the other, and several getting round with their gaffs, they shoved it, by main force, under the adjoining ice. Smashing, breaking, and pounding the smaller pieces in the course the vessel wished to take, room was afforded for the motion of the larger pans. Laying out great claws on the ice ahead, when the wind was light the crew warped the vessel on. If a large and strong pan was met with, the ice-saw was got out. Sometimes, a crowd of men clinging round the ship's bows, and holding on to the bights of ropes suspended there for the purpose, would jump and dance on the ice, bending and breaking it with their weight, shoving it below the vessel, and dragging her on over it with all their force. Up to their knees in water, as one piece after another sank below the cutwater, they still held on, hurraing at every fresh start she made, dancing, jumping, pushing, shoving, hauling, hewing, sawing, till every soul on board was roused into excited exertion. After looking on some time, I could stand it no longer: so, seizing a gaff, I jumped overboard, but soon got a damper, as, in my first essay to cross before the vessel, I did not distinguish the sound pieces from the mere broken mash and lolly, and in I went to my middle before I was aware of it. One of the men caught hold of me, and I scrambled up the side of the vessel, a little cooler than I went down. Every fresh hand, they said, has to pay his footing for his first dip: so I was obliged not only to lose my footing in water myself, but give it afterwards in rum to the crew. They continued their exertions the whole of the day, relieved occasionally by small open pools of water; and in the evening we calculated we had made about fifteen miles.

It continued foggy all day, and at night it began to rain. We had seen no vessel since the morning – nothing but a dreary expanse of ice and snow stretching away into the misty horizon...

March 10th: At dawn a gale from the south brought rain and dirty weather, and we lay all day fast in the ice with our sails furled. In the afternoon we filled all the watercasks that had up to this time been emptied with beautifully clear fresh water, collected in the hollow of a pan alongside of us. After dark the wind fell, and the clouds gradually cleared off before a light westerly breeze, unfolding a most lovely sky studded with bright stars, and adorned by the presence of the young moon, and the brilliant flickering streamers of a fine aurora in the north. The ice too opened, and we sailed gently through calm water, among numberless fairy islets of glittering ice and wreaths of snow, with shining pinnacles and fantastic forms floating calmly about us, and 'Quietly shining to the quiet moon.' Everything was still, and even the sailors hushed their noisy clamour, insensibly silenced by the influence of this most lovely scene. Even the hoarse voice of the master of the watch as he sung out, from the foretop, brief orders to the helmsman, was not out of harmony with the feelings of the time, while, sounding at intervals, it served but to make the silence of all nature around us more deep and solemn...

March 12th: Again foggy, with a southeast wind. As we stood on deck this morning before breakfast, we heard a cry down to leeward, like the cry of a gull, which some of the men said it was. It became, however, so loud and continued, that both Stuwitz and I doubted its being the cry of any bird, and one of the men took a gaff and went to look. We watched him for some distance with our glasses as he proceeded slowly through the fog till he suddenly began to run, and then struck at something, and presently returned dragging a young seal alive over the ice, and brought it on deck. It was of a dirty white colour, with short close fur, large dark expressive eyes, and it paddled and walloped about the deck fierce and bawling. A Newfoundland dog called Nestor, belonging to the captain, approached it, but it snapped at his nose and bit him, though its teeth were just beginning to appear. After taking it down below to show the captain and demand the usual quart of rum for the first man who caught a seal, one of the men knocked it on the head and skinned it. Stuwitz then cut off its 'fippers' or paws and its head, and after breakfast we took it into the 'after-hatch,' or steerage, where he drew and dissected it. In the middle of the day we heard from some of the men who had been out on the ice, that a vessel a few miles ahead of us had already 2500 seals on board, so we pushed on through the ice, and shortly came into a lake of water. On the borders of this many young seals were lying, and two or three punts were hoisted out to despatch and collect them. I shot one through the head that was scuffling off a pan of ice, but the crew begged me to desist, as they said the balls might glance from the ice and injure some of the men who were about. Having picked up the few which were immediately about us, we hoisted in our punts again, as there were several vessels near us, and more coming up, and bore away farther north through an open pool of water. In passing through a thin skirt of ice, one of the men hooked up a young seal with his gaff. Its cries were precisely like those of a young child in the extremity of agony and distress, something between shrieks and convulsive sobbings. It thrilled one's nerves at first, but when I found that their sole employment, when alone on the ice, was uttering similar cries, and that nearly the same cry was expressive of enjoyment or defiance as of pain and fear, I became more reconciled. We soon afterwards passed through some loose ice on which the young seals were scattered, and nearly all hands were overboard slaying, skinning and hauling. We then got into another lake of water and sent our five punts. The crews of these joined those already on the ice, and dragging either the whole seals or their 'pelts' to the edge of the water, collected them in the punts, and when one of these was full brought them on board. The cook of the vessel, and my man Simon, with the captain and myself, managed the vessel, circumnavigating the lake and picking up the boats as they put off one after another from the edge of the ice. In this way, when it became too dark to do any more, we found we had got three hundred seals on board, and the deck was one great shambles. When piled in a heap together the young seals looked like so many lambs, and when occasionally, from out of the bloody and dirty mass of carcasses, one poor wretch still alive would lift up its face and begin to flounder about, I could stand it no longer; and arming myself with a hand-spike I proceeded to knock on the head and put out of their misery all in whom I saw signs of life...

[March 13]: The ice to-day was in places very slippery and in others broken and treacherous, and as I had not got my boots properly fitted with 'sparables' and 'chisels' I stayed on board and helped the captain and the cook in managing the vessel and whipping in the pelts as they were brought alongside. By twelve o'clock, however, my arms were aching with this work, and on the ice side of the vessel we stood more than knee deep in warm seal skins, all blood and fat. Some of the men brought in as many as sixty each in the course of the day, and by night the decks were covered, in many places the full height of the rail. As the men came on board they occasionally snatched a hasty moment to drink a bowl of tea, or eat a piece of biscuit and butter; and as the sweat was dripping from their faces, and their hands and bodies were reeking with blood and fat, and they often spread the butter with their thumbs, and wiped their faces with the backs of their hands, they took both the liquids and the solids mingled with blood. The deck of course, when the deck could be seen, was almost as slippery with gore as if it had been ice. Still there was a bustle and excitement in the scene that did not permit the fancy to dwell on the disagreeables, and after a hearty refreshment the men would snatch up their gaffs and hauling ropes, and hurry off in search of new victims: besides, every pelt was worth a dollar!...

[March 18]: I went with one punt, taking my double-barrelled gun and some seal-shot. I got several shots at old seals, but found the charges from my fowling-piece not heavy enough for them, as, though I wounded several severely, most of them got away, and I only killed one or two dead on the spot. Even the young ones, unless hit about the head or in the heart, will carry off a good deal of shot. I knocked over one young one that was shuffling off a pan, but notwithstanding this he popped into the water, and swimming about ten yards, crawled on to another pan, when I gave him the other barrel: he again got into the water, and on his crawling out one of the men fired a sealing-gun at him, but the contents only striking him about the tail he again got away, and it was only by shooting him in the head as he raised it from the water, that I succeeded in killing him at last. Generally, however, the young ones did not attempt to stir as we approached them, and quietly suffered themselves to be knocked on the head with the gaff, and skinned on the spot. I saw one poor wretch skinned, or sculped, while yet alive, and the body writhing in blood after being stripped of its pelt. The man told me he had seen them swim away in that state, and that if the first blow did not kill them, they could not stop to give them a second. How is it one can steel one's mind to look on that which to read of, or even to think of afterwards, makes one shudder? In the bustle, hurry, and excitement, these things pass as a matter of course and as if necessary, but they are most horrible, and will not admit of an attempt at palliation. As this morning I was left alone to take care of the punt while the men were on the ice, the mass of dying carcasses piled in the boat around me each writhing, gasping, and spouting blood into the air nearly made me sick. Seeking relief in action, I drove the sharp point of the gaff into the brain of every one in which I could see a sign of life. The vision of one poor wretch writhing its snow-white woolly body with its head bathed in blood, through which it was vainly endeavouring to see and breathe, really haunted my dreams. Notwithstanding all this the excitement of being out in the punt, forcing our way through narrow channels between the ice-pans into lakes of water where old seals were sporting on every side, filling our boat with pelts, engineering so as to sweep over a mile or two of new ground, and return to the vessel by a different way from that we came, clearing the ice of seals as we went along, and the hunting spirit which makes almost every man an animal of prey, and delight in the produce of his gun or his bow, kept me in the punt till a late hour in the afternoon.

NOTE

1 Jukes was accompanied by a Norwegian, Professor Stuwitz, professor of natural history in the University of Christiania, and by a servant named Simon.

'A BAPTISM OF VIOLENCE' (1840)*

In May 1837, Thomas Talbot (1818-1901) arrived in Newfoundland from Ireland, and settled in Harbour Grace, where his father, 'having retired from the business of the fisheries,' was engaged in farming. By 1882, when his *Letter Addressed to a Friend in Ireland* was published, Talbot had spent forty-five years in Newfoundland and had been at various times a farmer, teacher, journalist, politician, and Sheriff of St John's and of the central district of the island. He was also a poet and classical scholar.

SCARCELY HAD I time to get acquainted with the character of the country, and the various pursuits and interests of its inhabitants, before an opportunity presented itself of obtaining an insight into its political condition. The colony had but recently [in 1832] acquired the privilege of a legislature. Only two general elections had taken place since that event; the second only a few months before my arrival. One of the members for Conception Bay having vacated his seat by accepting the office of stipendiary magistrate at Carbonear, a writ was issued for the election of a member in his place. Two candidates presented themselves to the constituency, one a resident of Harbour Grace, the other of Carbonear; both were Roman Catholics, and belonged to the Liberal party. Even at this early stage of their parliamentary government the population had divided themselves into two political parties, the one called Tory or Conservative, the other Liberal. Derisively they were called respectively, the Merchants' party and the Priests' party. And most extraordinary parties they were. After sufficient inquiry, however, I soon found that the one party (the Merchants' or Conservative) had for their guiding principle the resistance to all innovation, a name which they gave to the promotion of any measure that had not the especial benefit of the fisheries for its sole object. Taxation of every kind was ignored by their creed; and so of consequence was every civil institution, and every improvement that implied the expenditure of money. The other party (the Liberal or Priests' party) steered by a principle directly opposite. Hence the unavoidable collision between

* Thomas Talbot *Newfoundland; or, A Letter Addressed to a Friend in Ireland* (London 1882)

the two parties. But, in justice to both, in commenting upon their ways and doings, I must say, as things appeared to me then, and as I afterwards found by personal experience, the Liberal party were by no means remarkable for adhesion to the principle of moral force in carrying out their objects. Conception Bay at this time formed but one electoral district, having a shore line of over 100 miles, and a population of about 24,000. This population has doubled itself since. The polling was carried on from town to town, and village to village, beginning at Harbour Grace, the chief town, and ending at Carbonear, the second town of importance in the district. Thus the polling occupied three weeks or so; and very naturally, when a sharp contest occurred, the hostile feelings of parties rose as they went along. In this particular contest, as I have said, the two candidates were of the same party – both Roman Catholics; the Liberal party being chiefly composed of Roman Catholics, a circumstance almost unavoidable, seeing that the priests were the chiefs of the party, or at all events generally regarded as such. The Harbour Grace man, who was a more popular man, and, in a political sense, perhaps a better man, was not a favourite with the priests. He was, it might be, not pliant enough, and consequently the priests opposed him, and supported the Carbonear man. The party then split, and it became a contest between Harbour Grace and Carbonear, the respective places of birth and abode of the two candidates.

The merchants of Harbour Grace, and indeed the influential classes generally in both towns, supported the Harbour Grace candidate, who consequently headed the other all along the line until they arrived at Carbonear. Here the polling was to terminate; but as the Harbour Grace man was in an immense majority at the opening of the poll here, and his success was certain, his opponents felt that nothing remained for them but to nullify the election by creating a riot. Accordingly the polling-booth was invaded by the rioters; the returning officer was knocked down, and the poll-books carried away and destroyed. Then ensued a scene of confusion and disorder not easily described. The Harbour Grace men were struck at with sticks and stones, and all sorts of weapons and missiles that came to hand. They defended themselves in vain, for their assailants were too numerous, and evidently well prepared for the occasion. They fought desperately, however, and occasionally drove back the enemy with irresistible force, inflicting a severe retaliation. Some pistol-shots were said to have been delivered during the *melee*, which had the effect only of increasing the fury of the combatants. The fight was continued along the Harbour Grace road, the Harbour Grace men retreating towards their home until they came within a mile or so of it, when they were met by a number of their fellow townsmen who had come out to their assistance. Then the Carbonear men began to give way, and to retreat towards their home. Here they attacked all those belonging to Carbonear who had supported the Harbour Grace man. They set fire to one house, and broke in the windows and doors of several others. The night set in, and amid the darkness which followed were heard all through the town the ferocious shouts of the depredators, and the shrieks of women and children running from house to house for protection. It was a fearful scene – a living pandemonium. The lofty and wide-spreading flames, and crackling sounds of the large house on fire in the midst of the little town, joined to the crashing and reverberating noises of the stones that were hurled against the windows and doors on either side of the street, with the combined roaring, shouting, and screaming of the assailants and the assailed, formed such an extraordinary scene that a stranger unacquainted with its origin, and the motives which inspired it, would have fancied that a party of savages had suddenly come out from the forests and made a raid on the inhabitants of the town for the purposes of murder and plunder. Many persons were severely injured in the course of the onslaught; among others two middle-aged gentlemen, the heads of the two principal commercial houses at Harbour Grace, were fearfully maltreated. One was confined to his room for several weeks before he recovered from the effects of his wounds and injuries; and the other though temporarily restored to health, yet never fully recovered from the effects of the injuries he had received; and died within a few years afterwards. My share in the business was simply being a Harbour Grace man, and a friend of the Harbour Grace candidate, and having been present at his nomination, and otherwise known as one who was favourable to his election. I was not a voter; nor was I in any way interested in the result. However, I did not escape in the mad affray, having barely got off with my life. How often have I thought since, as in the case of the impending shipwreck at the little fishing village of Portugal Cove, how near I was to having my life ingloriously cut off just at its threshold, in a senseless and silly affray in the little town of

Carbonear. But the fury of the storm did not subside for three or four days afterwards; nor until a company or two of soldiers had been sent over from St John's by the governor. The consequence of this interruption to the polling, and of the destruction of the poll-books, was that no return was made, and consequently neither candidate was elected. Such was the manner in which I was inducted into the mystery of politics in Newfoundland. It was a baptism of violence.

THE CLASS STRUCTURE IN NEWFOUNDLAND (1842)*

Richard Henry Bonnycastle (1791-1847) studied at the Royal Military Academy, Woolich, and in 1809 became a lieutenant in the Royal Engineers. He served in the War of 1812 and in the Canadian rebellions of 1837-9. He later became commanding engineer in Newfoundland. He retired from the service in 1847, having attained the rank of lieutenant-colonel. In the same year that he published his work on Newfoundland from which the following extract is taken, he also published *The Canadas in 1842.*

THE UPPER CLASS, which at home would almost without exception be the middle class, consists of the clergy, judges, councillors, and officers of the state, with the oldest and most wealthy of the merchants holding office.

The middle class – that class so well named in England as the 'shield of society' – consists here of the newer merchants, the conductors of the business of the extensive firms at home, and a growing, most important, and rapidly-increasing number of the sons and daughters of those respectable men who have chosen Newfoundland as the country of their children. It is only necessary to attend at a public charitable ball to see these excellent people in their real character; it strikes every unaccustomed beholder with admiration, for a finer, healthier, or better dressed and behaved colonial 'gentry' there does not exist. Professional men, lawyers, and medical men, belong, as in every other colony, to both these classes.

* R.H. Bonnycastle *Newfoundland in 1842* (London 1842)

The third class I have no name for, as neither that of labourer nor that of peasantry is applicable.

The third class in Newfoundland are small farmers, small shopkeepers, and fishermen, or fishermen exclusively. They are well clothed, and usually wear a distinctive habit, which is a blue jacket and trowsers, of good cloth, and a lowcrowned glazed hat. To see these people in a public procession, one is tempted to observe, with the Emperor of Russia, when he first saw the English in mass, on the occasion of the visit of the allied monarchs, 'Where *are* the poor?' I have seen them in every possible situation, and have uniformly observed them quiet, orderly, and respectable; even in the pit of the theatre, which is frequently during winter filled with them, not a word nor an indication of row or noise occurs.

In the towns, of course, there is a still lower class, which is engaged, as elsewhere, in domestic or in menial offices, or employed in hewing wood and drawing water, or as carters, farm servants, etc.

But still, with all these advantages, there are miserable and destitute citizens enough in St John's, and plenty of poverty in the out-harbours, for which two causes may be assigned.

The fisherman, formerly, during seven months of winter weather, had no resources but idleness or drink. If he was industrious, it is true, he might employ himself, when he resided near the towns, in cutting and hauling fuel with his dogs, from the woods, which have hitherto been looked upon as common property; but since the opening of the coal-mines in Nova Scotia and Cape Breton even this source of profit has been diminished at the capital, for those who can afford it always use coal for firing, the hard wood being scarce, and the sparkling and crackling spruce and fir kinds of soft wood not pleasant to burn in an open grate, and too expensive in close stoves, which are not in general use, as in Canada, for that reason.

The periods of hauling by men or dogs on the snow are very short, and very precarious and difficult, as, the climate being one in which high winds and rain prevail, one night or one day of wind will lay bare all the approaches to the town; the poor, therefore, who only use the wood fuel, frequently suffer much from not being able to procure it in severe and changeable winters. The consequence has been, until the successful introduction of temperance pledges and societies, that those unfortunates, from the accidental causes of a failure in the fishery, from constitutional idleness, sickness, or inability, either took to drinking, or suffered indescribable miseries.

The other cause has been the want of roads and the extensively scattered nature of the coast population. There, if the fishery was unproductive, or the winter very rainy, the solitary settler had no means of answering the cries and wants of his family, however industrious.

But a change is coming over the nature of society here. Temperance has made great progress where it is most requisite, and that is amongst the industrious poor. Agriculture is patronized by the government, and no man presumes any longer to assert that the necessaries for a poor man's existence – potatoes, hay, and oats – cannot be successfully raised, whilst, with common attention, every 'tilt,' as the wretched dwelling of the extremely poor is here called, might be supplied from a small garden with cabbage, and all other common vegetables and herbs.

No person who has travelled much, not even in those districts in Ireland where the mud hut is scarcely cover for the inhabitant, can fancy the extreme wretchedness of the accommodation of the very poor in this island. I walked yesterday, with some gentlemen of St John's, along the shore in the village of Portugal Cove, not ten miles from the capital, and found a family, consisting of a woman and seven children, in a hut of which the following is a feeble description: It was, perhaps, about eighteen feet long by fourteen in breadth, for I did not measure it correctly, as it was surrounded by fences and snow, and consisted of one apartment only, in which the whole family, excepting the father, who had gone with his dog to the woods for fuel, were squatting round a scanty fire, and were of all ages, from that of womanhood to the nursed infant, and they were all females excepting a very young boy or two.

This dwelling, which was as lofty as a barn, was built of poles or sticks of very small diameter, placed upright, irregularly together, and braced every here and there. The chimney, formed of rough unmortared stone, adjoined the roof, which was also of poles at one gable end, and was finished above the ridge pole with boards, or short slabs of wood. The roof had been covered with bark and sods, and some attempts had originally been made to stop or caulk the crevices between the poles, both of the roof and walls, with moss or mud; but these substances had generally disappeared, and in every part of this wretched dwelling, was the light of heaven visible, and everywhere must the rain have fallen in it, excepting towards the gable, opposite the chimney, which had some pains taken with it, and where the unfortunate family slept on their rags. And yet these people neither solicited nor expected charity, and we had sought the man, in order to engage his services for an hour or two profitably. The miserable mother looked lean and yellow; but, strange to say, in a climate where the thermometer was then not many degrees above zero, the children appeared, although clothed in light summer rags, healthy and strong.

The house had evidently been built in better days, upon too large a scale; but even this hut is good, compared with some of the summer tilts, which are constructed to carry on the fishery in the little harbours and coves, where, very often, a huge boulder or projecting rock forms the gable, or actual reredos, as our ancestors called the only chimney, or substitute for a chimney, and from this chimney-rock, a few slight poles built up erect in an oblong form, with a pole-roof sloping against a bank, or rock, the whole covered with bark, when it can be had, which is seldom, or with turf; and with turf piled up against the side walls, without a window, and with only an apology for a door; and the whole interior scarcely affording standing room; compose the only habitation which often contains the poor fisherman, and his generally numerous family, the smoke escaping always from an old barrel, or a square funnel of boards placed over the fire.

When winter sets in, or as soon as the fishing is over, this tilt is abandoned, and the family retire to the woods, and erect another somewhat better. There they are rather more comfortable, as the woods afford fuel and shelter, and they live on fish dried or salted, and potatoes, if they have been provident enough to raise them, with occasionally the milk of a goat numbers of these animals being kept, and suffered, like the dogs, to forage for themselves.

These are the very poor, and I am sorry to say, they are somewhat numerous; but even in the capital, they are not clamorous nor obstinate beggars, and to the credit of the higher and middle classes be it said, every exertion is made to ameliorate their condition.

DROWNING A DOG (1846)*

Philip Tocque (1814-99) was born in Carbonear, Conception Bay. He spent much of his life as a teacher and justice of the peace, but in 1864 took orders in the Anglican Church, having studied at Berkeley Divinity School in Connecticut. He served as a minister in the United States and in Nova Scotia, Quebec, and Ontario. He died in Toronto. The extract below is taken from his first book. In 1878 he published *Newfoundland, As It Was and As It is in 1877,* and a collection of his essays, edited by his daughter, Annie Tocque, was published in 1895 under the title *Kaleidoscope Echoes.*

NO ANIMAL IN Newfoundland is a greater sufferer from man than the dog. This animal is employed during the winter season in drawing timber from the woods, and he supplies the place of a horse in the performance of several duties. I have frequently seen one of these noble creatures drawing three seals (about one hundred and thirty pounds' weight) for a distance of four miles over huge rugged masses of ice, safe to land. In drawing wood the poor animal is frequently burdened beyond his strength, and compelled to proceed by the most barbarous treatment. Of the cruel conduct of many an unfeeling master I have often been a witness, and I have seen the poor creatures left dead on the side of the road. I have twice seen the head of this sagacious animal stuck upon the stump of a tree, exhibited as a memorial of the cruel and inhuman conduct of his master. Nor does the horse at this season escape being over-loaded, and treated with great barbarity. I have seen a man beating this admirable creature with a stick larger than a man's arm, until one of his eyes was knocked out of his head. Some of these animals die from the cruel treatment they receive...

I well remember seeing some boys taking a poor dog to drown him. It is almost a general practice in Newfoundland, that after the poor animal has faithfully served his master, and is no longer able to draw wood, there is a large stone sufficient to sink him, fastened firmly round his neck, and he is then thrown into the sea to die. The boys were engaged in this most cruel and unfeeling practice when I

* Philip Tocque, *Wandering Thoughts and Solitary Hours* (London 1846)

saw them, but in this instance instead of taking him to the sea, where there was deep water, they were endeavouring to drown him in a brook with hardly sufficient water to cover the poor animal. The owner of the dog was looking on, and appeared pleased to see his children practising such cruelty. I remonstrated with him on the impropriety and inhumanity of such a procedure. He said, 'I thought as every body else drowned their dogs when they got too old to work, it was no harm for me to do so.' I said, 'But do you not conceive it to be unfeeling and sinful to take away the life of your poor dog, after having laboured for you all his life? and do you not think that your children, from practising such cruelty, will gradually become insensible to all sorrows but their own? and if the practice be continued in, it is very probable that they would witness unmoved your own death, as they would the dying agonies of the poor animal they are now endeavouring to drown. Therefore, you ought to give a different direction to their feelings, teaching them not to be thoughtless of the sensations of any thing that has life, and guarding them against any sport or amusement wherein either the larger animals or birds, or even insects, may be treated with cruelty.' He said, 'I never before heard that it was sinful to drown a dumb animal; if I had thought so I am very sure I should never have done it.' I replied, 'Cruelty to animals is a sin very little thought of. It is certainly a transgression of God's law; the scriptures say, "A merciful man regardeth the life of his beast"; this means, that he will be attentive to provide for the wants of those animals that contribute to his pleasure and advantage; not to overload and work them beyond their strength; not to drown them when old, nor to beat or unmercifully injure them in any way.' He said, 'I am sorry I never thought of this subject before, for I have drowned many dogs during my life; we will, if you please, go and rescue the dog from the hands of the children.'

We found the poor dog nearly choked from the pressure of the rope around his neck, to which the stone was attached, in order to sink him when thrown into the water. After cutting off the rope, I was glad to find he was still able to walk, though the boys had been endeavouring to drown him for nearly half an hour. It is now nearly four years since this occurrence took place, and the dog was living the last time I was at Carbonear, although not able to draw wood in the winter season; and the person who owned him exceedingly regretted that he should have ever been the cause of taking the life of an animal.

THE PETTY HARBOUR BAIT SKIFF (1852)*

The ballad of the Petty Harbour bait skiff was written by John Grace, a sailor from Riverhead, St John's. It was based on an actual disaster which occurred on 8 June 1852, during a year noted for particularly stormy weather. The lone survivor of the crew clung to the jib boom of the skiff, which luckily remained afloat.

GOOD PEOPLE all both great and small
  I hope you will attend,
To those few simple verses
  That I have lately penned.
They are concerning dangers
  That we poor seamen stand,
Whilst sailing by the stormy shores
On the [coast] of Newfoundland.

It happened to be in the summer time
In the lovely month of June,
When fields were green, fair to be seen,
And valleys were in bloom
When silent fountains do run clear,
Caressed by Heaven's rain,
And the dewy showers that fall at night
To fertilize the plain.

We bid Adieu unto our friends.
And those we held most dear
Being bound [from] Petty Harbor
In the spring-time of the year.
The little birds as we sailed on
Sung o'er the hills and dales,
Whilst Flora, from her sportive groves,
Send forth her pleasant gales.

On Saturday we sailed away,
Being in the evening, late;

* James Murphy, comp. *Songs Their Fathers' Sung* (St. John's 1923)

Bound unto Conception Bay,
All for a load of bait
The sea-gulls flying in the air,
And pitching on the shore,
But little we thought 'twould be our lot
To see our friends no more.

The weather being fine, we lost no time
Until we were homeward bound;
The whales were sporting in the deep;
And the sword fish swimming round,
And Luna bright, shone forth that night
To illuminate the 'say.'
And the stars shone bright, to guide us right,
Upon our rude pathway.

We shook our reefs and trimmed our sails,
Across the bay did stand;
The sun did rise, all circle-ized
Like streamers o'er the land
The clouds lay in the atmosphere
For our destruction met;
Boreas blew a heavy squall,
Our boat was overset.

When we came to the 'Nor'ad' head,
A rainbow did appear.
There was [every] indication
That a storm was drawing near,
Old Neptune riding on the waves
To windward of us lay.
You'd think the ocean was on fire
In Petty Harbor Bay.

John French was our commander,
Mick Sullivan second-hand,
And all the rest were brave young men
Reared up in Newfoundland.
Six brave youths, to tell the truth

Were buried in the sea,
But the Lord preserved young Menchington's life
For to live a longer day.

Your heart would ache, all for their sake,
If you were standing by,
To see them drowning, one by one
And no relief drawing nigh.
Struggling with the boisterous waves,
All in their youth and bloom,
But at last they sank, to rise no more,
All on the eighth of June.

Jacob Chafe, that hero brave,
And champion on that day,
They boldly launched their boat with speed
And quickly put to sea.
They saved young Menchington from the wreck
By their united skill,
Their efforts would be all in vain
But for kind Heaven's will.

Out of that fine young crew you know,
There was one escaped being drowned,
He was brought to Petty Harbor
Where good comforts there he found
He is now on shore, and safe once more,
With no cause to complain,
He fought Old Neptune up and down
Whilst on the stormy main.

When the sad news arrived next day
In dear old St John's town,
There was crying and lamenting
On the streets both up and down.
Their mothers were lamenting,
Crying for those they bore,
On the boisterous waves they found their graves
Where they n'er shall see them more.

Now to conclude and finish
Those few lines I write in pain.
Never depend out of your strength
Whilst sailing the main.
But put your trust in Providence,
Observe the Lord's command,
And He'll guard you right, both day and night,
Upon the sea and land.

AN OFFICIAL EXAMINATION FROM WHICH SOMETHING APPEARS (1858)*

Robert Traill Spence Lowell (1816-91), son of the distinguished Unitarian clergyman Charles Lowell, and older brother by three years of James Russell Lowell, was born in Boston and educated at Harvard University. In 1843 he was ordained priest in the Episcopal Church. His novel *The New Priest in Conception Bay* was based on his experiences as a missionary of the English Society for the Propagation of the Gospel at Bay Roberts, Conception Bay (1843-7). The book was reprinted in McClelland and Stewart's New Canadian Library in 1974.

The novel deals in part with the relationship between Protestants and Roman Catholics in 'Peterport' and neighbouring communities. Skipper George Barbury's daughter, Lucy, thought to be attached to the young Roman Catholic James Urston, becomes seriously ill and, at the height of her illness, mysteriously disappears. The charred remains of Lucy's prayer book are found outside the home of Thomas Urston, James' father, and Mrs Bridget Calloran, another Roman Catholic, is apparently implicated. Mr Bangs, a visiting American merchant, and Captain John Nolesworth of the brig *Spring-Bird*, report seeing a number of nuns in the vicinity of Skipper George's house, carrying 'something' with them. A Roman Catholic plot to abduct Lucy is suspected. Accordingly, Constable Gilpin[1] (accompanied by a posse consisting of William Frank, called locally 'Billy Bow', Zebedee and Nathan Marchant, Skipper George's nephew Jesse Barbury, called locally 'Jesse Hill', and Isaac Maffen) arrest Mrs Calloran, James Urston, and Thomas Urston and bring

* Robert R. Lowell *The New Priest in Conception Bay* (Boston 1858)

them before the stipendiary magistrate Ambrose Naughton, for official questioning. Also appearing or mentioned in the scene which follows are the Reverend Arthur Wellon, the Anglican minister at Peterport, who had picked up an apparent trace of Lucy, a white cap marked 'L.B.,' in a local cove called the Worrell; Mr Williamson, the parish clerk; Fr Nicholas, parish priest at neighbouring 'Bay-Harbour'; and Fr Debree, the mysterious 'new priest' who has turned up at Peterport.

THE MAGISTRATE'S HOUSE, to the party now approaching it, looked as a house might look, which, built in very ungainly style and of no large dimensions, was dignified by its association with the magistracy, and now clothed in all the awfulness of an official want of animated life. Not much impression seemed to settle upon 'Mr Gulpin,' or his prisoners, who walked, with little apprehension, up to the front door; unmindful how the gravel-stones were scattered from their heels; but to the valiant Jesse and the valiant Isaac an awful figure of spectral personation of Authority or Indiction seemed to possess the gate and plant its shadowy terrors directly in the way. They drew off to each side; accounting for their movements by the remark: 'He don't want none of we yet, I don't suppose, do 'e? '

On the arrival of a second squad, however, the first, as if they had received a sudden summons, anticipated the new-comers by a hasty movement, which brought them to the door in time to make their way into the kitchen; while their official leader and his captives went, under the guidance of Mr Naughton's maid-of-all-work, into the presence of the magistrate; if presence it could be called, where he sat with his back broadly towards them.

'Please your worshipful,' said the usheress, 'it's Mr Gulpin, sir; wi' some that 'e've caressed, most like, sir.'

'Directly!' answered the official voice; which then proceeded to read in a low tone, and hastily, out of some book before him, ' "both houses of parliament, and" – I must look at that again; seven hundred and twenty-seventh page.'

Meanwhile, the constable leaving his charge, for a moment, standing at the stipendiary's back, went out long enough to give a message, of which the last words were heard, as he enforced them:

'And mind ye, Jesse, bring un along: don't come without un; and come back as quick as you can.'

The ermine, or other fur of the magistrate, set itself up at this, and he intimated to his subordinate that 'order and silence were necessary at that investigation.' With a large dignity, he invited the minister, who was entering, to a seat.

Having, at length, received the constable's return, he proceeded to business by ordering that officer to swear the prisoners at the bar. Gilpin looked, with twinkling eye, at his prisoners, and then at the magistrate:

'What'll I swear 'em to, Mr Naughton?' he asked.

'There's a copy of the Holy Evangelists here,' said the stipendiary.

'I can find Bibles fast enough, sir: but they're not witnesses.'

'I may ask them some questions and desire their answers to be under the solemn sanction of an oath,' answered the magistrate; but when Mr Urston had the Sacred Volume held out to him, he decidedly objected; insisting that if he and the others were there as prisoners, they were not there as witnesses; and desiring that the accusation might be read, and the witnesses examined.

The magistrate assured him, with dignity, that that was not the regular order of judicial proceedings, but that he would waive the point.

Having, in his own way, made the prisoners acquainted with the charge, he said, 'There must be a record of the proceedings of this court! Mr Williamson, you will act as clerk. Constable, qualify Mr Williamson, and summon the witnesses.'

The constable having qualified the clerk, called 'Jesse Hill!' but there was no answer; and he called Jesse Hill again, and again with no answer.

'I sent him after Mr Banks,' explained Gilpin.

'Sending one witness after another is quite irregular; I trust that it will not occur again. It will be my duty to suspend the proceedings until you can produce Mr Hill, or Barbury.'

At this moment, Mr Naughton noticed Father Debree near the door, attending by a shuffling of feet and a low buzzing of the waiting public. The magistrate with dignity invited him to a seat, but the priest preferred standing. Mr Wellon attempted conversation with his new neighbor, but found him this day so reserved or preoccupied as to give little encouragement to the attempt.

Mr Wellon, during the absence of the constable, was entertained by the stipendiary with an argument for having a 'lychnoscope' introduced, as a sacred accessory, into the new chancel of the church; the earnest advocate for ecclesiological development claiming that the thing was so old that its very object and purpose were entirely unknown.

Gilpin, as he returned with Jesse (and Isaac) behind him, said, in an under voice, 'I told un not to come without Mr Banks; an' so he stuck to his orders. I found un sitting on one rock and Isaac Maffen on another, neither one of 'em sayin' a word.'

The Stipendiary now crowned his brow with the awful rigors of justice once more and sat as the chief figure of the scene. The witness, having been sworn, was questioned:

'Mr Barbury, proceed. Are you a witness?'

'Is, sir, ef it's wantun, I'll tell what I knows.'

The noise of heavy shoes on the feet of those of the public furthest back in the entry, testified to the unabated interest with which Jesse's story was expected.

'What's your name? is the first question.'

Jesse was redder than usual; but he saw his way, and gladly opened his mouth.

'Oh! 'ee wants it that w'y, do 'ee, sir? "N or M" is what it says.'

'Ha! *you're* not much acquainted with legal proceedings,' said the magistrate, throwing a sentence loaded with about the usual amount of official wit, of about the usual quality, and glancing at the Minister to see if he took the joke.

'What *is* your name? that's all,' said he again, to the simple-minded testifier.

'Jesse Barbury's my name, sir. I sposed 'ee knowed that, sir!'

'The Law knows nothing, Mr Barbury. Our information is from the evidence. Have you any alias, Mr Barbury?'

'No, sir; I drinkt a morsel o' tay – Izik Maffen an' me, sir, afore we comed!' answered Jesse, mistaking the magistrate's technicality.

'Are you ever called any thing else, the Law means.'

'They calls me Hill, sir; I suppose 'ee knows that, sir.'

'Mr Barbury, what is your occupation?'

'Fishun, sir, fishun.'

'Have you any other occupation, Mr Barbury?'

'I follys the Church, sir, ef that's what 'ee manes.'

'That's a respectable occupation,' said the Parson, parenthetically.

'Ah! abstract questions seem to confuse the witness's mind; we will therefore come to the point. Mr Barbury, do you know any thing of this affair of Mr George Barbury's daughter, in connection with any of the prisoners at the bar?'

'No, sir. Skipper George is my connexion, sir.'

'Yes; well, tell all you know.'

'There, that won't take ye long, Jesse,' said the constable, by way of encouragement. 'Go at it your own way, Mr Naughton means.'

'Let us preserve decorum, Mr Constable,' said the magistrate. 'Let the witness proceed, without fear or favor. Which side is he on?'

'Are you for or against, Jesse?' asked the constable.

'Oh! agen harm comin to Lucy, surely, Mr Gulpin.'

If the solemnity and sadness connected with the maiden's loss did not prevail in this examination, it might have consoled right-minded spectators to reflect that this whole scene appeared entirely separated and apart from that calamity, after it had proceeded a little while.

The witness being now encouraged to go on (all difficulties being taken out of the way), proceeded as follows, the magistrate ostensibly neglecting to listen, and studiously, with much flutter of leaves, comparing one place with another in his great book.

'I was aw'y over, t'other side, a-jiggin squids, I was; and Izik Maffen was along wi' I; and I says to un, "Izik," I says, " 'e knows Willum Tomes," I says, "surely." "Is, sure," 'e says, "I does," to me, agen. "Well, Izik," I says, "did 'ee hear, now, that 'e 've alossed 'e's cow?" I says.'

The magistrate officially cleared his throat of some irritation; the Minister wiped his face with his handkerchief, a circumstance that seemed to have an encouraging effect upon the witness. He went on:

'So Izik 'e says to I agen, "No, sure," 'e says, "did un, then Jesse?" "Is, sure," I says, " 'e've alossed she, surely." With that 'e up an' says to I, "A loss is a loss, Jesse," 'e says. "That's true," I says.'

This moral reflection brought the Minister's handkerchief suddenly to his face again. The constable received the saying with less self-control, though it was as true as any sentence of the Philosophers. William Frank, who was further off, commented: 'Wull, wisdom is a great thing; it's no use!' Jesse continued.

' "Izik," I says to un, agen, "Izik," I says, "do 'ee think, now, would n' the squids do better a little furderer up?" I says. With that we takes an' rows up tow'rds Riverhead, a bit. Wull, after bidin' there a spurt, I axes Izik what e' thowt such a cow as that might be worth. I says – '

'You must remember, Mr Barbury,' interposed the Stipendiary, 'that the time of a magistrate is valuable, not to speak of the time of the others that are here.'

'Be 'e, now, sir?' said the poor fellow, getting abashed, 'so 'e must be, surely; that's a clear case. That's a'most all I've agot to s'y, sir.'

'Begin just where you're going to knock off, Jesse,' suggested the constable.

'Wull, Mr Gilpin, I were goun to tell about what I sid myself.'

'That's the very thing,' said Mr Naughton; 'no matter what you said, or what was said to you, you know.'

With these directions, the witness paused a little, handling his sou'wester (hat).

'Whereabouts was we, Izik?' he asked of his adjutant.

' 'Ee was talkun about the cow, Jesse, 'ee was,' answered Isaac, anxious that Jesse should do justice to himself.

'Wull, sir.' Then the straightforward witness for the Crown began: 'I was jest a sayin to Izik, I was – '

'Your observations and those of your companion (or friend) are of comparatively little consequence, Mr Barbury,' said the magistrate, who must have had a standard for estimating speech.

'He means, he doesn't care what you and Isaac said,' the constable prompted.

' 'Is, sir, surely. Wull, Izik says to I – '

'Never mind the sayins, you know,' persisted the constable.

The witness looked like some animal in an inclosure; but he did hit upon the opening in it.

'Wall, sir, I sid a some'at all in white clothes a comin' down Backside-w'y (an' Izik Maffen, 'e sid the same, so well), like a woman or a mayd, like, an' it comed right along tull it goed right aw'y, like, I dono how. I never sid no more of it.'

'Did you stop to look?'

'Is, sir, surely; I says to Izik, "Izik," I says, as soon as ever I could speak – for I was dumb-founded entirely, first goun off – "Izik," I says, "Did 'ee ever see 'e'er a angel, Izik?" "No, sure, Jesse," he says, "how should I?" "Wull then," I says, "that was a some'at looked very like one, seemunly, to my thinkin," I says, "O, Lordy!" he says – that's his way, you know, sir – what 'ave abecomed of 'un? Jesse," he says. "Mubbe" I says, "it was a goun somewhere, tull it sid we; an' now it's adone a doun of it, for a notion its abad I says; sartainly we tookt swiles, of a Sunday, last spring," I says. "Howsever," I says, "mubbe we'd best knock off now," an' so we done, sir, an' comed right home, sir, round the land-head. That's all the witness I knows.'

'You may retire, Mr Barbury (unless any of the prisoners at the bar desire to question you).'

This privilege the prisoners did not claim.

There was a monstrous discharge of pent-up breaths at the conclusion of this evidence, showing that a good many of Jesse's friends were in the passage communicating between the kitchen and the parlor, who felt that Jesse had more than satisfied the highest expectations that could have been formed about his testimony, and had contributed to the fund of information which the magistrate was gathering, as wonderful an ingredient as any that was likely to be produced that day. To his friends, as he modestly withdrew from the blaze of importance, he gave the information for the hundredth time, perhaps, that it was Friday evening that this occurred; that he did not hail the apparition; that it did not come within hail; that 'he shouldn't have a know'd what to say to it, ef he'd awanted to.'

'No more 'ee would'n; that's a sure case,' said Isaac Maffen.

'Any evidence as to the credibility of Mr Barbury and his friend, will now be admissible,' said the magistrate, with dignity tempered by condescension.

'Haw! H–' burst from the constable, very untimely; a laugh cut off in the middle.

Mr Wellon, at this point withdrew.

'Call the next witness!' said the magistrate, waiving further interruption.

'I dono how to call un, exactly; I believe his name is Nathan; but he's got an "L," stuck before it, I thinks, from the way he spoke it.'

'– L., Nathan Banks! L., Nathan Banks!' Gilpin called, making his comment also. 'Well, if that isn't a way of writing a name! I've sid L's and D's stuck at the end, but sticking 'em at the beginning 's noos to me.'

Our readers have seen the world some days farther on than Gilpin had, and are familiar enough with a fashion of which Mr Bangs, whose name happened to be Elnathan, was quite innocent.

Mr Bangs did not appear. 'I thought surely he'd turn up, as he did t'other night,' said Gilpin. 'I didn't tell un he'd be summonsed; but he's got a sharp nose.'

'I understood that Mr Wellon could testify,' said the stipendiary.

'Ay; but without Mr Banks you can't weld the evidence together, sir.'

'You'd best summon him; and that point can be determined.'

' 'E's just out in Tom Fielden's house,' timidly suggested Nathan, or Zebedee, or some one of them, not thinking his voice fit to intrude in so awful a presence. ' 'E went there, however, a bit sunce.'

'Present my compliments to him then, please, one of you; "compliments of his worship, the Stipendiary Magistrate, to the Reverend Mr Wellon," and ask if he'll please to step here for a few moments.'

The 'one' who undertook this errand must have had an unusual number of feet, or of shoes upon his feet, if one judged by the multitudinous clatter that followed.

The Minister, on coming in again, gave his short account of finding the little cap at the Worrell; and that was all. The stipendiary spoke:

'The evidence just received may go towards establishing the nature of the crime by which Mr Barbury's daughter has been assailed; but, in my judgment, it would be insufficient to fix the guilt with unerring certainty upon any individual.'

'I shall proceed to examine the remaining witnesses?'

The case had assumed an entirely different look, since the beginning of this investigation, from that which it had worn when the Parson and the constable put together the facts and conjectures, like bits of a torn letter. In the present condition of things, Gilpin's evidence about the Prayer-book, and Mrs Calloran, and Father Nicholas, amounted to little, unless in its effect upon the public within hearing; an effect testified to by moving of feet, hard breathing, whispers, and low-toned remarks, Captain Nolesworth was not called.

Mr Urston was indignant at the listening which Gilpin confessed to, and which the latter justified by the grounds of suspicion existing against Mrs Calloran, at least. The Stipendiary Magistrate took a new view of the case at this point: 'That, being the trusted depositary of justice, he had consulted the convictions of the community in entering upon this Investigation; but that, as important witnesses for the crown were absent, and the prisoners at the bar asserted their own innocence, he judged it best, employing that discretion which the crown and nation necessarily bestowed upon the administrators of the Law, to postpone the farther examination for one calendar month; in the mean time binding over the prisoners at the bar to keep the peace with sufficient sureties.'

Mr Urston very pertinently suggested that 'until some sort of show of evidence appeared against them, it was unreasonable to treat them formally as suspected persons; and why they were to be bound over to keep the peace, he could not understand.'

The magistrate explained that ' "keeping the peace" was merely a legal expression; the object being to prevent prisoners from escaping. He would say fifty pounds each, for Mr Urston and his son; and would consider them responsible for the appearance of Mrs Calloran. The day to which he had adjourned the court,' he said, 'would be appreciated by the persons chiefly interested; it was the fifth from that of the Exaltation of the Holy Cross, and following that of St Lambert, Bishop and Martyr. In consideration of the result of the patient and deliberate investigation which had afforded him peculiar gratification, he would himself be responsible for the usual costs.'

The Minister offered himself as surety, and was at once accepted.

Gilpin, on getting into the open air, as he did very speedily, surrounded by the open-mouthed and eager public, did not prevent himself from exclaiming (while he looked flushed and chagrined), 'Well, if that isn't law, with a tail to un!'

An irreverent voice from among the public (strongly resembling Billy Bow's) asserted that 'The King (ef 'twas the king 'isself that doned it) might as well take a squid or a tom-cod for a magistrate, as some 'e'd amade,' and then proposed 'three cheers for Mr Charles Gulpin, Constable of his majesty in this harbor and the neighboring parts.'

The cheers were begun lustily, though at Gilpin's mention of Skipper George's loss, they broke off, and just as they were dying away, the door of the Magistrate's house opened, and he appeared, looking from side to side, and with a modesty that sate gracefully upon dignity and authority, said that 'Words would fail him to express his sense of the generous confidence of the people of Newfoundland; that he was glad that his humble efforts had met the applause of his fellow-subjects, which was next to the award of an approving conscience. He looked with confidence to the approval of his sovereign. In conclusion, he begged all present to partake of a little coffee, which he had given orders to have prepared.'

'Three cheers for 'e's woshup, the Sti-pendery of Peterport'; cried the voice again, 'and may the King soon be so well plased to put un in a berth better fittun to his debilities!' Over this there was more subdued laughter than shouting.

NOTE

1 Gilpin has been eavesdropping on Mrs Calloran in an effort to gain information.

A PARSON AND HIS PEOPLE (1863)*

The English divine Julian Moreton was born at Chelsea in 1825. He was appointed to the Greenspond mission of the Anglican Church in October, 1849. He described the work from which the following extract is taken as 'an extension of an Address delivered at St James's, Picadilly, at Hursley, at St Peter's, Rochester, and on several occasions in the parish of Romford, Essex.' He worked in Newfoundland 'for upwards of thirteen years.'

MANY AN AMUSING anecdote might be told of dull apprehension, which is so like perverse misapprehension and clever evasion, that you cannot be sure of which kind it is. I was told of one of my predecessors in Greenspond, that in trying with much earnestness and labour to correct the sordid temper of an aged parishioner, he cited as an exemplar the conduct of the martyr Cranmer. 'He might have saved his life, John, if he would. All he need do to save himself from the fire would have cost him nothing, but he would not do wrong for any gain. It was only to write his name on a piece of paper, and he would not.' The old man, much interested exclaimed, 'Why, he must have been a proper fool!'

Alas, how often are our words spent to as little purpose! I was once labouring to impress upon a man the duty of the flock to maintain its church and minister, and his own duty in particular to contribute to my yearly collection of dues. He replied that the Society (for the Propagation of the Gospel in Foreign Parts) maintained me, and that if my salary were not sufficient, the Society was

* Julian Moreton *Life and Work in Newfoundland* (London 1863)

to blame for having reduced it. To exculpate the Society, I asserted the ability of the flock, and showed how much the Society had done in wholly maintaining the mission for so many years, and paying its several successive ministers in that time no less a sum than so much. I now forget the time and sum. My argument resulted only in the man's astonished exclamation, 'My! there's a sight of money the parsons had.' I had but confirmed him in the common and most unreasonable notion that the parson is a rich man...

My own hopes have sometimes been excited by a request for information, usually prefaced with many apologies for making it: 'I hope it's no harm what I'm going to ask, sir, but I said I'd ask you. Excuse my boldness.' Then came some question about a passage of Scripture. Too commonly it proved to be only an idle inquisitiveness upon some point which could have no bearing upon their own faith and practice. I have been taken aside from a journey, and detained in a house by the way, solely to satisfy an inquiry as to who were those sons of God that allied themselves with the daughters of men. One day, while on a journey in my last mission, I saw a woman sitting outside her house, looking very thoughtful over a book which I had lately given her. I stayed to talk with her, and she told me that she was in perplexity about the subject on which she was reading. 'I know it's very stupid of me, sir; but I'm thinking and stud'ing, and I can't make it out. And I've asked Aunt Rachel too, and she's a very knowledgeable woman, but she can't resolve me.' The difficulty was first that she could not discover who was the mother of the Blessed Virgin. When I had helped her out of this trouble, she told me next that she could not find out to what tribe and family the Virgin belonged. I said, 'The tribe of Judah, and the house of David.' 'Yes, sir, I know it's said she was of the house and lashens [lineage] of David, but what I can't find out is which of Judah's sons she came of.' It was now time to point out to her the unprofitableness of such inquiries, and direct her to more useful thoughts, which ended our conversation...

The practice of choosing unusual names for children from Holy Scripture, or from other books, is well known amongst the poor every where. My people in Newfoundland were much given to it, and often my utmost power of conjecture or invention was tried to find and give the proper names to infants at their baptism. The word spoken by the sponsors was often unlike any known name, and when with difficulty I discovered what it was intended for, it sometimes proved so objectionable as to oblige me to require a substitute. I was asked to name one child Lo Ruhamah, and its mother was much displeased that I disliked her choice. In her family there had been both this name and Lo Ammi. Jerusha, Abi, Keren-Happuch, and other equally unusual names from Scripture were often given. The names of evil characters were as much in request as those of holy persons, and it may be supposed the parents could not appreciate the feeling which objected to them. The choice made from other sources was sometimes more puzzling. Idgnia was the name appointed by one man to be given to his child. The mother rightly hesitated to reject his choice in his absence, so I taxed my memory to find the name intended, and after much conjecture adopted Eugenia. For another child I changed Hemmony to Hermione. Pertilda was a mispronunciation of Matilda, and Familia of Pamela. Diana, a very frequent choice, I rejected as heathen, and substituted Dinah. A woman whom I knew as Bertha was married years before as Bathsheba, while the register of her baptism gave the name Beersheba. Once when entering a baptism, the babe's mother gave her own name for entry as Blizer. Much puzzled I asked her to spell it. 'Well, sir,' she replied, 'it's strange that you don't know it. Why that's not all my name. I'm Anna Bliza.' This gave me a clue, and I entered her name Annabella Eliza. The process of contraction had been first, Bell Liza, and then Bliza. One woman asked me to name her child Eeplet, and I discovered the intention to be Hypolite. The choice was her husband's, and he was a Frenchman. Once I found a child bearing the hateful name of Cain...

At services held in dwelling-houses, where no church or school is in being, strange interruptions often arise, not only from the necessary presence of the younger members of the family, and the continuance during the service of some culinary processes, but also from the fact of the poor people's being unaccustomed to religious assembling, and not being under the peculiar solemn feeling which the very appearance of a sacred building serves to excite and foster. Immediately before beginning a service I have been disturbed by a woman near me, who intended no offensive familiarity, lifting my surplice to examine it, and remarking aloud upon it. My predecessor was once interrupted, in the midst of his sermon I believe, by the mistress of the house exclaiming to her grandchildren, 'Lotte, hook out the lamp. Jack, drive out the dog.'

A poor man in my mission, whilst once reading the Church prayers, and a sermon for a little congregation where no reader was appointed, was similarly annoyed by an old woman in the chimney corner calling to some young ones, 'My gracious, girls, I've forgot the loaf. Julia, go out to the next house and hang on the bakepot.'

'THE POOR MAN'S ROAD' (1880)*

Daniel Woodley Prowse (1834-1914) was born at Port de Grave, Conception Bay, and was educated at Miss Beenland's school at St John's and also at the Collegiate School in Liverpool. Called to the bar of Newfoundland in 1859, he was a member of the House of Assembly (1861-9) and from 1869 to 1898 was a judge of the Central District Court. A wit, scholar, eccentric, and bon vivant, Prowse was the author of *The History of Newfoundland* (1895), still the most comprehensive history of the island.

THE INCEPTION of the railway in Newfoundland met with great opposition. The merchants were specially hostile to the new departure; one old business man used to stand on the head of his wharf, and tell the people how 'a tall gate' (tollgate) would be placed at the western entrance to St John's; every one with a horse and cart would have to pay 2s 6d, and whenever the surveyor's tape was passed over their land it was gone from them for ever. In consequence of these stories the people were stirred into a state of frenzy and madness. When the railway surveyors began their work at Topsail, at least five hundred insane men and women followed them about constantly insulting and threatening them. I was sent out with a small body of police to talk to the people, and explain all about the railway. For days and days I sat on the hillside, and told them all about the advantages of the new line. It was all in vain; I could not overcome their dread of the new and dangerous enterprise. At last one morning they made a murderous assault on the surveyors, took all their instruments, and they had to run for their lives. As soon as I had

* D.W. Prowse, quoted in J.C. Millais *Newfoundland and Its Untrodden Ways* (London: Longmans 1907) 79-81. Reprinted by permission of Longman Group Ltd

taken the deposition of these frightened officials, I hurried back to where the crowd were rejoicing over their victory. The leader in the assault on the surveyors was a fisherman farmer called Charley Andrews. We had some difficulty in carrying out his arrest. After he had been conveyed to the city jail, I met him on one of my usual rounds of inspection. 'Well, Charley,' I said, 'how are you getting on?' 'I am all for the railway now, Judge.' 'How has that change come over the spirit of your dream?' said I. 'Well,' he answered, 'it was this way. An English sailor chap got drunk and he were put into my cell; when he wakes in the mornin' he says to me, "Well, old chap, what in the name of heaven brought you here?" I told 'un it were fer fightin' agen a railway. "What an infernal old bloke you must be," he said, "to do the like o' that. Why, the railway is the poor man's road," and then that sailor chap he up and explained to me all about en, so I'se all for the railway.' 'But, Charley,' I said, 'did I not explain all this to you over and over again? Did I not explain all this to you over and over again? Did I not tell you all the work it would give the people, how it would bring all the goods to your doors, and quick passages in and out to town?' He hung his head in confusion for some time. At last he took a sly glance up at me: 'Yes, Judge, but we knowed you was paid for sayin' dem tings.'

WINTER SCENES FROM THE GREAT NORTHERN PENINSULA (1882-4)*

Frederick Lloyd was born at Milford Haven and educated at Dorchester College. In 1882, having taken Anglican orders, he was appointed to the mission of the Strait of Belle Isle in the diocese of Newfoundland. His mission field embraced 'the whole of the Northern and a portion of the Eastern coast of Newfoundland, together with about forty miles of the coast of Labrador.' There were fifty-two settlements in the mission, extending over a costline of approximately two hundred miles. Lloyd worked on the mission until 1884 when he was transferred to the diocese of Quebec. When he wrote the account from which the following extract is taken, he was rector of Lévis and south Quebec.

* F.E.J. Lloyd, *Two Years in the Region of Icebergs* (London 1886)

AT THE BEGINNING of November, all eyes are turned in the direction of the winter houses, which are snugly built on a clearing in the midst of the sheltering woods. These houses are very necessary, the summer houses being universally placed as near the sea as possible, where the situation is bleakest and most exposed to the severity of the weather. They are merely log huts, but are always rendered warm and comfortable. The chinks between the logs are calked, or 'stogged,' as they say, with moss previously gathered and dried. The hut usually consists of four apartments, two downstairs, and a similar number upstairs. These apartments are severally known as 'the house' (kitchen), 'room' (which may for sake of distinction be called a parlour), 'outside loft' (room over kitchen), and 'inside loft' (over parlour); in addition to which there is a small 'back house' or 'porch,' built on the warmest side of the hut, in which firewood is kept. In the kitchen near the partition stands a huge stove, like an engine boiler, in which there is always a fire like a furnace. The other kitchen furniture comprises benches, water-barrel, a table, hen-coop, a small dresser, and a 'gun rack.' At a short distance from the house stands the 'wood pile,' where 'one hand is kept cuttin' all the day.' ...

In the winter a considerable number of weddings take place, the festivities accompanying them being the only break which occurs in the monotonous routine of a northern Newfoundlander's life. A hunting expedition ... always precedes a wedding, to provide food for the guests, who come in crowds, whether invited or not. It seems an understood thing that all the men, women, children, and babies of the neighbourhood should assemble at every wedding feast. ... At the conclusion of the marriage ceremony, instead of the merry pealing of the marriage bells, a great firing of guns ensues in honour of the happy couple. At home all is bustle and confusion, in preparing for the hungry company which will soon arrive. Plum puddings, which are known as 'figgy pudden,' are in great demand, as is also what is called 'sweetcake,' a concoction of flour, yeast, and molasses. The fare provided for a wedding feast at which I was an honoured guest, consisted of twenty-seven enormous puddings, seven beavers, several hares and ptarmigan, a corresponding supply of vegetables, some rum, I regret to say, and cake *ad infinitum.* The houses being for the most part small, the guests are usually served in relays, and I must give them credit for possessing the most alarmingly prodigious appetites I ever saw or heard of; but probably, like children in view of the 'tea party,' they denied themselves the pleasure of breakfasting in order to sharpen their appetites, and enlarge their digestive capabilities. The feasting over, dancing begins, and is kept up at intervals during three or four days, or sometimes a week...

The arrival of the mail was always a time of great rejoicing. Thanks to the generosity and thoughtfulness of good friends in England, I always received a liberal supply of newspapers, magazines, and other interesting reading matter. ... All the reading matter I received I used to distribute amongst those of my people who could read, who in their turn communicated its contents to their brethren who could not read. They were very fond of news, and the more exciting it was the more acceptable. They loved most of all to hear about 'the war.' Their first question after the mail arrived was invariably, 'How's the war gettin' on, Sir?' or, if there was no war, 'Is there any war, Sir?' A negative reply to this question was always received with dissatisfaction, I regret to say. They are a most loyal people, and faithful subjects of England's gracious Queen. Nothing used to grieve them more than to hear of the English army suffering a defeat in battle; and, on the other hand, it was truly delightful to witness their enthusiasm and the glow of their patriotism on the occasion of an English victory. They were extremely indignant with the Mahdi and his followers, whom they regarded as villainous and reprobate; and there was little love lost between them and the French.

THE GREAT FIRE OF 8 JULY 1892*

Moses Harvey (1820-1901) was born in Armagh, Ireland, and attended the Royal College, Belfast. In 1852 he went to St John's and for twenty-five years served as Presbyterian minister of St Andrew's Free Church. He was perhaps the foremost publicist of Newfoundland in his day. One of his best known works, *Newfoundland, the Oldest British Colony: Its History, Its Present Condition*

* Moses Harvey *The Great Fire in St Johns* (Boston 1892)

and Its Prospects in the Future, was written in 1883 in collaboration with Joseph Hatton.

ON THE AFTERNOON of that dark day in the annals of Newfoundland I attended a meeting in the basement of St Andrew's Church, for the distribution of prizes to the pupils of the General Protestant Academy. Little did I imagine that this would be the last meeting in that fine, substantial building, and that when I next saw it, only shattered walls and smoke-begrimed ruins would greet the eye.

The meeting closed at a quarter past four, and in company with a friend I went for a walk in the direction of the Parade Ground. About five o'clock I noticed the glare of fire some distance beyond, near Fresh Water Road, and hastening to the spot I found three houses on fire. I remarked to my friend that this was a bad day for a fire. A high wind from the north-west was blowing, hurling the sparks far and wide on the roofs of the clusters of wooden houses. For a month previous hardly any rain had fallen, and the shingled roofs were like tinder. The firemen were soon on the spot, but the supply of water was feeble, and their efforts to arrest the progress of the flames produced little effect. By a strange fatality the water had been turned off in the morning in order to make some new connections of mains, and though it had been turned on again its force on this high ground was slight. A tank which was usually full had been emptied the previous evening by the firemen, when practising with their hose, and by some stupid carelessness had not been filled.

Soon half a dozen more houses were on fire, then twenty. The volume of flames increased, and the roaring wind hurled the burning brands in all directions, which, alighting on roofs at a distance, created fresh centres of fire. Then it became evident that an alarming conflagration had broken out, but no one yet dreamed of the terrible results that were to follow. The force of the wind was increased by the heat, and the fire was now steadily eating its way down Long's Hill into the very heart of the city. The firemen were overpowered, their hose burned, and the flames got beyond control. On the high ground to the right of Long's Hill stood a mass of wooden buildings, consisting of the Methodist College and schools, with dwelling-houses, the Masonic Temple, and the Presbyterian manse. In a few minutes the roof of the college began to smoke, and in half an hour the whole group of buildings was an enormous mass of flames. The fiery torrent, thus swollen, now rushed on, growing by what it fed on. The Methodist Gower Street Church, the Orange Hall, the Synod Hall and schools of the Church of England, the residence of Bishop Jones, went down before the avalanche of fire; and now the beautiful Cathedral of the Church of England – the pride of the city – was surrounded by a ring of flames. No one imagined that such a solid stone structure could be burned; and for an hour before the terrified people around had been carrying their valuables to it as a place of safety. Bishop Jones had placed in it all his household treasures. The fiery tornado swept on. The intense heat melted the lead around the panes of glass, and the destroyer having found an entrance, the stately Cathedral, with all its contents, was soon a glowing mass of fire. The beautifully moulded arches and massive pillars crumbled, and with a crash the lofty roof fell in. The flames leaped up, as if exulting, a hundred feet into the air, and resumed their destructive march. Now came the turn of St Andrew's Presbyterian Church, which was only two or three hundred yards below the Cathedral. It was a massive brick building and supposed to be invulnerable to fire from the outside; but the fierce heat soon melted the glass of the windows, and in an incredibly short space of time nothing remained of St Andrew's but the tower and blackened walls, shattered as with shot and shell.

Opposite St Andrew's Church stood the Athenaeum. Desperate efforts were made to save it, but all in vain. It was a handsome structure, containing a fine concert and lecture hall, the Savings Bank, the Surveyor General's office, a public library, containing seven thousand volumes. The cost of the building was $60,000. It was the institution on which the city prided itself most, and indeed it would have been a credit to any community.

The fiery giant rushed on. The Court House, the Commercial Bank, with the surrounding buildings, speedily shared the common fate. The Union Bank made a stout resistance, and being favorably situated, and well protected by iron shutters, managed to escape. The conflagration now set to work on Duckworth Street, and soon it had all the streets above it in its grasp. Garrison Hill had gone some time before, and all efforts proved futile to save St Patrick's fine hall, with the schools of the Christian Brothers on its ground floor. The Congregational Church, at no great distance, speedily succumbed; and all the area of houses in front of the Catholic

Cathedral and onward towards the east end of the city furnished food for the flames.

The destroying force which had started so advantageously from the heights about the head of Long's Hill, overlooking the city, had here divided itself and sent a strong detachment down towards Water Street, a little east of Carter's Lane. Ere long this column burst into Water Street – the business part of the city – at Beck's Cove, cutting it in two, and leaving one-third untouched to the westward. Now the work of destruction commenced in earnest. Bowring's huge premises, shops, stores, warehouse, wharves, were soon enveloped in sheets of flame. The beautiful shops, full of valuable goods; the stores behind, containing thousands of barrels of flour and provisions of all kinds; the fish stores; the wharves, which it had cost immense sums to erect – disappeared one by one into the maw of the destroyer. Goodfellow's, Ayre & Sons', Baird's, Baine Johnston's, Thorburn & Tessier's, immense premises; Marshall & Roger's, Job Brothers' great block – all fell a prey to the flames, and the whole of Water Street, on both sides, was 'swept with the besom of destruction.'

I had been watching the progress of the fire down Long's Hill, and afterwards as it spread to Scotland Row and attacked the Cathedral and St Patrick's Hall, and I had been helping some friends to remove their goods. When I saw that it had burst into Water Street and was sending out great flakes of fire and tornadoes of fiery particles, like an advanced host of skirmishers, while the solid mass of fire steadily advanced, I then knew that the city was doomed. I began to think of my own home in Devon Row, and for the first time realized that in all probability it would be included in the general destruction. Through a suffocating atmosphere, laden with burning sparks and blinding smoke, I wended my way homeward, and found that all the inhabitants of Devon Row were packing their goods and preparing to remove them to places of safety, as it was believed to be impossible to save the Row. I followed the general example, and we continued the work for two hours and a half, and were successful in carrying to a place of safety all that was portable – thanks to the aid of numerous kind friends. Meantime the fiery torrent was bearing straight down upon us. Devon Row consists of six brick houses, four stories in height, with a tarred asphalt roof – a projecting wooden cornice under the roof, and a wooden balcony behind, so that it presented many vulnerable points. The inmates were all doing their best to fight the fire, and a strong force was assembled at No 5, the house next the fire. The roof was kept wet – wet blankets placed at the end of the balcony, and brooms in active service to sweep off the sparks as they fell in myriads. Still, we had little hope of escaping, as far stronger buildings and better protected had perished. The torrent approached; the house next the Row blazed up, and the blood-red tongues of fire shot out, licking the gable-end and mounting towards the roof. We stood looking on, expecting every moment to see the roof or the windows on fire. We held our breath, waiting for the final catstrophe; but the fiery bombardment did not take effect; the sparks flew off without getting a lodgment; the flames from the burning house next it began to collapse after the roof fell in, and with a sigh of relief we realized that Devon Row was saved. Had it gone, all the houses below it, with the railway station, would have been destroyed.

By this time it was half-past two o'clock in the morning. The sight of the burning city when the conflagration was at its height was appalling. A roaring, tossing sea of fire, its waves at intervals leaping high into the air, as one great building after another collapsed, lighting up the country all around, and the thick smoke canopy overhead; the crackling of burning beams; the crash of falling roofs; the roaring of the wind, now increased to a gale; the fierce heat and suffocating smoke; the terror-stricken inhabitants flying before the destroyer, trying to save some wrecks of their furniture and household goods; the cries of weeping women, hurrying with their children to places of safety – all constituted a scene which not even the pen of a Dante could describe.

The next morning I took a walk around the awful scene of devastation. It was heart-rending. Nothing visible for a mile from Devon Row but chimneys and fallen or tottering walls. The thick smoke, from the smouldering ruins, still filled the air. Where yesterday stood the homes of fifteen thousand people, there were only ashes and debris, or walls and chimney-stalks, ghastly in their nakedness. The wrecks of the fanes of religion stood out, the broken walls pointing heavenward, as if in mournful protest against the desecration that had been wrought.

And the poor inhabitants, where were they? It made the heart ache to see the groups of men, women, and children, with weary, blood-shot eyes and smoke-begrimed faces, standing over their scraps of furniture and clothing – some of them asleep on the ground from utter exhaustion – all with despondency depicted on their faces. They filled the park and grounds around the city. Many hundreds escaped with nothing but the clothes they wore; others had caught up some small wrecks of their property. They had no shelter for their heads, and in many cases had lost all. At least twelve thousand people were burnt out. The value of the property destroyed is estimated at from fifteen to twenty millions of dollars, of which about one-third is covered by insurance. The middle class are the greatest sufferers. Hundreds of families, from comfort and independence, are now brought to penury, and have to begin life afresh. The burnt area is a mile in length, and from a quarter to half a mile in breadth, being more than two-thirds of the city, and that by far the better portion.

St John's has received a terrible blow, and of course it will affect the whole colony and its trade and industries. The fire of 1846 was not to be compared with this in regard to the value of the property destroyed. The city had made very great progress within the past thirty-five or forty years. I had watched its advance with pride and pleasure during that time, and admired the energy and industry of its noble-hearted people. Now I gaze sadly on the wreck of the results of forty years of toil and endeavor – of civilization and progress.

But St John's will rise from its ashes, improved and beautified, I hope, but not in my day.

LOITERERS (1897)*

Henry Beckles Willson (1869-1942) was born in Montreal and went to England in 1892 to make his name in the world of letters. Of particular interest among his numerous books are three regional studies, all based on his own travels: *The Tenth Island* (1897), later revised under the title *The Truth about Newfoundland* (1901); *Nova Scotia: The Province That has been Passed By* (1911); and *Quebec: The Laurentian Province* (1913).

* Henry Beckles Willson *The Tenth Island* (London 1897)

AFTER EACH VISIT I paid to the provincial building, I remarked a numerous body of fishermen and nondescripts loitering in the vicinity. They were dressed in every conceivable shape and style of garment, with some quite inconceivable details as to fit, colour, and patch, with tanned, whiskered countenances, and chewing tobacco, for the most part. These, I was informed, were influential electors come up to demand work and favours. Rough, hardy, and unlettered mariners these, who had smelt of politics from afar, and seemed to have acquired a zest for the banquet. And so they came up, and chewed and spat on the Ionic porticoes and exchanged stories of marine adventure, patiently waiting until they could unfold their grievances or their demands to the 'skipper,' as Sir William[1] is called. For they are 'afther having nothing else in the world to do.'

As I called to pay my respects at Government House I was struck by the beauty of the country about me, as far as eye could reach. Who would have believed this was Newfoundland? The rolling lands were bathed in the sunshine of Italy, and studded with trees and houses, and intersected with picturesque brooks and fine roads.

Pursuing my path, I caught a glimpse by the wayside of a finely-built, ruddy, white-bearded gentleman in a tweed cap toiling resolutely with a shovel.

It was the Governor, Sir Herbert Murray, KCB.

NOTE

1 Sir William Whiteway, prime minister of Newfoundland

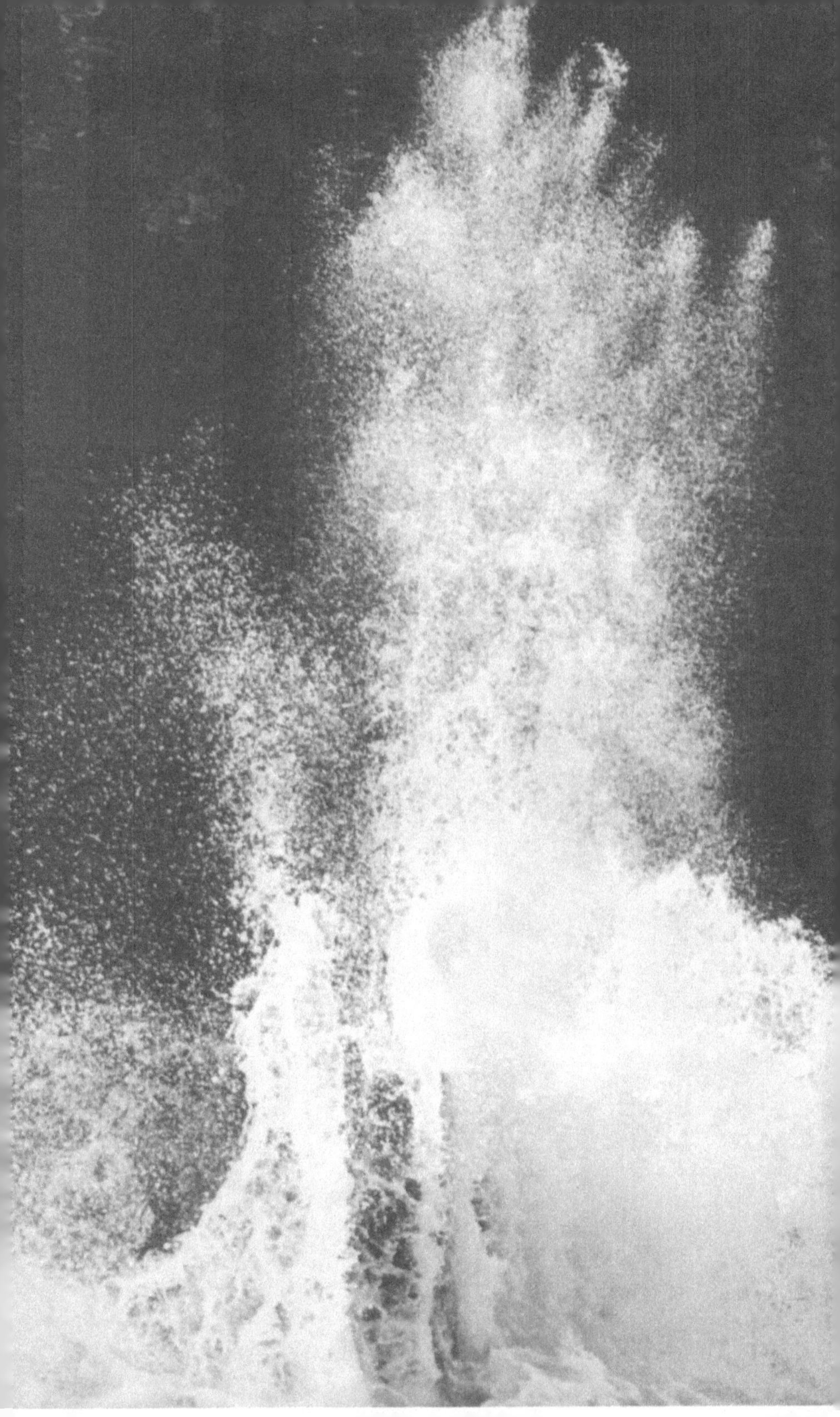

4 NORTH ATLANTIC DOMINION

REFLECTIONS ON THE DEATH OF SOLOMON STRIDE, FISHERMAN (1902)*

Norman Duncan (1871-1916) was born in Brantford, Ontario, and attended the University of Toronto. Beginning in 1895 he worked for a number of eastern American journals and in 1900 made his first trip to Newfoundland as a correspondent for *McClure's Magazine.* He made other visits to the island and Labrador between 1901 and 1906 while teaching at Washington and Jefferson colleges. Duncan was captivated by outport life, which he made the principal subject of his essays and fiction. His works include *The Way of the Sea* (1903), *Dr Luke of the Labrador* (1904), and *Dr Grenfell's Parish* (1905).

NOW THE WILDERNESS, savage and remote, yields to the strength of men. A generation strips it of tree and rock, a generation tames it and tills it, a generation passes into the evening shadows as into rest in a garden, and thereafter the children of that place possess it in peace and plenty, through succeeding generations, without end, and shall to the end of the world. But the sea is tameless: as it was in the beginning, it is now, and shall ever be – mighty, savage, dread, infinitely treacherous and hateful, yielding only that which is wrested from it, snarling, raging, snatching lives, spoiling souls of their graces. The tiller of the soil sows in peace, and in a yellow, hazy peace he reaps; he passes his hand over a field, and, lo, in good season he gathers a harvest, for the earth rejoices to serve him. The deep is not thus subdued; the toiler of the sea – the Newfoundlander of the upper shore – is born to conflict, ceaseless and deadly, and, in the dawn of all the days, he puts forth anew to wage it, as his father did, and his father's father, and as his children must, and his children's children, to the last of them; nor from day to day can he foresee the issue, nor from season to season foretell the worth of the spoil, which is what chance allows. Thus laboriously, precariously, he slips through life: he follows hope through the toilsome years; and past summers are a black regret and bitterness to him, but summers to come are all rosy with new promise...

* Norman Duncan *The Way of the Sea* (New York: Fleming H. Revell Co 1903)

In that night, when the body of old Solomon Stride, a worn-out hulk, aged and wrecked in the toil of the deep, fell into the hands of Death, the sea, like a lusty youth, raged furiously in those parts. The ribs of many schooners, slimy and rotten, and the white bones of men in the off-shore depths, know of its strength in that hour – of its black, hard wrath, in gust and wave and breaker. Eternal in might and malignance is the sea! It groweth not old with the men who toil from its coasts. Generation upon the heels of generation, infinitely arising, go forth in hope against it, continuing for a space, and returning spent to the dust. They age and crumble and vanish, each in its turn, and the wretchedness of the first is the wretchedness of the last. Ay, the sea has measured the strength of the dust in old graves, and, in this day, contends with the sons of dust, whose sons will follow to the fight for an hundred generations, and thereafter, until harvests may be gathered from rocks. As it is written, the life of a man is a shadow, swiftly passing, and the days of his strength are less; but the sea shall endure in the might of youth to the wreck of the world.

PRISONERS OF THE WIND (1903)*

Dillon Wallace (1863-1939) was born at Craigsville, New York. In 1903 he accompanied Leonidas Hubbard Jr (1872-1903), editor of the magazine *Outing*, on his Labrador expedition. The third member of the party was George Elson, a half-breed Cree Indian from James Bay. Hubbard's intention was to follow the trail of the Mountaineer Indians from the Northwest River post of the Hudson's Bay Company, situated on Lake Melville, to Lake Michikamau, and from there beyond that lake northward. Ultimately, he hoped to locate the headwaters of the George River, which flows into Ungava Bay. The initial and fatal mistake made by the party occurred early in the expedition when they mistook the barely navigable Susan River for the much larger Naskaupi. They were also poorly equipped, did not leave for the interior until mid-July, and mistakenly believed that

* Dillon Wallace *The Lure of the Labrador Wild* (New York: Fleming H. Revell Co 1905) 147-61. Reprinted by permission of Fleming H. Revell Co

they could live off the land. The result was catastrophe. They never reached, but only saw, the Michikamau. Hubbard perished, and Wallace, thanks largely to Elston's endurance, barely survived the agonizing journey back. The extract that follows is taken from Wallace's account of the expedition and describes a fateful moment.

IT WAS FOUR o'clock in the afternoon, when the sun was getting low, that I, near the base of the mountain and still industriously picking berries, heard a shout from Hubbard and George at the canoe on the shore of the lake below. I was anxious to hear the result of their journey, and hurried down.

'It's there! it's there!' shouted Hubbard, as I came within talking distance. 'Michikamau is there, just behind the ridge. We saw the big water; we saw it!'

In our great joy we fairly hugged each other, while George stood apart with something of Indian stoicism, but with a broad grin, nevertheless, expanding his good-natured features. We felt that Windbound Lake must be directly connected with Michikamau, and that we were now within easy reach of the caribou grounds and a land of plenty. It is true that from the mountain top Hubbard and George had been unable to trace out the connection, as Windbound Lake was so studded with islands, and had so many narrow arms reaching out in the various directions between low, thickly-wooded ridges, that their view of the waters between them and Michikamau was more or less obscured; but they had no doubt that the connection was there.

'And,' added Hubbard, after I had heard all about the great discovery, 'good things never come singly. Look there!'

I looked where he pointed, and there on the rocks near George's feet lay a pile of ptarmigans and one small rabbit. I picked them up and counted them with nervous joy; there were nine – nine ptarmigans, and the rabbit.

'You see,' said Hubbard reverently, 'God always gives us food when we are really in great need, and He'll carry us through that way; in the wilderness He'll send us manna.' On similar occasions in the past Hubbard had made like remarks to this, and he continued to make them on similar occasions in the future. Invariably they were made with a simplicity that robbed them of all cant; they came from the man's real nature.

While George dressed three of the birds, Hubbard and I built a fire on the rocks by the shore. Since early morning, when we had a breakfast of thin soup made with three thin slices of bacon and three spoonfuls of flour, we had had nothing to eat, and our hunger was such, that while dinner was cooking, we each took the entrails of a bird, wrapped them as George told us the Indians did, on the end of a stick, broiled them over the fire and ate them greedily. And when the ptarmigans were boiled what a glorious feast we had! In using a bit of bacon for soup in the morning we had drawn for the first time on our 'emergency ration' – the situation seemed to warrant it; nevertheless, we were as bent as ever on hoarding this precious little stock of food.

At five o'clock we paddled up the lake to the northeast, to begin our search for the connection with Michikamau. Hubbard dropped a troll as we proceeded, and caught two two-pound namaycush [lake trout], which, when we went into camp at dusk on a small island, George boiled entire, putting into the pot just enough flour to give the water a milky appearance. With this supper we had some of the blueberries stewed, and Hubbard said they would have been the 'real thing if we only had a little sugar for them.'

All day on September 10th we continued our search for the connection with Michikamau, finally directing our course to the southwest where a mountain seemed to offer a view of the waters in that direction. It was dark when we reached its base, and we went into camp preparatory to climbing to the summit in the morning. We had been somewhat delayed by wind squalls that made canoeing dangerous, and before we made camp rain began to fall. We caught no fish on the troll that day, but Hubbard shot a large spruce-grouse. At our evening meal we ate the last of our ptarmigans and rabbit.

'George,' said Hubbard, after we had eaten our supper, 'you have a few more of mother's dried apples there. How would it be to stew them to-night, and stir in a little flour to thicken them? Wouldn't they thicken up better if you were to cook them to-night and let them stand until morning?'

'Guess they would,' replied George. 'There ain't many of 'em here. Shall I put them all to cook? '

'Yes,' said Hubbard, 'put them all to cook, and we'll eat them for breakfast with that small trout Wallace caught and the two ptarmigan entrails.'

In the morning (September 11th) we drew lots for the trout, and George won. So he took the fish, and Hubbard and I each an entrail, and, with the last of the apples before us that Hubbard's mother had dried, sat down to breakfast.

'How well,' said Hubbard, 'I remember the tree on the old Michigan farm from which these apples came! And now,' he added, 'I'm eating the last of the fruit from it that I shall probably ever eat.'

'Why,' said George, 'don't you expect to get back to eat any more?'

'That isn't it,' replied Hubbard. 'Father signed a contract for the sale of the farm last spring, and they're to deliver the property over to its new owners on the fifteenth of this month. Father wanted me to come to the farm and run it, as he's too old to do the work any longer; but I had other ambitions. I feel half sorry now I didn't; for after all it's home to me, and always will be wherever I go in the world. How often I've watched mother gathering these apples to dry! And then, the apple butter! Did you ever eat apple butter, boys?'

George had not, but I had.

'Well,' continued Hubbard, 'there was an old woman lived near us who could make apple butter better than anybody else. Mother used to have her come over one day each fall and make a big lot for us. And, say, but wasn't it delicious!'

'I've told you, Wallace, about the maple sugaring on the farm, and you had some of the syrup I brought from there when I visited father and mother before I came away on this trip. We used to bring to the house the very first syrup we made in the spring, while it was hot – the first, you know, is always the best – and mother would have a nice pan of red hot tea biscuits, and for tea she'd serve the biscuits with cream and the hot new syrup. And sometimes we'd mix honey with the syrup; for father was a great man with bees; he kept a great many of them and had quantities of honey. He had a special house where he kept his honey, and in which was a machine to separate it from the comb when the comb was not well filled. In the honey house on a table he always had a plate with a pound comb of white clover honey, and spoons to eat it with; and he invited every visitor to help himself.'

'Once, I remember, a neighbour called on father, and was duly taken out to the honey house. He ate the whole pound. "Will you have some more?" asked father. "Don't care if I do," said the neighbour. So father set out another pound comb, which the neighbour proceeded to put out of sight with a facility fully equal to that with which he demolished the first. "Have some more," said father. "Thanks," said the neighbour, "but maybe I've had enough." I used to wonder how the man ever did it, but I guess I myself could make two pounds of honey disappear if I had it now.'

Hubbard poured some tea in the cup that had contained his share of the apple sauce, and after carefully stirring into the tea the bit of sauce that clung to the cup, he poured it all into the kettle in which the sauce had been cooked and stirred it again that he might get the last bit of the apples from the tree on that far-away Michigan farm. Then he poured it all back into his cup and drank it.

'I believe it sweetened the tea just a little,' he said, 'and that's the last of mother's sweet apples.'

Breakfast eaten, we had no dinner to look forward to. Of course there was the 'emergency ration,' but we felt we *must not* draw on that to any extent as yet. Hubbard was much depressed, perhaps because of his reminiscences of home and perhaps because of our desperate situation. We still had to find the way to Michikamau, and the cold rain that fell this morning warned us that winter was near.

The look from the mountain top near our camp revealed nothing, owing to the heavy mist and rain. Once more in the canoe, we started southward close to the shore, to hunt for a rapid we had heard roaring in the distance. Trolling by the way, we caught one two-pound namaycush. The rapid proved to be really a fall where a good-sized stream emptied into the lake. We had big hopes of trout, but found the stream too shoal and rapid, with almost no pools, and we caught only a dozen small ones.

Towards evening we took a northwesterly course in the canoe in search of the lake's outlet to Michikamau. While paddling we got a seven-pound namaycush, which enabled us to eat that night. Our camp was on a rock-bound island, partially covered with stunted gnarled spruce and fir trees. The weather had cleared and the heavens were bright with stars when we drew our canoe high upon the boulder-strewn shore, clear of the breaking waves. The few small trout we had caught we stowed away in the bow of the canoe, as they were to be reserved for breakfast.

Early in the morning (September 12th) we were awakened by a northeast gale that threatened every moment to carry our tent from its fastenings, and as we peered out through the flaps, rain and snow dashed in our faces. The wind also was playing high jinks with the lake; it was white with foam, and the waves, dashing against the rocks on the shore, threw the spray high in the air. Evidently there was no hope of launching the canoe that day, and assuming indifference of the driving storm that threatened to uncover us, we settled down for a much-needed morning sleep. At ten o'clock George crawled out to build a fire in the lee of some bushes and boil trout for a light breakfast. Soon he stuck his head in the tent, and, his face told us something had happened even before he said:

'Well, that's too bad.'

'What's too bad?' asked Hubbard and I together.

'Somebody's stole the trout we left in the canoe.'

'Who?' asked Hubbard and I together.

'Otter or somebody – maybe a marten.' (George always referred to animals as persons.)

We all went again to look and make sure the fish were not there somewhere; but they were really gone, and we looked at one another and laughed, and continued to make light of it as we ate a breakfast of soup made of three little slices of bacon, with two or three spoonfuls of flour and rice.

We occupied the day in talking – visiting, Hubbard called it – and mending. Hubbard made a handsome pair of moccasins, using an old flour sack for the uppers and a pair of skin mittens for the feet. George did some neat work on his moccasins and clothing, and I made my trousers look quite respectable again, and ripped up one pair of woollen socks to get yarn to darn the holes in another. Altogether it was rather a pleasant day, even though Hubbard's display of his beautiful new moccasins did savour of ostentation and thereby excite much heartburning on the part of George and me.

Our second day on the island was Sunday, September 13th. We awoke to find that the wind, rain, and sleet were still with us. Our breakfast was the same as all our meals of the previous day – thin bacon soup. The morning we spent in reading from the Bible. Hubbard read Philemon aloud and told us the story. I read aloud from the Psalms. George, who received his religious training in a mission of the Anglican Church on James Bay, listened to our reading with reverent attention.

Towards noon the storm began to moderate, and in a short stroll about the island we found some blueberries and currants, which we fell upon and devoured. At one o'clock the wind abated to such an extent that we succeeded in leaving the island and reaching the mainland to the northeast. The wind continuing to abate, we paddled several miles in the afternoon looking in vain for the outlet. In the course of our search we caught a namaycush, and immediately put to shore to eat it. While it was being cooked we picked nearly a gallon of cranberries on a sandy knoll. We camped near this spot, and for supper had a pot of the cranberries stewed, leaving enough for two more meals.

For several days past now, when George and I were alone, he had repeated to me stories of Indians that had starved to death, or had barely escaped starvation, and a little later he spoke of these things in Hubbard's presence. To me he would tell how weak he was becoming, and how Indians would get weaker and weaker and then give up to it and die. He also spoke of how he had heard the big northern loons cry at night farther back on the trail, which cries, he said, the Indians regarded as sure signs of coming calamity. At the same time he was cheerful and courageous, never suggesting such a thing as turning back. His state of mind was to me very interesting. Apparently two natures were at war within him. One – the Indian – was haunted by superstitious fears; the other – the white man – rejected these fears and invariably conquered them. In other words, the Indian in him was panicky, but the white man held him fast. And in seeing him master his superstitious nature, I admired him the more.

Until this time it had been Hubbard's custom to retire to his blankets early, while George and I continued to toast our shins by the fire and enjoy our evening pipe. Then George would turn in, and I, while the embers died, would sit alone for an hour or so and let my fancy form pictures in the coals or carry me back to other days. In our Sunday night's camp on Windbound Lake, however, Hubbard sat with me long after George was lost in sleep, and together we talked of the home folks and exchanged confidences.

I observed now a great change in Hubbard. Heretofore the work he had to do had seemed almost wholly to occupy his thoughts. Now he craved companionship, and he loved to sit with me and dwell on his home and his wife, his mother and sister, and rehearse his early struggles in the university and in New York City. Undoubtedly the boy was beginning to suffer severely from homesickness – he was only a young fellow, you know, with a gentle, affectionate nature that gripped him tight to the persons and objects he loved. Our little confidential talks grew to be quite the order of things, and often as the days went by we confessed to each other that we looked forward to them during all the weary work hours; they were the bright spots in our dreary life.

A tremendous gale with dashes of rain ushered in Monday morning, September 14th. Again we were windbound, with nothing to do but remain where we were and make the best of it. A little of our thin soup had to serve for breakfast. Then we all slept till ten o'clock, when Hubbard and I went out to the fire and George took a stroll through the bush on the shore, in the hope of seeing something to shoot. While I cleaned my rifle and pistol, Hubbard and I chatted about good things to eat and the days of yore.

'Well, Wallace,' he said, 'I suppose that father and mother are to-day leaving the old farm forever, and that I never can call it home again. I dreamed of it last night. Over fifty years ago father cleared that land when he was a young man and that part of Michigan was a wilderness. He made a great farm of it, and it has been his home ever since. How I hate to think of them going away and leaving it to strangers who don't love it or care more for it than any other plot of ground where good crops can be raised! Daisy [his sister] and I grew up together there, and I used to tell her my ambitions, and she was always interested. Daisy gave me more encouragement in my work than anyone else in the world. I'd never have done half so well with my work if it hadn't been for Daisy.'

After a moment's silence, he continued:

'That hickory cleaning rod for the rifle we lost on a portage on the big river [the Beaver] father cut himself on the old farm and shaped it and gave it to me. That's the reason I hated so to lose it. If we go back that way, we must try to find it. Father wanted to come with me on this trip; he wanted to take care of me. He always thinks of me as a child; he's never quite realised I'm a grown man. As old as he is, I believe he could have stood this trip as well as I have. He was a forty-niner in California, you know, and has spent a lot of his life in the bush.'

When George returned – empty-handed, alas! – we had our dinner. The menu was not very extensive – it began with stewed cranberries and ended there. The acid from the unsweetened berries made our mouths sore, but, as George remarked, 'it was a heap better than not eatin' at all.'

Perhaps I should say here that these were the hungriest days of our journey. What we suffered later on, the good Lord only knows; but we never felt the food-craving, the hunger-pangs as now. In our enforced idleness it was impossible for us to prevent our thoughts from dwelling on things to eat, and this naturally accentuated our craving. Then, again, as everyone that has had such an experience knows, the pangs of hunger are mitigated after a certain period has been passed.

In the afternoon George and I took the pistols and ascended a low ridge in the rear of the camp to look for ptarmigans. Soon George exclaimed under his breath:

'There's two! Get down low and don't let 'em see you; the wind blows so they'll be mighty wild. I'll belly round to that bush over there and take a shot.'

He crawled or wriggled along to the bush, which was the nearest cover and about forty yards from the birds. With a dinner in prospect, I watched him with keen anxiety. I could see him lying low and carefully aiming his pistol. Suddenly, bang! – and one of the birds fluttered straight up high in the air, trying desperately to sustain itself; then fell into the brush on the hillside below. At that George raised his head and gave a peculiar laugh – a laugh of wild exultation – an Indian laugh. He was the Indian hunter then. I never heard him laugh so again, nor saw him look quite as he did at that moment. As the other bird flew away, he rose to his feet and shouted:

'I hit 'im! – did you see how he went? Now we'll find 'im.'

But we didn't. We beat the bushes high and low for an hour, and finally in disappointment and disgust gave up the search. The bird lay there dead somewhere, but we never found it, and we returned to camp empty-handed and perhaps, through anticipation, hungrier than ever.

On Tuesday (September 15th) the high west wind had not abated, and the occasional sleet-squalls continued. We were dreary and disconsolate when we came out of the tent and huddled close to the fire. For the first time Hubbard heard George tell his stories of Indians that starved. And there we were still windbound and helpless, with stomachs crying continually for food. And the caribou migration was soon to begin, if it had not already begun, and there seemed no prospect of the weather clearing.

We made an inventory of the food we were hoarding for an emergency, and found that in addition to about two pounds of flour, we had eighteen pounds of pea meal, a little less than a pint of rice, and a half a pound of bacon. Geroge then told another story of Indians that starved. At length he stopped talking, and we sat silent for a long while, staring blankly at the blazing logs.

Slowly the minutes crawled. In great gusts the wind swept down, howling dismally among the trees and driving the sleet into our faces. Still we sat cowering in silence when Hubbard arose, pushed the loose ends of the partially burned sticks into the fire and stood with his back to the blaze, apparently deep in thought. Presently, turning slowly towards the lake, he walked down through the intervening brush and stood alone on the sandy shore contemplating the scene before him – the dull, lowering skies, the ridges in the distance, the lake in its angry mood protesting against his further advance, the low, wooded land that hid the gate to Michikamau.

Weather-beaten, haggard, gaunt and ragged, he stood there watching; then seemed to be lost completely in thought, forgetful of the wind and weather and dashing spray. Finally he turned about briskly, and, with quick, nervous steps, pushed through the brush to the fire, where George and I were still sitting in silence. Suddenly, and without a word of introduction, he said:

'Boys, what do you say to turning back?'

THE DRAWN SHUTTERS (1905)*

James Brendan Connolly (1868-1957) was born in South Boston, Massachusetts. Having worked for three years with a corps of United States' Engineers in Georgia, he entered Harvard in 1895. He left the university when he was refused leave of absence to compete in the 1896 Olympic games, where he set a 'triple jump' record. He fought in the Spanish-American War and in 1902 published *Out of*

* From James B. Connolly *The Crested Seas* (New York: Charles Scribner's Sons 1907). Used by permission of Charles Scribner's Sons. Copyright 1907 Charles Scribner's Sons.

Gloucester, the first of many sea stories. In 1944 Connolly published an autobiography entitled *Sea-Borne: Thirty Years Avoyaging.*

NO SOONER HAD the *Midnight* let go her anchor in the cove than a door opened in the topmost little house on the rocks. Carefully an old man came down to the beach, with some difficulty launched his boat, and presently was alongside.

The skipper himself took the old man's painter. 'Come aboard, Mister Kippen,' he said heartily.

'Thankee, Captain, but not this mornin'.' He hesitated perceptibly ere he put the question. 'No word, Captain?' There was more of inquiry in the old man's eyes than in what came from his faltering lips – worn old eyes, in which was a pitiable plea for hope. 'No word yet o' the *Pallas*, Captain Butler?'

'None yet, Mister Kippen.'

'Wh-h-h –' the sigh shook the old body. 'Such a fine, able vessel as she was, too. My boy thought he was made when he got her, Captain.'

'And well he might, Mister Kippen.'

'And the proud man I was when I saw him sail out o' Carouge Cove that day. I followed him across the bay to old Weebald, you mind, in my little jack, Captain, though 'twas a risin' gale and I had to lay to Lark Harbor for two days after afore it moderated so I could put back. But the grand American schooners, they'll make easy work of this, I says, and warn't I proud to think of him sailin' that able American vessel! The first Bay of Islands boy that ever went master of a Gloucesterm'n. They'll few o' 'em show *him* the course to Gloucester, I says. Aye, I did. And –' again the eyes dulled – 'and no word o' him since, you say, Captain? Sure there's no word?'

'Well, not when we left home, Mister Kippen, though we didn't come straight from Gloucester. We stopped at St Pierre on the way. Maybe Murray, who's just come to anchor below, has some word. He left home two days after we did.'

'Did he, now? Two days? Yes, yes. I'll drop below and see him. Thankee, Captain, but not this mornin'. Ay, I could one time, and dance as I drinked, but my bitters be'n't what they were to me. No, my bitters don't taste right now; but thankee, Captain, for all that.'

The old man reseated himself in his little boat, resumed his oars, and was off. Captain Butler watched him until he had reached the side of Murray's vessel.

'There, he's aboard. He'll ask the same question, and Murray'll give him the same answer. Nobody with the heart to tell him the truth.'

'And what *is* the truth, Captain?'

'The truth? The whole story? Well, you must go back some little way for that – back to six weeks yesterday, when three of us were on this very spot ready to leave for Gloucester – Wesley Marrs in the *Lucy Foster*, old Kippen's son in the *Pallas*, and myself in this one. We were all of one tonnage, and there was rivalry between us to see who'd take the biggest load of herring. Each of us 'd took on two thousand barrels salt herring, and I know I thought that for our tonnage we all had enough. Well, that night the three of us met at a dance, and after the dance there was supper and a few drinks of smuggled stuff. There was more or less talking too, you know, before the girls, and somebody remarked how deep the vessels were loaded – too deep for that time of the year. We were, as a matter of fact, pretty deep; but Wesley said: "Deep hell! the *Lucy* could take another two hundred and fifty barrels and not know she had 'em." '

'Well, you know there are people in the world who are made of meanness and envy. There was a fellow there who was quite a little man when the American skippers weren't around. He'd been in the rear row for some time, but now he comes to the front again. He looks across at Wesley. "That's good talk, Captain. Could – you say you could, but *would* you?" '

' "Would? Yes, and *will*," fires back Wesley. "Have you two hundred and fifty barrels handy?" '

' "I will have 'em alongside in the morning." '

' "Then in the afternoon they'll be aboard," says Wesley.'

' "I'll have 'em there. That's certainly something *like* a load of herring," goes on this chap. "I wonder now if any of our people here would –" and looks over to young Kippen.'

' "What's that," asks Kippen, "about carryin' a load of herrin'?"

'The fellow repeated what he'd said, and Kippen flares right up. Bring him another two hundred and fifty barrels and see what he'd do with them! You see, he had double reasons for it. There was the girl that he was trying to work to windward of, and making good weather of it, too, naturally – a husky, good-looking young skipper – and this the night before he was to leave on what was generally reckoned a hard trip to Gloucester at this time of year. And then, too, he was the first man out of this place ever went master of a first-class American fisherman. And the natives hereabout were that proud of him! "H-m!" they'd say, "and so they has to come here to wild Newf'undland for skippers as well as men?" and could hardly keep from shouting, some of 'em, at our fellows as they went by. And maybe 'twas from knowing something of that spirit that Wesley Marrs was so quick to make his boast.'

'Anyway, whatever Wesley Marrs says drunk he'll make good sober. So when our friend was there with any quantity of salt herring next morning, Wesley took his two hundred and fifty barrels. And you may be sure the *Lucy* did set something scandalous in the water when she'd got 'em on deck – a good plank deeper than any vessel leaving Bay of Islands that month.'

' "I misdoubt you'll ever get her home, Captain Marrs, if you meets heavy weather," was the cheerful word of one native.'

' "No?" says Wesley. "no? Well, we'll see," and goes around with an auger plugging up her regular scuppers and boring new ones under the top rail. The natives couldn't keep their admiration to themselves when they saw that.'

'Simon Kippen, the old man's son, listened to that talk for a while, and then for the honor of the Bay of Islands – and the thought of the girl, too, I guess – he said he'd stand by what he said the night before. "What one man could do another man could do," and also went around plugging up the regular scuppers and boring holes under his top rail.'

'Tried to stop him, did Wesley. "Now you don't need to do that, Sim," he says, "just because you had a glass of liquor in you last night." '

' "Why not, as well as you?" says Sim, stung you see. "Why can't a Newf'undlander do what any American-born can do?" '

' "Why, no reason at all why he can't, gen'rally speaking, if he's got the right stuff in him, which I know you have; but I'll tell you why, and no discredit to you, Sim, that in this partic'lar case you can't. It's true I'm no older than you but I've been handling big fishermen ten times as long. I've been carrying sail since I was a boy 'most. I know what a vessel c'n do. I know what no man learns except by hard experience, and then he's lucky if he lives to brag about it afterward. I know just how far a vessel c'n roll down before she rolls down to stay. And partic'larly do I know what the *Lucy* c'n do. You don't learn that in one year, or two years, or five years of driving. And you're damn lucky if, after you've learned it, you don't get lost yourself – yourself and your vessel and all hands – some day, experimenting further. And more than that, Sim," says Wesley. "I've been making passages from here to Gloucester for eight or ten winters now. I know every foot of the road, and no credit to me, while this is your first passage as master." '

' "Maybe so," says Simon Kippen to that; "but I've been hand for many a passage – as many as you, for that matter." '

' "Maybe you have," says Wesley; and through it all he was good-tempered as could be. I mind how he looked, standing with one foot on the quarter-rail and smiling, though we all knew it might be no smiling matter soon. "Maybe you have, Sim," says he, smiling over at young Kippen, "but when you're master and the whole responsibility on you alone, you get to thinking a little deeper. So if you take my advice, and no harm meant, you won't take aboard that deck-load of herring." '

' "You put ashore your deck-load and I won't take mine aboard," says Sim.'

' "No," says Wesley. "I've shipped mine – it is in the papers now – and what I've shipped I'll take home or wash overboard – or," he added after a little pause, "go down with." '

' "Well, maybe I'll go down with mine, too." '

' "Maybe you will, too," says Wesley; "but what good will that do!" '

'So they put out. I warn't quite ready to sail – had to reeve a new main-sheet – and I remember I cast off – we were all three tied together – first Kippen's line, and then Wesley's.'

' "Good-by!" calls out Sim to me.'

' "Fair wind," I answered.'

' "I'll see you in Gloucester," was Wesley's word – "that's if all goes well," he added. Wesley was always like that, adding little last words after a little study. He'd lived too long on the sea, I s'pose, to make the mistake of ever saying he'd surely do this or cert'nly do that. But Sim warn't that way. He was drunk with the pride of sailing the *Pallas* out of the Bay of Islands, where all his old chums could see him, and his father, too – to say nothing of the girl he was in love with. To the dock she'd come to see him off. And there he kissed her and hopped aboard the *Pallas.* "Good-by, dad," he hollered back to the old man. "I'll be back in a month, and maybe be in Gloucester in three or four days; certainly in a week with anything like a fair chance. Maybe somebody'll be showing you a Gloucester paper with an account of the trip in it before I get back." '

'They sailed out, and I followed next day. And, of course, what further happened to them I didn't learn till afterward. But they had it out from the beginning. They were no sooner clear of the bay, hardly into the gulf, with Kippen maybe a mile or two in the lead, than they drove into a westerly gale. And all the way down this tough west coast to Cabot's Strait they had it. Both of 'em had on more sail than they should, more than was any mortal use to 'em; but after two days and two nights together, sometimes so close they could hail each other, they warn't either of 'em taking any of it in. Kippen ought to have, because – I meant to have said before – the *Pallas*, while as fine and able-looking a vessel as almost any man would want to see, was what's called a crooked vessel. Her deck wasn't flat enough, and she was too low in the waist – the kind that would fill up amidship and sometimes not get rid of it in time, while the *Lucy*'s flat as a ball-room floor. That was the biggest reason why we didn't want to see Sim load too deep. But you couldn't tell Kippen there was any fault with the *Pallas* – he'd eat you alive.'

'Well, Kippen held on, the gulf behind them, till they butted into the Atlantic and into that hard south-easter, the hardest gale in maybe two winters. I met it two days later, and though I warn't loaded near so deep as Wesley and Kippen, I was glad enough to put into Sydney for a harbor. And I warn't carrying any whole mans'l, either. So you can imagine what weather they made of it. Loaded deep with salt herring a vessel might's well be fastened with a long rod to the bottom of the ocean. There's no lift or heave to her. The sea breaking over her gives her no chance at all. Well, the bother in a case like that – a logey cargo, a big sea, a gale of wind, and a press of canvas – is that you're most sure to get caught sooner or later and hove down; and a vessel hove down with an overload of salt herring is in a bad way. Gen'rally she don't leave you long in doubt. That's what must have happened to the *Pallas* with her crooked deck. Up to five o'clock that particular afternoon, after twenty-four hours in the south-easter, those on the *Lucy Foster* could easily make out the *Pallas* astern. She'd hung on well up to that time – Wesley didn't pass her till they were clear of the Newf'undland coast; but now coming on dark this day the *Pallas* began to drop back, and soon after, when he'd put up her lights, they could hardly be seen from the *Lucy*. Now all this time they'd been having desp'rate times aboard the *Lucy*. There was forty times they thought she was going, but somehow or other, just like her, she'd come up just in time. Then the deck-load of two hundred and fifty barrels began to loosen up under the battering. Now it would have been a great blessing all around if the deck-load had gone – to all but the owners, that is, and even they'd rather lose the deck-load than the vessel and the two thousand barrels in the hold, not to speak of the crew. But Wesley wouldn't let 'em go. "No," he says, "I'll get 'em home. Nobody'll have it to say in Gloucester we got scared so soon. I know Kippen. He'll try and hang on to *his* deck-load long's he can." And with lines about them Wesley and his gang went into the swash and put extra lashings to the barrels on deck. By the time they got that job done 'twas good and dark, and they could barely see the staggering red light of the *Pallas* astern. After that they had no time for anybody but themselves. The worst of it was on them then. And it was well Wesley did get his deck-load double-griped. But tough as it was on the *Lucy* it must have been tougher still on the vessel that was lurching along behind them. And thinking of that, after two terrible seas had all but finished the *Lucy*, Wesley looked back for the lights of the *Pallas* again.'

'Wesley looked long to where he had seen the red light before. He brushed the spray from his eyes and looked again. No light could he see. He sent men into the rigging – he was lashed to the wheel himself – and they looked back over the water. No light anywhere – nothing but what looked like a patch of foam.'

'And though he dreaded it, Wesley hove to his vessel. "Suppose she isn't gone, and suppose she's not hove to and he keeps her goin', he'll cert'nly have the laugh on Wesley Marrs, but what of that? We may not be a bit of use, but we'll wait here till morning." '

'Which they did. But no *Pallas*, not even a bit of wreckage. Like a rock she must have gone down, as a vessel loaded like that and caught wrong is bound to. Anyway, Wesley was satisfied she was gone, and next day went on his way, and after another ten days of head winds battled into Gloucester.'

'Is she gone? Of course we all know she's gone. Six weeks ago that was. Her list was published in the Gloucester papers just before we left, but nobody here will tell that to old Kippen. He still thinks she was blown out to sea or maybe clear back into the Gulf of St Lawrence, where she is now drifting around dismantled and unable to help herself, but still afloat and the boy that left here six weeks back still walking her battered hulk.'

The master of the *Midnight* glanced down toward Murray's vessel. From there his eyes roved toward the little old house perched high up on the rocks, and back then to Murray's vessel, where now old Kippen could be seen shoving off his boat. The old man made but feeble progress, and the tide set him over toward the *Midnight.* Clearly he was very tired, but when he called out to Captain Butler there was a more hopeful ring to his words:'Captain Murray says 'tis possible the *Pallas* was drove clear back through the gulf to the Labrador coast, drove ashore like, and they might be there now, he says. Hard livin' on that coast, Captain, in winter.'

'It must be.'

'Aye, but they has their herrin', and what fresh fish they can ketch. Simon will make out.'

'I hope so, Mister Kippen.'

The old man rowed on to the beach, where, after drawing his boat above high-tide mark, he laboriously made the ascent of the rocks. Now they could see him, and again he would disappear beyond some intervening shack in the winding path. Neighbors were evidently hailing him on the way, for here and there he would halt and, half turning, nod his head, say a few words, of further hope doubtless, and pass along. Twice he paused, apparently for breath.

Arrived at his house he did not at once enter, but turned and gazed out over the bay. He stood so until the door opened and his old wife appeared; and together they stood on the flat rock that served for a doorstep and gazed over the water. It gave one a shiver to see their old gray heads bared to the cold winter air.

Not until the old woman clutched him by the arm did he turn his face from the sea, and even then he returned to it, sweeping his thin arm toward the north-west with hopeful emphasis. She bent her head to his ear then, and evidently asked a distrubing question, for he dropped his arm and shook his head, whereat, stepping heavily, she went within the door. The old man lingered for one more long look across the bay and out toward the Gulf of St Lawrence. Then he, too, went within.

The master of the *Midnight* sighed heavily. 'Isn't that tough? The old woman hasn't his faith, you see. But he'll go on hoping and praying, and none of us with courage to tell him. Maybe 'twould 've been better to tell him.'

As he spoke a neighbor was seen to stop at the door of the house on the hill and knock. The old man came to the door. The neighbor handed him a newspaper and was about to make off, but the old man called after him. The neighbor opened up the paper, pointed hurriedly to something in it and rushed away. The old man gazed after him and then at the paper, before he closed the door. 'He can't read,' commented the master of the *Midnight*, 'but his wife can. God! she'll get it first and have to tell him – what we might have told him before!'

In perhaps an hour the door of the little shack reopened. It was the old woman who came out. With some effort, for the wind was high, she closed all the shutters, and without further look around, stepped within the door again.

Presently another woman, a younger woman this, was seen to climb the winding path and stop at the door. The master of the *Midnight* unconsciously bent over the rail. 'See now – the poor girl!'

After some hesitation the young woman knocked. Again she knocked. And yet once more. No answer coming, she rapped on one of the closed shutters, and still receiving no response, stood on her toes in an effort to peek through the diamond opening. She was not tall enough for that, and, stepping back, again she essayed the door. She rattled the latch; but no word.

Throwing back her head, she stared anew at the blank walls; but nothing coming of that, she made a despairing gesture with her hands, resettled her shawl about her shoulders, and came away. Neighbors, from behind jarred doors, peered out on her, but none spoke to her; and so still was it that from the deck of the *Midnight* they could hear her heels clicking as she hurried down the rocky pathway.

'A GREAT LOTTERY OF HOPE AND FORTUNE' (1905)*

Norman Duncan (1871-1916) was born in Brantford, Ontario, and attended the University of Toronto. Beginning in 1895 he worked for a number of eastern American journals and in 1900 made his first trip to Newfoundland as a correspondent for *McClure's Magazine.* He made other visits to the island and Labrador between 1901 and 1906 while teaching at Washington and Jefferson colleges. Duncan was captivated by outport life, which he made the principal subject of his essays and fiction. His works include *The Way of the Sea* (1903), *Dr Luke of the Labrador* (1904), and *Dr Grenfell's Parish* (1905).

IN THE EARLY spring – when the sunlight is yellow and the warm winds blow and the melting snow drips over the cliffs and runs in little rivulets from the barren hills – in the thousand harbours of Newfoundland the great fleet is made ready for the long adventure upon the Labrador coast. The rocks echo the noise of hammer and saw and mallet and the song and shout of the workers. The new schooners – building the winter long at the harbour side – are hurried to completion. The old craft – the weather-beaten, ragged old craft, which, it may be, have dodged the reefs and outlived the gales of forty seasons – are fitted with new spars, patched with new canvas and rope, calked anew, daubed anew and, thus refitted, float brave enough on the quiet harbour water. There is no end to the bustle of labour on ships and nets – no end to the clatter of planning. From the skipper of the ten-ton *First Venture*, who sails with a crew of sons bred for the purpose, to the powerful dealer who supplies on shares a fleet of seventeen fore-and-afters manned from the harbours of a great bay, there is hope in the hearts of all. Whatever the last season, every man is to make a good 'voyage' now. This season – *this* season – there is to be fish a-plenty on the Labrador!

The future is bright as the new spring days. Aunt Matilda is to have a bonnet with feathers – when Skipper Thomas gets home from the Labrador. Little Johnny Tatt, he of the crooked back, is to know again the virtue of Pike's Pain Compound, at a dollar a bottle,

* Norman Duncan *Dr Grenfell's Parish* (New York: Fleming H. Revell Co 1905)

warranted to cure – when daddy gets home from the Labrador. Skipper Bill's Lizzie, plump, blushing, merry-eyed, is to wed Jack Lute o' Burnt Arm – when Jack comes back from the Labrador. Every man's heart, and, indeed, most men's fortunes, are in the venture. The man who has nothing has yet the labour of his hands. Be he skipper, there is one to back his skill and honesty; be he hand, there is no lack of berths to choose from. Skippers stand upon their record and schooners upon their reputation; it's take your choice, for the hands are not too many: the skippers are timid or bold, as God made them; the schooners are lucky or not, as Fate determines. Every man has his chance. John Smith o' Twillingate provisions the *Lucky Queen* and gives her to the penniless Skipper Jim o' Yellow Tickle on shares. Old Tom Tatter o' Salmon Cove, with plea and argument, persuades the Four Arms trader to trust him once again with the *Busy Bee.* He'll get the fish *this* time. Nar a doubt of it! *He'll* be home in August – this year – loaded to the gunwale. God knows who pays the cash when the fish fail! God knows how the folk survive the disappointment! It is a great lottery of hope and fortune.

When, at last, word comes south that the ice is clearing from the coast, the vessels spread their little wings to the first favouring winds; and in a week – two weeks or three – the last of the Labradormen have gone 'down north'...

At Indian Harbour where the *Strathcona*[1] lay at anchor, I went aboard the schooner *Jolly Crew.* It was a raw, foggy day, with a fresh northeast gale blowing, and a high sea running outside the harbour. They were splitting fish on deck; the skiff was just in from the trap – she was still wet with spray.

'I sails with me sons an' gran'sons, zur,' said the skipper, smiling. 'Sure, I be a old feller t' be down the Labrador, isn't I, zur?'

He did not mean that. He was proud of his age and strength – glad that he was still able 't' be at the fishin'.'

' 'Tis a wonder you've lived through it all, ' said I.

He laughed. 'An' why, zur?' he asked.

'Many's the ship wrecked on this coast,' I answered.

'Oh no, zur,' said he; 'not so many, zur, as you might think. Down this way, zur, *we knows how t' sail!*'

That was a succinct explanation of very much that had puzzled me.

'Ah, well,' said I, ' 'tis a hard life.'

'Hard?' he asked doubtfully.

'Yes,' I answered; ' 'tis a hard life – the fishin'.'

'Oh no, zur,' said he, quietly, looking up from his work. ' 'Tis just – just *life!*'

They do, indeed, know how 't' sail.' The Newfoundland government, niggardly and utterly undependable when the good of the fisherfolk is concerned, of whatever complexion the government may chance to be, but prodigal to an extraordinary degree when individual self-interests are at stake – this is a delicate way of putting an unpleasant truth – keeps no light burning beyond the Strait of Belle Isle; the best it does, I believe, is to give wrecked seamen free passage home. Under these difficult circumstances, no seamen save Newfoundlanders, who are the most skillful and courageous of all, could sail that coast: and they only because they are born to follow the sea – there is no escape for them – and are bred to sailing from their earliest years.

'What you going to be when you grow up?' I once asked a lad on the far north-east coast.

He looked at me in vast astonishment.

'What you going to *be*, what you going to *do*,' I repeated, 'when you grow up?'

Still he did not comprehend. 'Eh?' he said.

'What you going to work at,' said I, in desperation, 'when you're a man?'

'Oh, zur,' he answered, understanding at last, 'I isn't clever enough t' be a parson!'

And so it went without saying that he was to fish for a living! It is no wonder, then, that the skippers of the fleet know 'how t' sail.' The remarkable quality of the sea-captains who come from among them impressively attests the fact – not only their quality as sailors, but as men of spirit and proud courage. There is one – now a captain of a coastal boat on the Newfoundland shore – who takes his steamer into a ticklish harbour of a thick, dark night, when everything is black ahead and roundabout, steering only by the echo of the ship's whistle! There is another, a confident seaman, a bluff, high-spirited fellow, who was once delayed by bitter winter weather – an inky night, with ice about, the snow flying, the seas heavy with frost, the wind blowing a gale.

'Where have you been?' they asked him, sarcastically, from the head office.

The captain had been on the bridge all night.

'Berry-picking,' was his laconic despatch in reply.

There is another – also the captain of a coastal steamer – who thought it wise to lie in harbour through a stormy night in the early winter.

'What detains you?' came a message from the head office.

'It is not a fit night for a vessel to be at sea,' the captain replied; and thereupon he turned in, believing the matter to be at an end.

The captain had been concerned for his vessel – not for his life; nor yet for his comfort. But the underling at the head office misinterpreted the message.

'What do we pay you for?' he telegraphed.

So the captain took the ship out to sea. Men say that she went out of commission the next day, and that it cost the company a thousand dollars to refit her.

'A dunderhead,' say the folk, 'can *catch* fish; but it takes a *man* t' find un.' It is a chase; and, as the coast proverb has it, 'the fish have no bells.' It is estimated that there are 7000 square miles of fishing-banks off the Labrador coast. There will be fish somewhere – not everywhere; not every man will 'use his salt' (the schooners go north loaded with salt for curing) or 'get his load.' In the beginning – this is when the ice first clears away – there is a race for berths. It takes clever, reckless sailing and alert action to secure the best. I am reminded of a skipper who by hard driving to windward and good luck came first of all to a favourable harbour. It was then night, and his crew was weary, so he put off running out his trap-leader until morning; but in the night the wind changed, and when he awoke at dawn there were two other schooners lying quietly at anchor near by and the berths had been 'staked.' When the traps are down, there follows a period of anxious waiting. Where are the fish? There are no telegraph-lines on that coast. The news must be spread by word of mouth. When, at last, it comes, there is a sudden change of plan – a wild rush to the more favoured grounds.

It is in this scramble that many a skipper makes his great mistake. I was talking with a disconsolate young fellow in a northern harbour where the fish were running thick. The schooners were fast loading; but he had no berth, and was doing but poorly with the passing days.

'If I hadn't – if I *only* hadn't – took up me trap when I did,' said he, 'I'd been loaded an' off home. Sure, zur, would you believe it? but I had the berth off the point. Off the point – the berth off the point!' he repeated, earnestly, his eyes wide. 'An', look! I hears they's a great run o' fish t' Cutthroat Tickle. So I up with me trap, for I'd been gettin' nothin'; an' – an' – would you believe it? but the man that put his down where I took mine up took a hundred quintal out o' that berth next marnin'! An' he'll load,' he groaned, 'afore the week's out!'

When the fish are running, the work is mercilessly hard; it is kept up night and day; there is no sleep for man or child, save, it may be, an hour's slumber where they toil, just before dawn. The schooner lies at anchor in the harbour, safe enough from wind and sea; the rocks, surrounding the basin in which she lies, keep the harbour water placid forever. But the men set the traps in the open sea, somewhere off the heads, or near one of the outlying islands; it may be miles from the anchorage of the schooner. They put out at dawn – before dawn, rather; for they aim to be at the trap just when the light is strong enough for the hauling. When the skiff is loaded, they put back to harbour in haste, throw the fish on deck, split them, salt them, lay them neatly in the hold, and put out to the trap again. I have seen the harbours – then crowded with fishing-craft – fairly ablaze with light at midnight. Torches were flaring on the decks and in the turf hut on the rocks ashore. The night was quiet; there was not a sound from the tired workers; but the flaring lights made known that the wild, bleak, far-away place – a basin in the midst of barren, uninhabited hills – was still astir with the day's work.

At such times, the toil at the oars, and at the splitting-table, whether on deck or in the stages – and the lack of sleep, and the icy winds and cold salt spray – is all bitter cruel to suffer. The Labrador fisherman will not readily admit that he lives a hard life; but if you suggest that when the fish are running it may be somewhat more toilsome than lives lived elsewhere, he will grant you something.

'Oh, ay,' he'll drawl, 'when the fish is runnin', *'tis* a bit hard.'

I learned from a child – he was merry, brave, fond of the adventure – that fishing is a pleasant business in the sunny midsummer months; but that when, late in the fall, the skiff puts out to the trap at dawn, it is wise to plunge one's hands deep in the water before taking the oars, no matter how much it hurts, for one's wrists are then covered with salt-water sores and one's palms are cracked, even though one takes the precaution of wearing a brass chain – that, oh, yes! it is wise to plunge one's hands in the cold water, as quick as may be; for thus one may 'limber 'em up' before the trap is reached.

' 'Tis not hard, now,' said he. 'But, oh – oo – oo! when the big nor'easters blow! Oo – oo!' he repeated, with a shrug and a sage shake of the head, ' 'tis won-der-ful hard those times!'

The return is small. The crews are composed of from five to ten men, with, occasionally, a sturdy maid for cook, to whom is given thirty dollars for her season's work; some hold hands will sail on no ship with a male cook, for, as one of them said, 'Sure, some o' thim min can't boil water without burnin' it! A good season's catch is one hundred quintals of dry fish a man. A simple calculation – with some knowledge of certain factors which I need not state – makes it plain that a man must himself catch, as his share of the trap, 30,000 fish if he is to net a living wage. If his return is $250 he is in the happiest fortune – richly rewarded, beyond his dreams, for his summer's work. One-half of that is sufficient to give any modest man a warm glow of content and pride. Often – it depends largely upon chance and the skill of his skipper – the catch is so poor that he must make the best of twenty-five or thirty dollars. It must not be supposed that the return is always in cash; it is usually in trade, which is quite a different thing – in Newfoundland.

The schooners take many passengers north in the spring. Such are called 'freighters' on the coast; they are put ashore at such harbours as they elect, and, for passage for themselves, families, and gear, pay upon the return voyage twenty-five cents for every hundredweight of fish caught. As a matter of course, the vessels are preposterously overcrowded. Dr Grenfell tells of counting thirty-four men and sixteen women (no mention was made of children) aboard a nineteen-ton schooner, then on the long, rough voyage to the north. The men fish from the coast in small boats just as the more prosperous 'green-fish catchers' put out from the schooners. Meantime, they live in mud huts, which are inviting or otherwise, as the womenfolk go; some are damp, cave-like, ill-savoured, crowded; others are airy, cozy, the floors spread deep with powdered shell, the whole immaculately kept. When the party is landed, the women sweep out the last of the winter's snow, the men build great fires on the floors; indeed, the huts are soon ready for occupancy. At best, they are tiny places – much like children's playhouses. There was once a tall man who did not quite fit the sleeping place assigned to him; but with great good nature he cut a hole in the wall, built a miniature addition for his feet, and slept the summer through at comfortable full length. It is a great outing for the children; they romp on the rocks, toddle over the nearer hills, sleep in the sunshine; but if they are eight years old, as one said – or well grown at five or seven – they must do their little share of work.

Withal, the Labradormen are of a simple, God-fearing, clean-lived, hardy race of men. There was once a woman who made boast of her high connection in England, as women will the wide world over; and when she was questioned concerning the position the boasted relative occupied, replied 'Oh, *he's* Superintendent o' Foreign Governments!' There was an austere old Christian who on a Sunday morning left his trap – his whole fortune – lie in the path of a destroying iceberg rather than desecrate the Lord's day by taking it out of the water. Both political parties in Newfoundland shamelessly deceive the credulous fisherfolk; there was a childlike old fellow who, when asked, 'And what will you do if there *is* no fish?' confidently answered: 'Oh, they's goin' t' be a new Gov'ment. *He'll* take care o' we!' There was a sturdy son of the coast who deserted his schooner at sea and swam ashore. But he had mistaken a barren island for the mainland, which was yet far off; and there he lived, without food, for twenty-seven days! When he was picked up, his condition was such as may not be described (the Labrador fly is a vicious insect); he was unconscious, but he survived to fish many another season.

The mail-boat picked up Skipper Thomas of Carbonear – then master of a loaded schooner – at a small harbour near the Straits. His crew carried him aboard; for he was desperately ill, and wanted to die at home, where his children were.

'He's wonderful bad,' said one of the men. 'He've consumption.'

'I'm just wantin' t' die at home,' he said, again and again. 'Just that – just where my children be!'

All hearts were with him in that last struggle – but no man dared hope; for the old skipper had already beaten off death longer than death is wont to wait, and his strength was near spent.

'Were you sick when you sailed for the Labrador in the spring?' they asked him.

'Oh, ay,' said he, 'I were terrible bad then.'

'Then why,' they said, 'why did you come at all?'

They say he looked up in mild surprise.

'I had t' make me livin',' he answered simply.

His coffin was knocked together on the forward deck next morning – with Carbonear a day's sail beyond.

The fleet goes home in the early fall. The schooners are loaded – some so low with the catch that the water washes into the scuppers. 'You could wash your hands on the deck,' is the skipper's proudest boast. The feat of seamanship, I do not doubt, is not elsewhere equalled. It is an inspiring sight to see the doughty little craft beating into the wind on a gray day. The harvesting of a field of grain is good to look upon; but I think that there can be no more stirring sight in all the world, no sight more quickly to melt a man's heart, more deeply to move him to love men and bless God, than the sight of the Labrador fleet beating home loaded – toil done, dangers past; the home port at the end of a run with a fair wind. The home-coming, I fancy, is much like the return of the viking ships to the old Norwegian harbours must have been. The lucky skippers strut the village roads with swelling chests, heroes in the sight of all; the old men, long past their labour, listen to new tales and spin old yarns; the maids and the lads renew their interrupted love-makings. There is great rejoicing – feasting, merrymaking, hearty thanksgiving.

Thanks be to God, the fleet's home!

NOTE

1 Sir Wilfred Grenfell's hospital ship on which Duncan travelled to Labrador

ARTHUR. IN MEMORIAM: CAPTAIN ARTHUR JACKMAN. DIED 31 JANUARY 1907*

Daniel J. Carroll (1865-1941) was born in St John's and educated at St Patrick's Schools. On leaving school, he learned the trade of woodcarving with Messrs Callahan & Glass. He was also a noted cover designer and political cartoonist. Much of his verse was published in *The Newfoundland Quarterly*, which was founded in 1901 by the St John's publisher John J. Evans (1861-1944), but he also published in *Chamber's Journal, Donahue's Magazine*, the *Boston Traveller*, and elsewhere. Arthur Jackman (1843-1907), the subject of the tribute below, was one of the greatest of Newfoundland seamen. Born at Renews on the Southern Shore and known as 'Viking Arthur,' his rivalry with Captain Samuel Blandford (1840-1908) in the seal fishery became part of the folklore of the island. His brother William (1837-77) had become an enduring Newfoundland hero in 1867 when, at Spotted Islands, Labrador, he swam twenty-seven times through a heavy sea, the last sixteen times with a rope around his waist, to rescue the twenty-seven persons trapped aboard the *Sea Clipper*, which had run aground.

SILENCE AND STARS and the night dreamed on,
In the realm where the North Gods reign,
And lo! the soul of a Viking passed
Majestically in.
Radiant Aurora, rising from her throne,
Flung all her brilliant banners to the sky
In welcome to the brave, and Thor – the hero
Of that hero-land – took Arthur's hand, and
Then; the harps by Sagas thrilled of yore, with
Songs of Sea-Kings grew in Northland fame,
Burst forth anew.

I heard the heart of a man bemoan
The strong man's death.

* Daniel J. Carroll 'Arthur. In Memoriam: Captain Arthur Jackman' *The Newfoundland Quarterly* St John's (July 1907). Reprinted by permission of *The Newfoundland Quarterly*

'The blood that won the sea's domain was his;
The winds of the North and the white floe's brood
Know of his bravery.
In danger's hour when dark shores loomed alee,
Where coward hearts would wither in white Fear's fell grip,
With foam-anointed forehead he stood forth a Leader true,
And wrought high deeds while maddened Ocean raged,
By manhood and the courage of his Soul.
Yes – full many a year shall pass ere he's
Forgot, and many a captain brave shall
Quote his name, as towards the North, proud prowed
The fleets advance, manned by the brawn and blood
Of Newfoundland – Captains brave. From headland
And from hamlet as they pass, a people's heart
Shall give them this good wish, *"May Arthur's luck
Be with them on the Sea."* '

ADRIFT ON AN ICE-PAN (1908)*

Wilfred Thomason Grenfell (1865-1940) was born at Parkgate, Cheshire, and studied medicine at the London Hospital Medical School and London University from 1883 to 1886. Inspired by a sermon by the American evangelist Dwight L. Moody, Grenfell chose a life of dedication and became a medical officer with the Royal National Mission to Deep-Sea Fishermen, serving in the North Atlantic from Iceland to the Bay of Biscay. In 1892 he was sent to Newfoundland and Labrador to assess the need for a similar missionary effort there. He returned convinced that such an enterprise was indeed badly needed. In 1893 he went to Labrador and established at Battle Harbour the first hospital of the Labrador Medical Mission. *Adrift on an Ice-pan* was the work which dramatically brought Grenfell's missionary zeal to the attention of the world.

On 19 April 1908, Grenfell set out from St Anthony to Brent Island in Hare Bay, a distance of some sixty miles, to treat a boy

* Wilfred Grenfell *Adrift on an Ice-Pan* (Boston: Houghton Mifflin 1909) 31-45. Reprinted by permission of Houghton Mifflin Co

who was in danger of dying from blood poisoning. His komatik was drawn by his eight best dogs. On the second day of his trip he had to travel ten miles over an arm of the sea on treacherously loose ice. A strong offshore wind further loosened the ice, and Grenfell was trapped with his team on a small pan, drifting towards the open sea. To stay alive during his first bitterly cold night adrift, Grenfell slaughtered three dogs and slept wrapped in their skins.

THE WIND WAS steadily driving me now toward the open sea, and I could expect, short of a miracle, nothing but death out there. Somehow, one scarcely felt justified in praying for a miracle. But we have learned down here to pray for things we want, and, anyhow, just at that moment the miracle occurred. The wind fell off suddenly, and came with a light air from the southward, and then dropped stark calm. The ice was now 'all abroad,' which I was sorry for, for there was a big safe pan not twenty yards away from me. If I could have got on that, I might have killed my other dogs when the time came, and with their coats I could hope to hold out for two or three days more, and with the food and drink their bodies would offer me need not at least die of hunger or thirst. To tell the truth, they were so big and strong I was half afraid to tackle them with only a sheath-knife on my small and unstable raft.

But it was now freezing hard. I knew the calm water between us would form into cakes, and I had to recognize that the chance of getting near enough to escape on to it was gone. If, on the other hand, the whole bay froze solid again I had yet another possible chance. For my pan would hold together longer and I should be opposite another village, called Goose Cove, at daylight, and might possibly be seen from there. I knew that the komatiks there would be starting at daybreak over the hills for a parade of Orangemen about twenty miles away. Possibly, therefore, I might be seen as they climbed the hills. So I lay down, and went to sleep again.

It seems impossible to say how long one sleeps, but I woke with a sudden thought in my mind that I must have a flag; but again I had no pole and no flag. However, I set to work in the dark to disarticulate the legs of my dead dogs, which were now frozen stiff, and which were all that offered a chance of carrying anything like a distress signal. Cold as it was, I determined to sacrifice my shirt for that purpose with the first streak of daylight.

It took a long time in the dark to get the legs off, and when I had patiently marled them together with old harness rope and the remains of the skin traces, it was the heaviest and crookedest flag-pole it has ever been my lot to see. I had had no food from six o'clock the morning before, when I had eaten porridge and bread and butter. I had, however, a rubber band which I had been wearing instead of one of my garters, and I chewed that for twenty-four hours. It saved me from thirst and hunger, oddly enough. It was not possible to get a drink from my pan, for it was far too salty. But anyhow that thought did not distress me much, for as from time to time I heard the cracking and grinding of the newly formed slob, it seemed that my devoted boat must inevitably soon go to pieces.

At last the sun rose, and the time came for the sacrifice of my shirt. So I stripped, and, much to my surprise, found it not half so cold as I had anticipated. I now re-formed my dogskins with the raw side out, so that they made a kind of coat quite rivalling Joseph's. But, with the rising of the sun, the frost came out of the joints of my dogs' legs, and the friction caused by waving it made my flag-pole almost tie itself in knots. Still, I could raise it three or four feet above my head, which was very important.

Now, however, I found that instead of being as far out at sea as I had reckoned, I had drifted back in a northwesterly direction, and was off some cliffs known as Ireland Head. Near these there was a little village looking seaward, whence I should certainly have been seen. But, as I had myself, earlier in the winter, been night-bound at this place, I had learnt there was not a single soul living there at all this winter. The people had all, as usual, migrated to the winter houses up the bay, where they get together for schooling and social purposes.

I soon found it was impossible to keep waving so heavy a flag all the time, and yet I dared not sit down, for that might be the exact moment some one would be in a position to see me from the hills. The only thing in my mind was how long I could stand up and how long go on waving that pole at the cliffs. Once or twice I thought I saw men against their snowy faces, which, I judged, were about five and a half miles from me, but they were only trees. Once, also, I thought I saw a boat approaching. A glittering object kept appearing and disappearing on the water, but it was only a small piece of ice sparkling in the sun as it rose on the surface. I think that the rocking of my cradle up and down on the waves had helped me to sleep, for I felt as well as ever I did in my life; and with the hope of a long sunny day, I felt sure I was good to last another twenty-four hours – if my boat would hold out and not rot under the sun's rays.

Each time I sat down to rest, my big dog 'Doc' came and kissed my face and then walked to the edge of the ice-pan, returning again to where I was huddled up, as if to say, 'Why don't you come along? Surely it is time to start.' The other dogs also were now moving about very restlessly, occasionally trying to satisfy their hunger by gnawing at the dead bodies of their brothers.

I determined, at mid-day, to kill a big Eskimo dog and drink his blood, as I had read only a few days before in *Farthest North* of Dr Nansen's doing – that is, if I survived the battle with him. I could not help feeling, even then, my ludicrous position, and I thought, if ever I got ashore again, I should have to laugh at myself standing hour after hour waving my shirt at those lofty cliffs, which seemed to assume a kind of sardonic grin, so that I could almost imagine they were laughing at me. At times I could not help thinking of the good breakfast that my colleagues were enjoying at the back of those same cliffs, and of the snug fire and the comfortable room which we call our study.

I can honestly say that from first to last not a single sensation of fear entered my mind, even when I was struggling in the slob ice. Somehow it did not seem unnatural; I had been through the ice half a dozen times before. For the most part I felt very sleepy, and the idea was then very strong in my mind that I should soon reach the solution of the mysteries that I had been preaching about for so many years.

Only the previous night (Easter Sunday) at prayers in the cottage, we had been discussing the fact that the soul was entirely separate from the body, that Christ's idea of the body as the temple in which the soul dwells is so amply borne out by modern science. We had talked of thoughts from that admirable book, *Brain and Personality*, by Dr Thompson of New York, and also of the same subject in the light of a recent operation performed at the Johns Hopkins Hospital by Dr Harvey Cushing. The doctor had removed from a man's brain two large tumors without giving the man an anaesthetic, and the patient had kept up a running conversation with him all the while the doctor's fingers were working in his brain. It had seemed such a striking proof that ourselves and our bodies are two absolutely different things.

Our eternal life has always been with me a matter of faith. It seems to me one of those problems that must always be a mystery to knowledge. But my own faith in this matter had been so untroubled that it seemed now almost natural to be leaving through this portal of death from an ice-pan. In many ways, also, I could see how a death of this kind might be of value to the particular work that I am engaged in. Except for my friends, I had nothing I could think of to regret whatever. Certainly, I should like to have told them the story. But then one does not carry folios of paper in running shorts which have no pockets, and all my writing gear had gone by the board with the komatik.

I could still see a testimonial to myself some distance away in my khaki overalls, which I had left on another pan in the struggle of the night before. They seemed a kind of company, and would possibly be picked up and suggest the true story. Running through my head all the time, quite unbidden, were the words of the old hymn:

My God, my Father, while I stray
Far from my home on life's dark way,
Oh, teach me from my heart to say,
Thy will be done!

It is a hymn we hardly ever sing out here, and it was an unconscious memory of my boyhood days.

It was a perfect morning – a cobalt sky, an ultramarine sea, a golden sun, an almost wasteful extravagance of crimson over hills of purest snow, which caught a reflected glow from rock and crag. Between me and the hills lay miles of rough ice and long veins of thin black slob that had formed during the night. For the foreground there was my poor, gruesome pan, bobbing up and down on the edge of the open sea, stained with blood, and littered with carcasses and debris. It was smaller than last night, and I noticed also that the new ice from the water melted under the dogs' bodies had been formed at the expense of its thickness. Five dogs, myself in colored football costume, and a bloody dogskin cloak, with a gay flannel shirt on a pole of frozen dogs' legs, completed the picture. The sun was almost hot by now, and I was conscious of a surplus of heat in my skin coat. I began to look longingly at one of my remaining dogs, for an appetite will rise even on an ice-pan, and that made me think of fire. So once again I inspected my matches. Alas! the heads were in paste, all but three or four blue-top wax ones.

These I now laid out to dry, while I searched about on my snow-pan to see if I could get a piece of transparent ice to make a burning-glass. For I was pretty sure that with all the unravelled tow I had stuffed into my leggings, and with the fat of my dogs, I could make smoke enough to be seen if only I could get a light. I had found a piece which I thought would do, and had gone back to wave my flag, which I did every two minutes, when I suddenly thought I saw again the glitter of an oar. It did not seem possible, however, for it must be remembered it was not water which lay between me and the land, but slob ice, which a mile or two inside me was very heavy. Even if people had seen me, I did not think they could get through, though I knew that the whole shore would then be trying. Moreover, there was no smoke rising on the land to give me hope that I had been seen. There had been no gun-flashes in the night, and I felt sure that, had any one seen me, there would have been a bonfire on every hill to encourage me to keep going.

So I gave it up, and went on with my work. But the next time I went back to my flag, the glitter seemed very distinct, and though it kept disappearing as it rose and fell on the surface, I kept my eyes strained upon it, for my dark spectacles had been lost, and I was partly snowblind.

I waved my flag as high as I could raise it, broadside on. At last, beside the glint of the white oar, I made out the black streak of the hull. I knew that, if the pan held on for another hour, I should be all right.

With that strange perversity of the human intellect, the first thing I thought of was what trophies I could carry with my luggage from the pan, and I pictured the dog-bone flagstaff adorning my study. (The dogs actually ate it afterwards.) I thought of preserving my ragged puttees with our collection of curiosities. I lost no time now at the burning-glass. My whole mind was devoted to making sure I should be seen, and I moved about as much as I dared on the raft, waving my sorry token aloft.

At last there could be no doubt about it: the boat was getting nearer and nearer. I could see that my rescuers were frantically waving, and, when they came within shouting distance, I heard some one cry out, 'Don't get excited. Keep on the pan where you are.' They were infinitely more excited than I. Already to me it seemed just as natural now to be saved as, half an hour before, it had seemed inevitable I should be lost, and had my rescuers only known, as I did, the sensation of a bath in that ice when you could not dry yourself afterwards, they need not have expected me to follow the example of the apostle Peter and throw myself into the water.

OUTPORT MAN REFASHIONED (1910)*

Horace Gordon Hutchinson (1859-1932) was born in London and educated at Charterhouse and Corpus Christi, Oxford. His life was dedicated almost exclusively to sport. He was an excellent golfer, an avid hunter, and a prolific author on shooting, fishing, natural history, and golf. Construction began in 1905 at Grand Falls on Newfoundland's first paper mill.

THERE IS THIS further problem – but it is in course of solution – to inculcate the habit of patient work inland in a population that has hitherto known only the hard, but less continuous, toil of the fisher. Ubiquitously in the island we hear this difficulty spoken of by those who have its improvement at heart. It is realised that for its future development it is essential that the people must realise the necessity of not living by fish alone. They must be farmers, pastoral and agricultural, miners, and so on. The workers of this Grand Falls factory, though the great majority are natives, are described by the superintendent as being as various of language as though they came straight from the construction of the Tower of Babel. But he hopes to have them practically all natives soon. The love of the sea and the fishing, however, is in the blood of the native folk, and they are apt to obey its call and get down to their fishing work again after a spell of this up-country labour. Still, it is thought that they will soon be broken of this, will realise the advantage of the good houses in which they are placed at the Falls, and the blessing of a constant employment and a steady wage. Lord Northcliffe [owner of the mill at

* Horace G. Hutchinson *A Saga of the 'Sunbeam'* (London: Longmans 1911) 412-13. Reprinted by permission of Longman Group Ltd

Grand Falls], in his liberal longsighted way, does all that can be imagined to make their life agreeable. He has made a present of a gramophone to each of the more important houses – we are not informed of the effect, if all are set going, with a different 'record' in each, at the same moment – and has also sent them out a large assortment of instruments of music, with a view to the institution of a town band. For lack of a bandmaster it appears that acertain discord, rather than the desired harmony, is the immediate result, but no doubt this will mend itself. And there is a cricket ground, of sorts; so what more have they to wish for? Speaking in all seriousness, life seems as good as can be expected for these workers at the Falls, and in a short while they will, no doubt, realise all its goodness.

'FORTY THOUSAND STRONG' (1913)*

The Fishermen's Protective Union was founded in 1908 and quickly became influential in politics under its dynamic leader, William Ford Coaker (1871-1938). Born in St John's of outport parents, Coaker attended Bishop Feild College and farmed for a time on an island in Green Bay. He began to organize the Fishermen's Protective Union at a meeting at Herring Neck on the day of the Newfoundland tie election, 3 November 1908. A man of immense energy, clear vision, and great courage, Coaker led what was probably the most imaginative and innovative political movement Newfoundland ever produced. His followers displayed great élan, and the song below, which was published in the union paper *The Fishermen's Advocate* on 20 September 1913, under the title ' "Forty Thousand Strong": Terra Nova's army of toilers respond to Coaker's appeal,' was one of their favourites. It was written by 'A Union Man.' Coaker died in Boston after a stormy but fruitful career. He is buried at Port Union, a town he and his followers created to embody their ideals.

WE ARE COMING Mr Coaker from the East, West, North and South,
    You have called us and we're coming to put our foes to rout,
By Merchants and by Governments too long we've been misruled,

* *The Fishermen's Advocate* (St John's 20 Sept. 1913)

We're determined now in future and no longer we'll be fooled,
We'll be brothers all and freemen and we'll rightify each wrong,
We are coming Mr Coaker and we're forty thousand strong.

We have proved that Reid[1] and Morris[2] are in love but with their purse,
That the treatment of the fishermen is daily getting worse;
They've been tried and been found wanting, so we'll surely turn them down,
For we now have got the Leader who upon us shall not frown.
It is you shall slay the Dragons who have cowed us down so long,
We are coming Mr Coaker and we're forty thousand strong.

We are coming Mr Coaker, men from Green Bay's rocky shore,
Men who stand the snow white billows down on stormy Labrador;
They are ready and awaiting, strong and solid, firm and bold,
To be led by you like Moses, led the Israelites of old.
They are ready for to sever from the merchant's servile throng,
We are coming Mr Coaker and we're forty thousand strong.

We are coming Mr Coaker Bonavista Bay will fight.
As their fathers ever foremost to give battle for the right,
Trinity Bay to-day is solid, you and our good cause to back,
While the bold Placentia Bay men sure you'll find they won't be slack,
We'll be firm and true and steady, and will help our cause along,
We are coming Mr Coaker and we're forty thousand strong.

We are coming Mr Coaker blood of Saxon and of Celt,
You arouse a feeling in us that before we never felt,
Valiant men from far Placentia whom the angry ocean braves,
They are with you heart and spirit, breasting Cape St Mary's waves,
They are with the fight for freedom and its union is their song,
We are coming Mr Coaker and we're forty thousand strong.

We are coming Mr Coaker and though sharp shall be the fight,
Yet we trust in you our Leader, and our God will do the right,
All our beacon fires are lighted and we see them brightly burn;
With our motto 'No Surrender' all our enemies we will spurn,

Led by you we'll never falter, God shall help our cause along,
We are coming Mr Coaker and we're forty thousand strong.

NOTES

1 Sir Robert Gillespie Reid (1842-1908), founder and first president of the Reid Newfoundland Company, the owner of the Newfoundland Railway

2 Edward Patrick Morris (1859-1935), founder in 1908 of the People's party; prime minister of Newfoundland 1909-18

JOSHUA STANSFORD CALLS ON FRIENDS (1910, 1916)*

Joshua Stansford (1892-1961) was born at Grates Cove, Conception Bay. He lived the life of fisherman, storekeeper, political organizer, and outport notable. He was also a diarist and versifier.

ON NOVEMBER the 7th [1910] we were picking up our shop things, and getting ready for home. Before noon, Mr W.F. Coaker telephoned me to come to dinner at 1 PM.

At noon I met him at his office, and shortly afterwards we went across to his residence and took dinner together. After leaving Mr Coaker's, I went along to Water Street, to do some shopping, where I met Sir John Crosbie [prominent merchant and politician]. He asked me how I had enjoyed my dinner with Mr Coaker, and I asked him how he knew I had been there. He replied laughingly that he knew by the stars, and asked me to call at his house that evening. I said I would be pleased to accept his invitation for tea, but as I had a lot to do I was afraid I was unable to stay for the evening.

At that time Sir John Crosbie and Mr Coaker were in opposition over politics.

The following morning Sir John Crosbie telephoned to me, asking me to meet him on his wharf at 11.45 AM. I kept the appointment, and Sir John took me to his home in Freshwater Road. After a long chat, Sir John went into the kitchen and brought in two

* Joshua Stansford *Fifty Years of My Life in Newfoundland* (Ilfracombe: Arthur H. Stockwell Ltd 1952). Reprinted by permission of Eldred Stansford & Leslie Stansford

dinners – one for himself and one for me. As we sat down to eat, Sir John jokingly said that he did not want women about when he was eating. It was only the Coaker women who dined with the men, he said.

After our dinner, he kindly drove me around the City, which was most interesting; and on parting he invited me to call and see him every time I visited St John's, and added, joking, that he hoped I would remember him in my prayers...

On December the 19th [1916] I made another trip to St John's. It was by rail, and my purpose was to buy stores for my shop. I arrived at St John's by 10 PM and went to Surgeon Peet's home, where I took boarding. Next day I went shopping, and met Mr A.E. Hickman, who was then Member for the Bay-de-Verde district. He invited me to call upon him at his office during the afternoon and we had an interesting chat for over half an hour.

On December the 22nd I visited the President's Office, and had a chat with Mr Coaker himself. His offices were now situated at Mr J.M. Devines's [a St John's merchant] premises at Water Street. On leaving, after a long and pleasant chat, he invited me to call at his house at 6 PM for tea, but I was busy that evening and unable to accept his invitation.

On December the 23rd, while going up Water Street before noon, I met Sir John Crosbie who insisted on my taking dinner with him. We went to his residence in 25, Forest Road, and by the time we arrived his family had finished their dinner. We sat in the dining room and Mrs Crosbie brought in his dinner. 'Don't trouble about this man's dinner,' he said, 'I will see about that myself,' and he returned shortly afterwards with a large plate of dinner – and on the edge of the plate was a ten dollar bill. On placing the plate before me, he said 'Now, Joshua, don't you eat all that is on the plate. Be sure and pocket some.' I enjoyed my dinner, and after we had finished the meal he took me through his house, and then drove me down to Water Street.

I thanked him most heartily for his hospitality, but he said 'Don't thank me, but thank the Stars; and whenever you are in St John's, do call and see me.'

At 3 PM I met Surgeon Peet, who told me that several important men were looking for me and that at dinner time Mr Coaker had telephoned through to his house asking for me, as he expected I should be there having dinner.

I did some more shopping, and at 5 PM I went along to Mr Coaker's office. On entering I met him coming down the stairs. He said he had been looking for me all day. We then went to his home, and after tea and about two hours conversation, he put a five dollar bill in my pocket and said 'Don't forget the FPU and keep the flag flying.'

THE BADGER DRIVE (1915)*

John V. Devine of Stephenville Crossing, an uncle of Gerald S. Doyle, a prominent Newfoundland merchant and collector of folk songs, wrote this ballad about the Anglo-Newfoundland Development Company's loggers for a St Patrick's day concert around 1915. Badger, a logging town, is approximately seventeen miles west of Grand Falls.

THE BADGER DRIVE

There is one class of men in this country that never is mentioned in song;
And now, since their trade is advancing they'll come out on top before long;
They say that our sailors have danger and likewise our warriors bold
But there's none know the life of a driver, what he suffers with hardship and cold.
With their pike poles and peavies[1] and bateaus and all
And they're sure to come out in the spring that's the time
With the caulks in their boots as they get on the logs and it's hard to get over their time

Billey Dorothey he is the manager, and he's a good man at the trade;
And when he's around seeking drivers, he's like a train going down grade,
But still he is a man that's kind-hearted, on his word you can always depend,

* From Gerald S. Doyle, ed. *Old-time Songs and Poetry of Newfoundland* (St John's 1940) 29. Reprinted by permission of Mrs Gerald S. Doyle

And there's never a man that works with him but likes to go with
him again.

I tell you today home in London, *The Times* it is read by each
man,
But little they think of the fellows that drove the wood on
Mary Ann,[2]
For paper is made out of pulpwood and many things more you
may know,
And long may our men live to drive it upon Paymeoch and
Tomjoe.[3]

The drive it is just below Badger, and everything is working grand,
With a jolly good crew of picked drivers and Ronald Kelly in
command,
For Ronald is boss on the river, and I tell you he's a man that's
alive,
He drove the wood off Victoria,[4] now he's out on the main
river drive.

So now to conclude and to finish, I hope that ye all will agree
In wishing success to all Badger and the AND Company,
And long may they live for to flourish, and continue to chop,
drive and roll,
And long may the business be managed by Mr Dorothey and
Mr Cole.

NOTES

1 Pike poles and peavies are kinds of gaffs used by loggers to maneuver logs in the water.
2 Mary Ann Lake is north of Badger.
3 Pamehac Brook and Tom Joes Brook are south of Badger.
4 Victoria River, south of Red Indian Lake

SPANISH 'FLU IN LABRADOR (1918)*

Henry Gordon arrived at Cartwright, Labrador, in 1915 to become the resident Anglican minister. His journal of the chilling events of the winter of 1918-19 was published through the enterprise of Anne Grenfell, the wife of the famous doctor. Gordon remained in Labrador until 1925.

TUESDAY, OCT. 29th: Ran out to Indian Harbour in dead calm. Off to the southward we could see a large schooner becalmed, and guessed that she was the *St Bernard*, Mr Clark's long expected vessel. After lunch and a short service, we crossed the North River Flats and anchored just off the Graveyard Point. Everybody gathered at old Jim Williams' for service. There is always one recognised house in each little settlement where the parson stays and where service is held. Returning on board *St Helen* for the night, Roly [Roly Bird of Dove Brook, Gordon's assistant] fell very sick, so I stayed up keeping the stove going all night.

Wednesday, Oct. 30th: During the night we had got aground, but fortunately the weather was calm. Early this morning we got clear and set off for Cartwright. Roly was feeling much better. Ran into the wharf at Cartwright about 10:00. Not a soul to be seen anywhere, and a strange, unusual silence. Going along the path to the parsonage, we met one of the Company's [Hudson's Bay Company] men staggering about like a drunken man, and from him learnt the news that the whole settlement was prostrated with sickness. It had struck the place like a cyclone, two days after the mail-boat had left. After dinner, I went on a tour of inspection among the houses, and was simply appalled at what I found. Whole households lay inanimate all over their kitchen floors, unable to even feed themselves or look after the fire. No one complained of any particular pain; a bad headache and an utter exhaustion seemed to be the prevalent symptoms. No one, so far, seemed in a dangerous state. The remarkable thing about the whole business was the fact that the entire settlement was down. It suggested most forcibly a tropical typhoon. I

* Henry Gordon *A Winter in Labrador, 1918-1919* (New York 1920 [?]) 18-22, 26-9, 33-4. Reprinted by permission of Mrs Henry Gordon

think there were just four persons in the place who were sound. The *St Bernard* lay at anchor in the harbour, making a slow business of unloading her cargo, for lack of local help. One seemed utterly incapable of dealing with the situation. The only thing one could do was to see that no one perished for want of food and firing. This I started in on straight away. A feeling of intense resentment at the callousness of the authorities, who sent us the disease by the mail-boat, and then left us to sink or to swim, filled one's heart almost to the exclusion of all else. The helplessness of the poor people was what struck to the heart. The one and only doctor on the coast (Dr Paddon of the International Grenfell Association) was one hundred and eighty miles away, and might have been ten thousand for what chance he could have of getting his assistance to us. We could only come to the conclusion that the Spanish influenza had come amongst us, and the newspapers were brim-full of its deadliness.

Friday, Nov. 1st: Health and strength are the only things of any value now, and they must be used to the utmost. Shortage of wood is the most serious menace that we have to face. The weather is getting bitterly cold. Very few of our people have any stock of fire-wood home, and scarcely a house with any sawed up. Roly and I set to work and sawed and split as hard as we could go. Roly is simply splendid, and I don't know what I would do without him. In the evening I paid another round of visits. Some of the sick are getting distinctly worse. One house is in an appalling state. We have only one log hut in the place, where an old couple have lived for some years. They left it last summer and we hoped it would then disappear. Late this fall, a family of seven arrived from the outside, too late to get up to their winter quarters. There were five little children, and another was soon expected. A sort of old nurse was with them, and her old man remained to take her up the bay when she would be free. A young man and a little girl of six were also of the party. All this crowd was jammed into this little tilt barely ten foot square. They were all struck helpless before anything could be done to sort them out, and now they lay in heaps on the dirty floor in a terrible mess. Mrs Parsons, the wife of the new agent of the HBC, who has been a trained nurse, is of tremendous assistance. She gets about among the sick and, with the few drugs at her disposal, does wonders. My head is beginning to get heavy. I hope against hope that I may be able to keep fit.

Saturday, Nov. 2nd: Feeling rotten, head like a bladder full of wind. Felt able to get up, however. Word came up that the little Tilt baby had been born, and was not likely to live, so I went down and baptised it. If things in this house had been bad before, they were worse now. The old man and the old woman were practically dying on the floor. About noon, I received word that young Howard Fequet had died. Epileptic in normal times, he had not been able to stand at all against this disease. Scarcely knowing what I was doing I rowed out to the *St Bernard*, now lying all to herself in the harbour, and begged the crew to come ashore to dig Howard's grave. This they very willingly did. Digging graves in the Cartwright cemetery is labour out of the ordinary. Good folk many years ago chose the spot, evidently for its prominence, quite forgetful of the fact that a prominent spot in this country means a nut that the glacier or the sea was not able to crack. About one foot of soil lies over the ground, then comes a layer of tightly compressed blackish gravel, which reminds me of nothing so much as the carbon that accumulates on the cylinder of a motor engine. Beneath this are huge boulders almost cemented in with the pressure. When, in addition to all these other difficulties, the ground is frozen, it may be imagined what the work entails.

Sunday, Nov. 3rd: Got up, took a dose of brandy and buried Howard Fequet at 1:30, then went back to bed again.

Tuesday, Nov. 5th: Can't remember very clearly what happened on these two days. Felt very sick. I know Mr Parsons came up to ask me about burying somebody or other. I thought it was myself at the time. Someone gave me some oranges, and someone gave me some chocolate. Mrs Parsons, I know, helped me out a lot. Roly stuck to me like a brick.

Wednesday, Nov. 6th: Feeling ever so much better, but rather groggy in the legs. Found out that the old man (Mr Garland Lethbridge) was dead and buried, also that his wife was *in extremis*, and worst of all Sam Learning, my churchwarden, a man of an unusually fine character, was in a serious condition. This last piece of information got me up in a hurry. One could scarcely believe that it was true. Physically, Sam was the equal of any man around. I could not help laughing as I walked or rather 'tacked' along the road. Several others were doing the same and it reminded one so much of the flies coming out of the cracks in the springtime. My merriment, however, was turned to dismay, when I reached Sam's bedside. He was undoubtedly dying, despite Mrs Parsons's magnificent efforts to save him. She had been up with him all night, poulticing and doing everything possible. He asked for the Sacrament. Going home to get ready, I could not help actually crying. I suppose one's nerves were a good deal overwrought, but in any case Sam's death would be nothing short of a disaster. I will never forget that Sacrament, and whenever afterwards I perform the sacred service, I shall picture dear old Sam, manfully trying to incline his aching head at the name of Jesus, just as he always did. Men like these, of course, justify Christianity, and I think they also justify the Church. Late in the evening, Sam passed to his rest, as also did old Mrs Garland Lethbridge.

Thursday, Nov. 7th: At this stage of the proceedings the last mail-boat of the season arrived (ss *Seal*). She would allow no one on board. She had no doctor, or anything to help us out. As it was blowing a full gale, no one was able to get out to her or to come in from her. Two graves were needed, and I entered on my apprenticeship of grave-digging – and that in a graveyard like this! By evening one grave was ready, and I buried Mrs Lethbridge. The wind lulled a bit towards nighttime, so that communication with the steamer was resumed. She had a most enormous freight for Cartwright. It was a serious question whether there would be anyone able to help to land it.

Friday, Nov. 8th: Finished Sam's grave and laid him to rest. The way his wife took the whole thing was nothing short of wonderful, especially as there was every possibility of her losing her eldest child as well. I have decided to close our old graveyard, and in the future only bury in the new part. All available hands were mustered to unload freight from the steamer, which remained at anchor all day. The three local traders agreed to land all their stuff on one wharf, and for this purpose joined in one gang. I signed on also for the day. It was nearly midnight before we had got the stuff landed on the Company's wharf.

Thursday, Nov. 21st: A fine, calm, frosty morning. The first real calm day for several weeks. Taking the opportunity whilst it was here, I got out a small boat and went across the harbour for a load of wood, returning with 25 good sticks. With a few days of weather like this, I shall be able to get home a fine stock of wood. On my return, I saw a boat coming round the point. We had been fully expecting to hear some news of the other places to-day, but were quite unprepared for the tale we soon were listening to. The visitor was Will Learning, from Indian Harbour. For several weeks he had been cut off from any connection with his neighbours. Last night he had got across the run to North River, and found the place in a terrible condition. Out of twenty-one people he found ten dead, two or three next door to death, and the rest too sick and dismayed to do a thing. Some of the people had died at the beginning of the month, and were still lying as they died, in their beds. In one house, about half a mile from the rest, four out of the family of five were dead. The one remaining soul, was the old mother of 72 years, whose fight with death is one of the most heroic stories I have ever heard. When she was found she had been living all alone for nine days, since the last of her family had died. All that time she had been without a fire (this in Labrador!), and practically without food. In the porch were two buckets of solid ice. From these she would chop fragments with the axe, and thaw them out in a cup under her arm-pits. Outside were the starving dogs, tearing everything within reach of them and watching the least chance of breaking into the house. She was now in one of the other houses, and doing well.

It was decided to send out a relief expedition at once, consisting of Messrs Parsons, Clark, Doan, Roland Macdonald and myself. By 4:00 we had stocked ourselves with grub and sleeping gear, and were ready to start. It was dark by the time we were off the mouth of the river, so that it was no surprise when we found ourselves hard aground on the flats. The tide was fortunately rising, so that in about an hour we were able to get clear again. Arrived at the settlement, we soon found that all we had heard was only too true. It was absolutely pitiable to behold the sorrow of the few people that survived. It was some time before we could convince them that they would not have to die themselves.

We had arranged to leave all work till the morrow, but such a sharp frost set in by nighttime, that we began to be afraid of being frozen in the river, if we made any long stay. Even now great sheets of ice were sweeping out on the stream, and there was no knowing the moment when our boat might be cut adrift. Accordingly, we decided to start in straight away with the grave. Crossing the river we anchored under the Burying-ground Point, and went ashore with lanterns and tools. One big grave was marked out (24 by 7 by 4), and all hands took their own section. After the first foot, which was frozen, it was simply a matter of shovelling the fine red sand out as hard as one could go. The huge pit was finished by midnight and we went out on board the boat for food and a short nap. The food was managed all right, but the nap was a failure. Soon after settling into our sleeping-bags, the drift-ice bore down on us and we had to get up anchor in a hurry and clear out into the run. After this it was too cold and wet to do any sleeping. Mr Clark seemed the only one who might get a few winks, but he was voted down at the very first snore.

Friday, Nov. 22nd: Daylight revealed the fact that the river was frozen over during the night. It looked as though we would be barred off from the settlement. Mr Doan, whose boat we were using, suggested trying to break through. By means of rolling the boat from side to side we worked our way gradually through, pushing away the sheets of ice as we cracked them. It certainly did the boat no good. Then started the gruesome task of collecting the dead. Some had lain in their beds for over a fortnight, and the stench was fearful. We wrapped them up just as they were, in their bedclothes, then wound them round with cord, and carried them out to the boat. There was no time to even think of such things as coffins. When we had six from the main settlement, we went across the river to the house that stood by itself, the place where the old woman had such a hard time. The first sight that greeted our eyes, was the entrails of a dog, which had been killed and partly eaten by its fellows. We also caught sight of one of the animals hiding like a wild creature among the woods. Roland had a shot at it but missed. In the porch were the two buckets, showing the scoured ice which had served the old woman for drink. Three bodies lay on the floor, the other was upstairs on the loft, and necessitated the removing of the floor before we could get it down. We finally got all four outside and on board the boats. Before leaving here, we hauled up three boats which were beating about in the landwash, significant of the suddenness with which the people must have been taken sick. In the course of this work, Mr Parsons strained his back quite seriously, so that we were now reduced to four, and had to lose one of our best workers. It was 11:00 by the time we had all the bodies collected. We then made out of the river to the Burying-ground Point, and began the task of carrying our freight to the grave. This, I think, was the hardest job of the lot. Quite a little distance separated the boats from the grave, and the ground was covered with several feet of snow, too soft to bear us up. At last all was accomplished, and about 4:00 we headed the boat for Cartwright, in the face of a good stiff breeze, which sent the spray flying on board, and where it fell it froze solid. Added to our number was old Mrs Williams, the woman already referred to. We had decided that it would be best to take her away from the scene of her trouble.

Saturday, Nov. 23rd: Time flies nowadays. Another week-end is upon us, and the eternal wood problem to be tackled. Sawed and split all morning. Two visitors came in from Goose Cove, with the news that the fourth Toomashie was now dead. I arranged with them to bring in the bodies as soon as possible. We would get to work on a big grave on Monday. The last of the boats was hauled up to-day, only just in time. The harbour is fast filling in with slob. I played the gramophone for some of the young fellows, this evening.

Wednesday, Dec. 11th: Charlie Bird was bound on an expedition up the bay, so we joined forces, rather more to my advantage than to his! Calling in at Longstretch we found all well, but learnt for the first time that Separation Point (on the north side of the bay) had been badly hit by the sickness. They had lost seven of their number, a heavy toll out of such a small community. We, accordingly, changed our plans and headed for the north side of the bay first. I shall never forget the experience we had meeting these people. We had grown so used to death that we had almost lost all sentiment about it. Some of the settlements up the bay had miraculously escaped the sickness, and the people were really afraid of us. Of course, we never tried to enter any of these places, but it seemed strange to see anyone we happened to meet out on the ice 'convey themselves away from us.' One ought to have realised that these folk had only just got the news of Cartwright and the other hard-hit places, and were naturally deeply shocked. Separation Point was the only place affected, and so we put up there for the night. Here also were tales of sorrow and woe. A boy of sixteen had pluckily buried the dead. I promised to read the full funeral service over them, when the people who had weathered the storm were able to get out.

COMING HOME FROM LABRADOR (1919)*

Nicholas Smith was born in 1866 at Brigus, Conception Bay, in its late nineteenth-century heyday a leading centre of the Labrador and seal fisheries. He first went to the Labrador coast to fish in June 1874. Eventually he became an established figure in the Labrador trade, obtaining his first command in 1888 when he was twenty-one. In 1900 he purchased a fishing room on the Labrador coast at Cutthroat. This lay in an area of the coast favoured by the itinerant Newfoundland fishermen from Conception Bay, whose relationship to Labrador at this time resembled the relationship their west country and Irish ancestors had established with Newfoundland. Smith made his last voyage northward in 1934.

ON SEPTEMBER 1ST all hands began washing out and making their fish, and on the 20th I went to Smokey to supervise the loading of the foreigner *Nellie Louise*, belonging to Barbadoes; she had discharged a cargo of salt and was taking a load of dry fish. We started loading on September 22nd and on the 15th October we had 5000 quintals on board. The ship was quite large and was chartered for 7400 quintals.

We then got ready to sail for Comfort Bight to take on board the balance of cargo. Meanwhile, while the vessel was loading the 5000 quintals at Smokey my men brought up their fish and shipped it on board; as their voyage was small they had it all shipped by the middle of October. On October 16th we left Smokey for Comfort Bight and arrived there the following morning at 10 AM; we hauled in to the wharf and the fish being all ready in the store, we began shipping at once. By 9 PM we had 1000 quintals taken on board; the next day we continued until we had all that was in the store on board, 1800 quintals, and then finished our cargo from motor boats. On the 21st we had the charter on board, 7400 quintals, and she was ready for sea that night.

Three of the sailors deserted the ship and ran away, and we spent the next day enquiring for their whereabouts, but to no avail. No

* Nicholas Smith *Fifty-Two Years at the Labrador Fishery* (London: Arthur H. Stackwell, Ltd 1936). Reprinted by permission of Mrs Helena E. Hiscock

trace of them could be found, and, meanwhile the ship was being held up for the want of a crew. The Captain wired Capt. Randall at St John's, the ship's broker, who replied with the instructions to ship three men there and proceed to St John's, where he (Capt. Randall) would have three sailors ready to join the vessel. I engaged three fishermen to help bring the ship to St John's, they agreeing with the Captain to be paid a certain sum and to go on the ship next morning, October 24th.

However, when the ship was nearly ready to sail the three men said they didn't care about going on board and said that they feared the Captain might bring them across and not to St John's at all. I laughed at their remarks, and they then said that if I would take passage also they would go. I said, 'All right, I would just as soon go by the *Nellie Louise* as by the mail boat.' And so the thing was fixed; they put their boxes and bags on board, and in less than half an hour I had all my belongings on board too, and we were all ready.

It was then 'Heave away on the windlass' and go to sea, the wind being favourable, from the westward. After getting clear of the rocks the captain gave the wheelman his course, SS East, which brought us a long way outside Bell Island [an island east of the Great Northern Peninsula], which we passed that night. We continued the same course, SS East, all next day, and on relieving the 4 PM watch I remarked to the captain that our course was a rather difficult one. I said, 'Don't you think that we will be a long way off with this course when we get up in the latitude of St John's?' His reply was that he liked plenty of sea room, and that the wind might be easterly the next day. I said 'I beg your pardon, Captain, you are the man.' He hauled her up one point S by East, and at midnight to South. We were then in the vicinity of the Funk Islands, but were too far to sea to get a sight of the island, which was just as I expected.

On October 26th the wind was light from the west; the ship close-hauled her course SS West, making three or four knots per hour. At sunset the captain said that he saw the land, but I doubted it. At midnight the wind dropped off and came from the south, and the captain said that we were then off St John's. He then gave orders to steer the ship West by South, the wind increasing to a gale and the barometer moving down rapidly. For three hours we came in all she could suffer, and the captain then gave orders to shorten sail. We began with the flying jib and spanker, and before we had them secured the rest of the sails were blown away, nothing remaining but the rope of our mainsail, foresail, jib and jumbo. The wind took all before it, and we were in a disabled condition with all our principal sails blown away.

The wind was blowing a hurricane, and we were running before it under bare poles. At 6 AM on the 27th the wind hauled around to the westward, and I have never seen anything like it, except for the big gale some years ago; we had to hold fast on deck for fear of being blown away, and the seas ran mountains high. The ship scudded dead before it under bare poles, the decks were flooded with water, and it was impossible to move about. We lost our two boats off the deck, one a small motor boat, and also all our lines and hawsers that were coiled on the cabin house.

On October 28th it was still blowing a hurricane, and the seas running clean over the ship; we lost our water tank, the bolts drawing up through the deck; this did considerable damage beating about the deck and chafing it, as well as knocking off a lot of the bulwarks, and, worst of all, damaging our tarpaulin on the main hatch, thus enabling the sea-water to enter the hold. The ring bolts that drew up through the deck left four holes and through these the water ran down freely. To add to our trouble, the ship was leaking badly, and the pumps were constantly working. We had two watches of four hours, three men to a watch, and during the watch we spent two hours at the wheel and two hours pumping, which was laborious work. The captain was my buddy pumping, the worst man of the lot for the job as he was not used to hard work, and I being much the same. When our two hours' pumping were up we were pretty well exhausted, and didn't much care whether we were washed overboard or not.

On October 29th the wind was still blowing a hurricane, and we were still scudded under bare poles, pumping all day, two men at a time lashed to the mainmast with a rope. At noon a huge sea boarded the ship and washed both men from the pumps; were it not for the ropes one of them would have been gone, but he was badly injured from washing about; his right side turned as black as tar from the bruises he received. The second man received no injury, and continued on duty. We took the injured man, James Simms, down in my room and laid him on my bed; I rubbed him with liniment and bathed him with hot water, as per the instructions from the ship's medical guide book. At 5 PM a sea struck the ship on the port quarter, flooding her with water and turning her head right about; she was then helpless in the troughs of the seas and nothing to be seen except the top of the cabin-house; all hands were clinging about the mizzenmast and the vessel wasn't moving. Mate Spearns, a thorough seaman (that voyage being his thirtieth across the Atlantic) said to the captain, 'We cannot live another hour like this; our only hope is to try to get the ship before the sea. We have a part of the jib, and if we could hoist it up it might stand so that we could get the ship before the sea.' The captain replied, 'Try to do it, mate.'

Four of us started to go forward to hoist the jib, and it took us a long time to do it; we had to watch the seas, and had to climb on the main gaff and fore gaff to get forward, the main deck being filled with water up to the rail. We landed on the forecastle deck and hoisted part of the jib, and the ship bore away before the sea. This was a little better, and we were running before the seas. At 8 PM a tremendous sea was coming after us, and the mate at the wheel called out for all hands to watch and to tie themselves securely with ropes in case the sea would board us, which it did, covering the mate with water, making a bridge of the ship, and rushing over the ballards; it was a dreadful sight. The sea broke open the cabin doors, flooding the cabin, breaking our cabin stove, smashing our compass and our cabin lamp. The captain's charts and clothing were washing around the cabin floor, and my chest, half full of water, was going from side to side. There was over a foot of water in the cabin, and it was a trying time clearing up the wreckage by the light of candles.

At 9:30 we went on deck again, the mate at the wheel. He said to the Captain, 'I cannot live another hour; I am soaked to the skin where the water went down my neck and inside my shirt.' The captain told him to go down and change his clothing, if he could, while 'Mr Smith (as he always called me) and myself will take the wheel.' The mate, chilled to the bone, went below, and, after an hour we heard another big sea roaring astern. The captain told me to lash myself securely, as he was doing, and as the sea drew near, he asked, 'Are you lashed firmly?' I said, 'Yes, sir.' He then said, 'Mr Smith, put your trust in Jesus Christ; He will save us.' I replied, 'This is the eleventh hour now, sir, and I have been a sinner all my lifetime, but I never knew what swearing and sin was until I came on board this ship, and if the Almighty doesn't help us no other can.' The captain said that Jesus Christ would save him for the sake of his wife and kiddies in Barbados. I said, 'We all have wives and children at home, sir, and the Man Above may spare us for their sakes.' By that time the sea struck us, and it was a repetition of the last sea, flooding the ship and making her tremble. The captain said, 'Are you all right, Mr Smith? Are you hurt?' I said, 'No, sir, are you?' 'No,' said he, 'only that I am full of water inside my clothes.' And I was in the same condition.

He called out, 'All hands safe?' and they replied 'Yes.' The cabin doors were broken in again and a lot more water went down; the wheel-house was carried away, and, to make matters worse, this last sea broke in the door of the men's quarters, flooding it with water and soaking all their belongings except what they stood in; it was all washed out through the door and was lost. We had to take all hands in the cabin and I had to divide my clothing between my men, James Simms, Jerry Flynn and Robert Rose, all thorough seamen belonging to Brigus.

We had a terrible night, still scudding before the sea and pumping when possible. At 2 PM our watch was over, and we went below, well exhausted, cold and hungry. I lay on my bed with oilskins on and barred my door, for the last time, I thought. I said a few humble prayers taught me by my dear old mother, and tried the door again to make sure it was barred, as I did not want the sharks to enter in case we went down while I was asleep. It was not long before I fell asleep, as I was worn out from pumping, and at 8 bells the mate was calling me again by kicking at my door and saying, 'We're still afloat, Mr Smith, and it is a little better.'

'MAN'S MARK AND SIGN AND SIGNAL IN THE NORTH' (1922)*

George Allan England (1877-1936) was born in Nebraska and graduated from Harvard in 1902. He became a journalist and traveller.

* George Allan England *Vikings of the Ice* (New York: Doubleday, Page 1924) 82-6. 'Man's Mark and Sign and Signal in the North' Extracted from *Vikings of the Ice* by George Allan England, originally copyrighted 1924, republished through special permission of the author's widow by Tundra Books Inc 1969 under the title *The Greatest Hunt in the World*

He first went to Newfoundland to gather material for a series of articles he was writing on islands. He went to the ice in 1922 in the *Terra Nova*, commanded by Abram Kean, 'The Admiral of the Fleet,' who in 1934, at the age of seventy-nine, brought in his millionth seal. In 1969 *Vikings of the Ice* was reprinted under the title *The Greatest Hunt in the World* with an introduction by Ebbitt Cutter. In the selections that follow England describes the hunt and a typical hunter.

AN INSTANT, breathlessness held us all in its vise. Then confusion burst like a shell. Cap'n, bosun, carpenter, master watches, all jumped up. The checkerboard was overturned; pieces rolled to the floor; no matter. On deck, louder yells summoned. Keen with the blood lust, all who could go on ice began heaving on their gear. Such a shouting, such a leaping to arms, such a buckling-on of sheath, knives, steels, belts; such a grabbing of tow ropes and murderous gaffs you never could imagine.

Young Cyril, the Cap'n's grandson, with flying leaps shot through the cabin, ducked into the cubicle I shared with him and Skipper Nat, snatched his gaff and nearly impaled me as I ran for my 'oppers' (spyglasses) and camera.

Even though I had no purpose to imbrue my hands in blood, my heart was drumming a bit, my temperature rising. For now the kill was close upon us.

Up tumbled all hands and out upon the coal-blackened decks. Spiked boots ground the planking. Forward, streams of hunters came milling from the to'gal'n' house, the 'tweendecks, the dungeon. A rapid spate of cries, questions, cheers, troubled the frozen air. Grimed faces appeared at galleys, at engine-room scuttle. Sealers lined the broad rails gesticulating out toward the illimitable plain of arctic ice that blazed, dazzling white, under the March sun.

The thrill that comes but once a voyage had arrived. For now we were to have 'a rally at de young fat.' We, first of all the fleet, had struck the longed-for whitecoats.

Already Cap'n Kean had gained the bridge. He seemed more like a 'gert, bear-lookin' stick of a man' than ever, as, bear-like, his furry arms waved over the weather-cloth.

'Overboard, me sons!' he shouted. 'Make a pier-head jump an' get into 'em! Over, me darlin' b'ys!'

But the men needed no urging. Even before the ship had bucked and ground, rearing, into the edge of the groaning floe they had escaladed the rail – dozens, scores of them.

They seemed now to have no organization. There was no gathering of 'goes,' or gangs, under command of master watches, as later in the old-fat kill. This was just a free-for-all scramble.

First of all actually to make the ice was Cyril. Not more than sixteen, he; but boys are daring in those hardy latitudes. He led the leaping, yelling crowd that jumped to the loose-broken pans; that scrambled with goat-like agility to solid floes, and in heavily spiked skinny woppers ran like mad demons, yelling, across that fantastic confusion.

At the rail, meantime, I watched; I, who by the grace of Bowring Brothers [St John's merchants] had been permitted to go 'to the ice.' My first interest was less with the hunters than the hunted. At the beginning of it all, the whitecoats looked to me like great white or whitish-yellow pincushions, woggling along, lying still, taking their blobby and full-fed ease, heaving around, blatting with a sort of puppy-like, kitten-like, lamb-like bawl, mew, bark, or what you choose to call it.

As the whitecoats passively awaited the attack, some of the old seals raised inquiring heads, began to get under way with a peculiarly sinuous motion. The dogs, to their shame be it said, were first to make for rifters and bobbing holes; for these were harps, and not the fighting hoods. Open waters thrashed with escaping seals. Up, down, and up again the old ones surged, with a startled and anxious air; glorious, sleek, brown-eyed creatures, gleaming and glistening. They seemed inquisitive, willing enough to find out what manner of thing this swift, two-legged animal might be that ran and laughed and yelled.

Some of the females lingered, but not long. They had to go, one way or the other – into the sea or under the sculping knife. I was astonished at the mother seals' lack of maternal devotion. Perhaps half fled. With a farewell wave of the scutters, scores of them vanished. But the young, the coveted whitecoats, still remained.

'Dere'm de fat, sir!' a grizzled old Notre Dame Bay man exulted to me. 'Ondly a little larry string, but dat'm a beginnin'!'

The kill was in full cry. Swiftly the men ran and leaped over rough ice. They caught seals, struck with their heavy, cruelly pointed and hooked gaffs. Cyril later boasted that he had slaughtered the first seal.

I beheld Cyril's feat. A fat dog was his prey. The dog faced round at him, raised its head, flashed sharp teeth – the sort of teeth that sometimes work havoc on incautious hunters. It flung a throaty 'Rrrrr-r-r-r-r-r!'

Whack!

The seal's head dropped. Far from dead the seal was; still thrashing; but never mind about that! Cyril jammed his gaff into the ice, flung off his coil of tow rope, jerked out his flensing knife and whetted it, all with the correct technique of a finished sealer. He rolled the seal over; with a long gash split it from throat to scutters, and, amid perfectly incredible floods of crimson, began skinning it. Colour? The ice glowed with it!

Everywhere men were going into action. Everywhere the gaffs were rising, falling; tow ropes being cast off; sealers bending over their fat booty of both young seals and old. Everywhere the seals were being rolled over and sculped.

Almost invariably the seals met death head-on. They might flee at man's approach, but once he was upon them, they would stand and show fight. Nearly always they would rear up, fling their growl, make show of biting. But one or two slashes with the long-handled gaff usually fractured the skull; the seal dropped, dying; and the knife expedited his departure to some world where perhaps polar bears, sharks, and men were not.

The actual work of blood at first – though later I grew used enough to it! – was rather shuddering to me. A seal is so extremely bloody, and that blood so extraordinarily hot. The fleshy whack-whack-whack, dully drifting in over the ice, isn't an agreeable sound, either. Nor is it pretty to watch seals die.

All over the ice, near, far, among clumpers and pinnacles and in sheltered seal nurseries, the hunters were shucking seals out of their sculps as deftly and almost as quickly as you would shell a peanut. Every sculp – the sculp is the skin with the fat adherent – had one flipper cut out, one retained. Spots of red dotted the ice-scape. Fwitt-fwitt-fwitt sounded the whetting of blades on steels; and rather horrifically the hunters wiped their dripping knives on their sleeves. Their clothing and the ice, alike, blossomed vividly. Their hands looked like gloves of red that dripped. All about pelted carcasses sprawled, twitched, steamed in crimson pools.

Afar off men were still running. From distances beyond leads dusked by catspaws, where seals were leaping, echoed shouts of the kill. Along the rail, those who had borne no hand in the exploit were gathered and tumult arose. Men clung in rig and ratlines. Officers peered from the bridge. Gibes, cheers, laughter rang into the thin and shining air.

Somebody yelled that this was the southeast 'carner' of the main patch; but in this wilderness, how could anybody know?

Now some of the hunters, having slain all they could make shift to get aboard, were returning. Open came the loops of the lines; swiftly the nimrods laced their 'tows.' They cut holes in the edges of the sculps, passed the ropes back and forth through these, and made a peculiar, complicated knot. A turn of rope served as a grip for the left hand. The long end was passed over the right shoulder, wrapped round the arm, and firmly held by the right hand. Lacing a tow is something of a trick in itself.

Through ice defiles and around pinnacles they toiled, each 'scotin' his tow,' bending far forward with the weight of the load. From every man's shoulder, thus toiling, swayed and swung his gaff. Over plaques of virgin white – white no longer when they had passed! – the hunters came labouring shipward. Long, wavering lines of colour formed; they joined to broader roads, all converging on the *Terra Nova.* Crimson trails, these, such as no otherwhere on earth exist. Man's mark and sign and signal in the North.

'AN EDGE FOR HUMAN GRIEF' (1923-32)*

Edwin John Pratt (1882-1964) was born at Western Bay, Conception Bay, and attended the Methodist College in St John's and Victoria

* 'The Ground Swell,' 'Erosion, 'Sea-Gulls,' 'The Drag-Irons,' and 'The Lee-Shore' from *Collected Poems* by E.J. Pratt, Second Edition, edited by Northrop Frye, reprinted by permission of The Macmillan Company of Canada Limited. 'Loss of the Steamship Florizel' from *Newfoundland Verse* by E.J. Pratt, reprinted by permission of The Macmillan Company of Canada Limited

College, University of Toronto. His poem *Rachel* was privately printed in 1917, and *Newfoundland Verse* was published in 1923. Within a few years he was an established literary figure and an eminent academic at the University of Toronto. In 1930 he was elected to the Royal Society of Canada. His *Collected Poems* appeared in 1944. A second edition was edited by his friend and colleague, Northrop Frye.

THE GROUND SWELL[1]

Three times we heard it calling with a low,
  Insistent note; at ebb-tide on the noon;
  And at the hour of dusk, when the red moon
 Was rising and the tide was on the flow;
 Then, at the hour of midnight once again,
  Though we had entered in and shut the door
  And drawn the blinds, it crept up from the shore
 And smote upon a bedroom window-pane;
Then passed away as some dull pang that grew
Out of the void before Eternity
  Had fashioned out an edge for human grief;
 Before the winds of God had learned to strew
 His harvest-sweepings on a winter sea
  To feed the primal hungers of a reef.

LOSS OF THE STEAMSHIP *FLORIZEL*[2]

What changed thy face from that of yesterday,
  Great Sea! that with thy mothering hands outspread
And smiling on our common life, didst lay
  The table covers for our daily bread?

To-day, held by the thresh of iron shocks
  Within the vortex of a lightless fate,
Thy hands are tearing seaweed on the rocks,
  And thou – a stark and wild inebriate.

EROSION

It took the sea a thousand years,
A thousand years to trace
The granite features of this cliff,
In crag and scarp and base.

It took the sea an hour one night,
An hour of storm to place
The sculpture of these granite seams
Upon a woman's face.

SEA-GULLS

For one carved instant as they flew,
The language had no simile –
Silver, crystal, ivory
Were tarnished. Etched upon the horizon blue.
The frieze must go unchallenged, for the lift
And carriage of the wings would stain the drift
Of stars against a tropic indigo
Or dull the parable of snow.

Now settling one by one
Within green hollows or where curled
Crests caught the spectrum from the sun,
A thousand wings are furled.
No clay-born lilies of the world
Could.blow as free
As those wild orchids of the sea.

THE DRAG-IRONS

He who had learned for thirty years to ride
The seas and storms in punt and skiff and brig,
Would hardly scorn to take before he died
His final lap in Neptune's whirligig.

But with his Captain's blood he did resent,
With livid silence and with glassy look,
This fishy treatment when his years were spent –
To come up dead upon a grapnel hook.

A LEE-SHORE

Her heart cried out – 'Come home, come home,'
When the storm beat in at the door,
When the window showed a spatter of foam,
And her ear rang with the roar

Of the reef; and she called again, 'Come home,'
To the ship in reach of the shore.

'But not to-night,' flashed the signal light
From the Cape that guarded the bay,
'No, not to-night,' rang the foam where the white
Hard edge of the breakers lay;
'Keep away from the crash of the storm at its height,
Keep away from the land, keep away.'

'Come home,' her heart cried out again,
'For the edge of the reef is white.'
But she pressed her face to the window-pane,
And read the flash of the signal light;
Then her voice called out when her heart was slain,
'Keep away, my love, to-night.'

NOTES

1 The first two poems are from *Newfoundland Verse* (1923) and the last four are from *Many Moods* (1932).

2 The SS *Florizel* was lost in a snowstorm near Cappahayden on the Southern Shore on 24 February 1918.

BOB BARTLETT'S BOYHOOD (1928)*

Robert Abram Bartlett (1875-1946) was born at Brigus, Conception Bay, and attended Bishop Feild College in St John's. In 1897 he sailed to the Arctic under the command of his uncle on the *Windward*, a ship Lord Northcliffe had presented to the American explorer Robert Peary. When Peary travelled north on his 1905-6 and 1908-9 expeditions aboard the *Roosevelt*, Bartlett was in command. It was on the second of these expeditions that Peary is said to have reached the pole. Bartlett commanded the whaler *Karluk* on the Canadian Arctic expedition of 1914 led by Vilhjalmur Stefansson.

* Robert Bartlett *The Log of Bob Bartlett* (New York: G.P. Putnam's Sons 1928). Reprinted by permission of G.P. Putnam's Sons

This vessel was lost on the mission but all hands were saved. Later Bartlett sailed for many years his own schooner the *Effie M. Morrisey*. He died in New York.

MY FATHER AND mother grew up when Brigus was at its best. Conditions there were then the same as in New Bedford, New London, Mystic, Stonington, and other New England places in their eras of prosperity. There was plenty of money in Brigus at the time; no unemployment; ten children to a family; and everywhere a great pervading happiness. It was the Golden Age of Newfoundland.

Grandmother Bartlett was boss in our tribe. Grandfather Bartlett, for all his ravings on the after deck, did not have much to say about the raising of his 'kids.' 'Abram, while I live, I reign,' was Grandmother Bartlett's ultimatum on the beach. And reign she did. A good, kind woman, but as full of authority as ever a skipper at sea. In family affairs she set the course and steered it, come fair or foul, to the bitter winter day she died.

It was in my grandparent Bartlett's home that I was born. The house had high ceilings, and was plastered with home-made lime from basement to roof. The large rooms were furnished with old English furniture, mostly brought from the old country. In the lower floor were French windows with long crimson curtains and heavy mahogany rods in well polished brass rings. I remember the rich Brussels carpet, the big mahogany table in the center of the room, the open fireplace with its brass fenders and andirons; the quaint marble clock on the matelpiece; the rich crimson and gold paper on the wall.

I can picture a snowy winter's evening with a lot of Brigus youngsters in to supper. The different games such as Bagatelle. The stories told. I can recall my grandmother asking us all about happenings at school, and listening attentively to every word of it. Much chatter about skating, coasting, hunting and trouting. The girls whispering their affairs. Never-to-be-forgotten days!

Evenings one of my sisters would play the piano. Up and down the long wide hall we would dance waltzes, mazurkas, reels, polkas, lancers and quadrilles. It was an open house and always had been. Indeed, some of the boys' and girls' parents had been entertained as youngsters there a generation before we were born!

Grandmother lived well but simply. We ate enormously of her milk and cream, hot biscuits and jams, poultry, vegetables and roasts; a provender that produced a hardy group...

Money was plentiful in those early days. With the many avenues for revenue open to a man, especially sealing, it was seldom that all of them failed during one season. And since, as I have just said, those were the days before prohibition, nearly every master had a well stocked cellar. As a result it was often a difficult thing for the poor women-folks to round up their lords at meal time since masters were always around sampling each other's stock. But this was also in the good old days when servants were plentiful and never thought of kicking either at late dinners or extra company and meals were seldom served on the dot.

Visiting these old scenes today, it seems impossible that they could have been the center of such open-hearted genial hospitality and gaiety. Alas, most of the fine old mansions have crumbled to dust with their owners.

Father's code was a terribly strict one even in other things besides drink. I never heard father curse, or saw either mother or father drink or smoke. Though both had been raised in homes where there was plenty of liquor, card playing and dancing, when mother got a home of her own she had none of it. Father read prayers morning and evening. When father was away sealing, mother read prayers. It was a stiff change from the freedom of Grandmother's place...

Growing up we were always in awe of our parents. 'Children should be seen and not heard' was the rule in those days. I never was chummy with my father until I grew up. He was a stern man. I have heard but few men or women ever call him by his first name, even those who, as boys and girls, played and grew up with him. It was always 'Captain' or 'Skipper.' I always had to 'sir' him; and, when speaking to mother, to say, 'Yes, mother' or 'Yes, ma'am.' I wouldn't dare to come in father's presence with my cap on, nor would I in any way be familiar or salacious.

As I was the eldest son my mother resolved that I should enter the ministry. So at fifteen I was sent to the Methodist College at St John's, Newfoundland. But the spirit of my fathers was in my blood. The sea was calling me.

At seventeen I gave up the struggle and went with my father to the seal fisheries. Sealing is still a hard life. As I have already described, often a blizzard sweeps down while the men are away from their ship. Then, with no shelter and frequently without food, they wander about for hours and sometimes days. As many a staunch Newfoundlander has become numb and dazed at such a time and has lain down and died, we have many 'sea widows' at home. Hard as it was, this was the life that ran in my blood.

Let me tell you a little incident in my own early experience to show how tough a young man has to be for that work. One time I was with a gang shooting old seals and we came to a lead of water separating us from a fine bunch of animals. As the lead was too wide to jump across I took off my clothes without hesitation and plunged in. Remember this was early spring, with the temperature close to zero. I wouldn't do the same thing now for a cask of gold.

The water was terribly cold, but I swam across. I was so numbed that I found it hard to climb up on the sharp ice on the other side. Finally I crawled out with shivering limbs and chattering teeth. The other fellows threw my clothes and rifle across. With shaking fingers I got dressed and ran hard in the direction of the seals to warm up. It was a tough twenty minutes, I tell you. That evening the captain offered me a tot of rum for the unusual number of seals I had killed. As I don't drink I didn't take it. But I remember how fine I felt when he looked me up and down and suddenly exclaimed: 'You'll do, boy! You'll do!'

SIR WILLIAM COAKER BOWS OUT (1930)*

The Fishermen's Protective Union was founded in 1908 and quickly became influential in politics under its dynamic leader, William Ford Coaker (1871-1938). Born in St John's of outport parents, Coaker attended Bishop Feild College and farmed for a time on an island in Green Bay. He began to organize the Fishermen's Protective Union at a meeting at Herring Neck on the day of the Newfoundland tie

* *Twenty Years of the Fishermen's Protective Union*, ed. W.F. Coaker (St John's: Advocate Publishing Co Ltd 1930) 388-9. Reprinted by permission of The Fishermen's Advocate Publishing Co Ltd

election, 3 November 1908. A man of immense energy, clear vision, and great courage, Coaker led what was probably the most imaginative and innovative political movement Newfoundland ever produced. His followers displayed great élan, and the song below, which was published in the union paper *The Fishermen's Advocate* on 20 September 1913, under the title ' "Forty Thousand Strong": Terra Nova's army of toilers respond to Coaker's appeal,' was one of their favourites. It was written by 'A Union Man.' Coaker died at Port Union, a town he and his followers created to embody their ideals.

LOOKING BACK OVER the 22 years passed since that memorable night of November 3rd, 1908, at Herring Neck, I observe great changes. The fishermen and working men have a far different conception of the part they now should make regarding national affairs. Where indifference and apathy prevailed in 1908, the keenest interest in commercial, political, governmental, educational, and social conditions is now manifested. A new era for Newfoundland was indeed initiated with the FPU movement of 1908. The work the FPU was organized to perform, has about been accomplished. The toilers of the North had seen a light and faithfully followed it for 22 years. It is now the duty of the faithful to take another step forward and raise the banner that was hoisted in 1908 a few feet higher and to develop the work of the past 22 years in a direction compatible with conditions that present themselves to-day. The toilers now realize their influence and responsibilities; they have been taught by the old guard how best to travel the journey. Present day conditions call for remedies somewhat different from what I advocated in 1908. More new men, clean, square, honest, sincere, experienced and level-headed must be found to go forward and lead the way. The toilers must be on their guard against the propaganda of professionals who have but one secret desire and motive and that is to use them to promote the game they would like to play. Any new movement will end disastrously unless led by one of their own comrades possessing the qualifications and reputation I have above referred to. I see the need of such a movement and I can see how it can attain to success, and continue the work initiated in 1908; but I am not so sure that I can locate the right type of a comrade that I would recommend as a leader. I know of several aspirants, but I candidly confess that I see nothing but disaster in the leadership of any of them. When the right man will appear, if I am alive, I will gladly bestow on him my blessing...

The country is anxious to see a number of reforms introduced into the body politic and the next general elections will be chiefly directed to securing these necessary reforms; and, if some leader has sufficient courage to make them the main plank in his platform, success will crown the effort. It will be in this direction that the influence of the toilers will have to be thrown in 1932, if they are to be faithful to their duty to the country generally.

For 22 years I have carried a burden that few comprehend. I have endeavoured to live up to the ideals preached in 1908. I may have failed in some respects, but I can honestly assert that I have sincerely endeavoured to do a man's part towards the country and towards those who trusted me, commercially and politically, since the eventful movement initiated at Herring Neck, November 3rd, 1908. My primest years have been given to the work. I am now nearing my sixtieth year and will gladly give place to a younger man if such can be found, who will be more able, and wise enough to escape from the storms that I had to encounter.

It will be someone's duty in coming years to write a history of our time, and when that is accomplished it will if impartial, bestow a mede of praise on the good work of the FPU. I wish our people were actuated to-day by the political ideals which made the FPU the power it became. I wish all the representatives of the House of Assembly were actuated by the sincere motives and ideals of the FPU candidates nominated in 1913. Cannot political leaders and patriotic electors make an effort to strangle political demoralization now so apparent throughout the greater portion of the country? A great work for country needs to be undertaken and accomplished. If I were as energetic as I was 15 years ago I know well the part I would endeavour to perform. I see the breakers ahead. I know the course I would steer to escape them. It is doubtful if a ship's crew could be secured who would be ready to steer the course I would consider safe. Even if I were well enough to become one of the crew I regard my labours of the past twenty-two years as my fair share of the burden and worries one man should be expected to shoulder as his portion of public responsibilities. My remaining days, be they few or many, I regard as belonging to myself, and I should be allowed to derive from them some relaxation from the strenuous labors of the past and a few rays of sunshine in my declining years. I thank all, some old friends, others new, who have stood by me through these years. I thank them from a full heart. Through good and evil report they were loyal. The confidence reposed by the North 22 years ago has continued without break or doubt up to the present. I am not unmindful of their confidence. It has again and again helped me to do my duty. They should never doubt that I have failed at any time to appreciate that confidence.

Thousands of friends and aquaintances have passed over the border since I established the FPU. One by one they passed over. They were sincere and true and knew from a life's experience the necessity of a work such as I attempted. Their children have but little conception of the treatment their fathers experienced and consequently cannot see the necessity now-a-days for a work such as the FPU accomplished from 1909 to 1923 and is performing to-day. These friends passed over and left me the poorer for as one by one passed I lost a true confiding friend and comrade of sterling worth, and each made a gap that was not filled. I compute that of the 25,000 toilers enrolled during my 18 years as president of the organization that 15,000 have passed over. Their work here ended as so will ours. Life even at 80 is but as yesterday. It soon passeth away and we are gone. What about it if our days here are misspent? What about it if we are false to our duties and responsibilities? What will misspent years avail us in that life to come when every wrong will have to be righted and our sole consolation will be the good done here in assisting our fellow men? Even a cup of water supplied the thirsty will then receive its reward.

5 BREAKERS AHEAD

NEWFOUNDLAND TODAY (1937)*

Joseph Roberts Smallwood was born at Gambo, Bonavista Bay, in 1900. He attended school in St John's and subsequently followed a varied career as journalist, traveller, union organizer, publicist, editor, author, radio announcer, co-operator, and politician. In 1929 he published *Coaker of Newfoundland: The Man Who Led the Deep-Sea Fishermen to Political Power,* a book which was dedicated to his son Ramsay Coaker 'by the Author of both.' In 1937 Smallwood edited and published a two-volume work, *The Book of Newfoundland,* from which the selection below is taken. This was the largest collection of information on Newfoundland and Labrador ever assembled. Two more volumes of the work appeared in 1967. The architect of Confederation, he was premier of Newfoundland from 1949 to 1972.

AFTER ALL THE bludgeonings of Fate Newfoundland's head may be bloody, but it is still unbowed. The economic blizzard has strewn the scene with considerable wreckage, but the spirit of the people is invincible. The wreckage will be cleared away. It is being cleared away. Newfoundlanders are the most tenaciously nationalistic and patriotic people in the world, and it takes more than a storm to destroy their pride.

Just a little bit ridiculous is their pride, perhaps. Their country is small, their numbers are few. Their history has been so tragic that Newfoundland was long ago called 'the Cinderella of the Empire,' 'the sport of historic misfortune.' Yet there is more stubborn pride of country in every cubic inch of the average Newfoundlander than will be found in a cubic foot of any other people.

The greatest wonder of it all is that there are any people living in Newfoundland at all. Why is it that Newfoundland is not merely a great summer playground for trouters, salmon fishermen, caribou hunters, from amongst the wealthy classes of the Empire and the world? It *is* that; but it is also a country with a resident population of three hundred thousand highly stubborn, compactly individualistic, colourfully personal men and women.

* J.R. Smallwood *The Book of Newfoundland* (St John's: Newfoundland Book Publishers 1937). Reprinted by permission of the author

Had the early governments of England had their way; had the swashbuckling merchants of the west coast of England been able to prevail against the love of liberty of our early settlers; had our own resident fish-merchants of two and three hundred years ago been able to overcome the wishes and desires of a pioneering race who did wish to settle in Newfoundland and carve homes of their own out of a wilderness – then would Newfoundland's resident population today be confined solely to a handful of gamekeepers, transatlantic cable operators, and a sprinkling of other necessary guardians and watchmen.

Newfoundlanders are great battlers. They must be great battlers: they have been battling against this or for that ever since the first settler landed here. Battling for the opportunity of getting a berth on one of the West-Coast English fishing-vessels coming on a summer voyage to Newfoundland in the early days of the Island's discovery; battling for an opportunity to desert the vessel before she returned to England with her cargo of codfish in the autumn of the year; then battling to hew a humble home out of the virgin forest that grew to the salt water's edge in some small cove far along the coast out of sight or knowledge of the English fishing-vessels coming to our coast each summer in those early years; battling against Nature and the elements to wrest a living from the sea and the forest while they were building homesteads; battling against the dreaded surprise attacks of pirates, English men-o'-war, 'Fishing Admirals'; battling against the merciless, ruthlessly determined efforts of the early fish-merchants to amass fortunes out of the toil of the Newfoundland fishermen: against official stupidity and private greed; against betrayal, treachery, double-dealing and downright theft: against all these and many other evils had the early Newfoundlanders to battle.

Nor has there been a time ever since when there seemed much less need to struggle and fight.

The much-advertised English bull-dog courage and the equally publicised Irish love of a fight have both found their greatest need of expression here in Newfoundland, from the dawn of our history to the very present.

Perhaps our trouble has been that we were mere 'fighting fools' who fought for the most part blindly, instinctively, without using those shrewd and wily tactics which make a fighter into a champion. Perhaps as a people we are not shrewd and wily fighters at all.

For the defence: it is a matter of a mere hundred years or so ago since they took enough interest in us to allow us to have our first school, to build our first mile of road, to own a piece of land or build a home without breaking the law. While they were giving nearby Nova Scotia all the fostering care and encouragement they were capable of giving, they were holding Newfoundland deliberately in check: sending us at first no governors at all, then ignorant 'Fishing Admirals' of strong thieving propensities, then naval governors of unimaginative dullness who thought they were honouring the colony by their willingness to spend two or three months out of the whole year amongst us: never making a move with regard to Newfoundland except at the behest of the powerful and wealthy fish-merchants of the English West Coast, who were interested only in squeezing the last possible farthing out of the island; giving away whole stretches of our coast to the French, to the Americans.

It would be unmanly and untruthful, however, to place all the blame for our backwardness upon others. We ourselves have failed to use many of the qualities necessary to make a success of our country. Perhaps the very nature of our struggle, of our methods of wresting a living from Nature, has helped to unfit us for creative and constructive effort.

It is a fact that for centuries we have lived by *killing* cod and other fish; by *killing* seals in the water or on the ice, and animals on the land; by *killing* birds, and *cutting down* trees. Has all this developed in us a trait of destructiveness, or narcotised what ought naturally to be an instinct of creativeness? Is it not true that we have been intensely, bitterly individualistic, each of us preferring, wherever and whenever possible, to paddle his own canoe and turn his back upon the other fellow? Have we not failed almost completely in the one virtue that the modern world has made an absolute essential: the ability and the desire to co-operate to achieve a commonly desired end?

Possibly it is a bit indecent to be washing our dirty linen in public – this book is likely to be read by many who are not Newfoundlanders at all, and it cannot be good 'publicity' for a country to dwell upon its weaknesses; although, to tell the truth, I do think we Newfoundlanders need to have something said to diminish our rather swashbuckling pride of country and militant patriotism. After all, if the world really knew us, it would not be Scotland or Ireland or Wales, or the Jews of the world, who would be cited as the *ones* most irrepressibly patriotic, but rather the people of Newfoundland.

If I argue that we ought to be less aggressively patriotic and proud of our country, I do so, I confess, quite half-heartedly. Always keeping one eye upon the possible accusation of the psychologist that such insistent patriotism must really denote the existence of an inferiority complex deep down within us, I hail this pride of the Newfoundlander in his country as one of the most promising *media* by which Newfoundland will overcome her troubles and carve a great future for herself.

We have the resources. God was good to us when He made Newfoundland. Our coastal waters are literally alive with fish of all kinds: why, if all the fish teeming in our waters were to swim at one time into our greatest bay – Placentia Bay – they would fill the great indraught until there was not a single drop of water left in it. A new mathematics would have to be invented to count them. We have the greatest seal-herds in the world. Our salmon are the best in the world. We have as yet barely scratched the surface of our fish resources. Our water powers, both in Newfoundland and Labrador, have already developed vast hydro-electric power for industrial and commercial purposes, and are capable of many times their present yield. We have great timber reserves on our Labrador territory and in Newfoundland – enough to supply two or three more great newsprint paper-mills, or artificial-silk or cellulose mills. As for minerals, it is not even half the story to say that we have, at Bell Island, the world's largest iron-ore reserves, which will become increasingly valuable as the Lake Superior reserves shrink in volume; that we have, at Buchans, the world's richest lead-zinc-copper-gold mine. Our whole Island is known to be valuably mineralised, and even as this is written a small army of trained geologists from various Universities of the United States are scouring the Island in an organised beginning at measurement and survey. Expert opinion inclines strongly to the belief that it is the mineral resources of Labrador, rather than its forest wealth, that will make our vast dependency; so much bigger than ourselves, a source of great wealth in the years to come.

We have the resources to make us one of the greatest small nations of the earth. Sportsmen and seekers of the quaint and unusual in countries have begun to 'discover' Newfoundland in the past half-dozen years. Jealously they keep their knowledge to themselves, lest others too learn their secret and come. Capitalists will discover our vast heritage of natural wealth, and their capital will pour in upon Newfoundland and Labrador to exploit these resources, make great profits for themselves, and bring enduring prosperity to Newfoundlanders. We were on the trembling edge of a breath-taking mineral boom just as the world depression plunged capitalists into the depths of pessimism and passivity. We depended a little too much upon the enterprise and 'push' of pioneering capitalists of the outside world to develop our mineral resources. Now we have set ourselves, by the help of these groups of officially directed geological survey parties, to the task of learning what we used formerly to leave it to others to learn: the actual facts about our mineral wealth. Soon we shall be in a position to tell the outside world in exact terms just what we have got in the mineral line.

Newfoundland is in the happy position of being able to say that the starting of two or three sizable new industries employing eight or ten thousand men would at one blow end unemployment in the Island; circulate enough wages to make the people self-supporting; end all need for dole or relief; enable the government to balance its budget; give the Newfoundland Railway, which has just declared its first operating surplus, a fat operating profit indeed.

Two or three new industries! It sounds easy, and it ought to be easy. We have the resources: the existence of the great Harmsworth newsprint paper-mill at Grand Falls and of the even greater International Power and Paper Company newsprint papermill on the Humber prove that paper-making in Newfoundland is not only possible, but capable of more economical production than elsewhere this side of the Atlantic Ocean. The existence of the two great mines operating at Bell Island and Buchans proves that mining can be successfully and profitably conducted in Newfoundland.

In a book [*The New Newfoundland*] which I wrote in 1931 I ventured to make several prophecies about Newfoundland. One of these had to do with air travel to and from the Colony. That particular prophecy is at this moment so near to fulfilment (I refer, of course, to the great Imperial Airways transatlantic air line now being arranged, with Cobb's Camp, Newfoundland, as the great connecting link) that I make this further prophecy with greater assurance than that with which those others were made – namely, Newfoundland, within the next half-dozen years, will have blossomed forth as a mining country whose importance will challenge the attention of the world. We shall be the third largest producer of newsprint paper in the world. We shall not have an unemployed man, but will need new immigrants. Our fisheries will have been completely transformed and made vastly more important and profitable by the introduction of considerable sums of new capital.

In other words, our country's onward march to industrial importance and prosperity, interrupted by the economic deluge which settled upon us and the world in 1929 and 1930, will be resumed with increased tempo and brightened by more knowledge than ever.

I am not one of those who consider that the particular form of government at any given time makes much difference of a fundamental nature in the process I have here sought to indicate. Newfoundland has known many forms of government. We were ruled by ignorant, illiterate 'Fishing Admirals' from the decks of visiting fishing-schooners; by itinerant governors who were sent here for a few months each summer; by a much abler class of naval governors who used to remain throughout the year; by a form of representative government; then by a form of government which was a formless amalgamation of representative and responsible government; by full responsible government. Now it is government by commission.

Governments come and governments go, but the people live on forever, their experience becoming ever more enriched by vicissitudes, failures and successes. The natural resources remain. Governments are artificial and superficial things at best. It is the genius of a people that counts. What will make Newfoundland great and prosperous is not this or that government, this or that form of government; but rather that unconquerable, invincible, dogged courage and spirit so eloquently typified by Basil Gotto's bronze statue in Bowring Park of 'The Fighting Newfoundlander.'

This government or that may indeed, by its policies and work, help or hinder the slow, upward march of the people whom it has been set to govern. That is about the limit of its power. Its function at best is that of *accoucheur.* It is the people who count; they, and their inherent qualities of mind and heart.

Governments come and go; depressions come and go. The Newfoundlander possesses more than his needed share of fighting spirit; his country possesses a more than generous share of God-given wealth. The combination is irresistible. Greatness Newfoundland deserves; greatness she shall have.

THE SIX-HORSEPOWER COAKER (1940)*

Arthur Reginald Scammell was born at Change Islands on 12 February 1913. He was educated at St Margaret's School, Change Islands, and at Memorial University College, McGill University, and the University of Vermont. He taught in Newfoundland schools for more than six years and afterwards in Montreal. He is best known as the composer of the ballad 'The Squid Jiggin' Ground.' He was a frequent contributor to and associate editor of the *Atlantic Guardian,* which was founded in 1945, and he also published extensively in *The Newfoundland Quarterly.* He published *Songs of a Newfoundlander* in 1940, *Mirrored Moments* in 1945, and *My Newfoundland,* a collection of his stories, poems, and songs in 1966. In November 1973, an album of his songs and poems entitled 'My Newfoundland,' sung and recited by the author, was released under the 'Audat' label.

THE SIX-HORSEPOWER COAKER

You fishermen free that go forth on the sea,
With engines of various makes,
This old jump-spark of mine, I would take every time
You can keep all your new make-and breaks.

She was tied up with twine, there were bits of tarred line
Round the timer to keep it in place.
Her compression was weak and the air used to leak
Where the packing was blown from the base.

She was easy on fuel, but she kicked like a mule,
For the screws on the beddin' were slack.
And we all of us swore, when she'd rise from the floor,
We feared that she'd never come back.

* Arthur Scammell *Songs of a Newfoundlander* (1940). Used by permission of Broadland Music Ltd – 1973

So we lashed her with wire and a motor car tire,
O, how we did labour and scote,
And with posts on each side, we earnestly tried
To keep her from leavin' the boat.

This motor of ours has miraculous powers,
One summer we broke our pump band,
Now they cost quite a lot, so when she got hot,
We cooled off that Coaker by hand.

One evenin' last fall we went out to our trawl
Though it looked like 'twas going to blow.
We turned to go in, in the teeth of the wind
With a cross-handed dory in tow.

Tom hove up the wheel, and he cussed a good deal,
He cranked till he found of his heart,
He tested the oil, examined the coil,
But the divil, a bit, would she start.

'Twas coming on night, with the seas feather white.
When up to us rowed a small skiff,
And a bedlamer boy with a cast in his eye,
Kindly offered to give us a lift.

The kid stepped aboard, with the air of a lord,
His movements unhurried and slow;
He noted the string and the window blind spring,
But he got that old Coaker to go.

Go, go, he made that thing go
At first he just ran her dead slow,
She has'nt much speed, cause the oil don't feed,
But he got that old Coaker to go.

Just a poor homeless lad, he had'nt a dad
And his name you may never have heard;
But the boat swung about, as he opened her out,
And she rose to the waves like a bird.

So we shipped on that kid, and we're sure glad we did,
Now 'tis seldom we ask for a tow;
And he gets a full share, which I think only fair
For getting that Coaker to go.

Go, go he makes that thing go.
How he does it I'm sure I don't know;
We can race with the Clyde, and we'll keep her 'longside
When he coaxes that Coaker to go.

THE HEALER (1941)*

Margaret Duley (1894-1968) was born in St John's. Her three novels set in Newfoundland – *The Eyes of the Gull* (1936), *Cold Pastoral* (1939), and *Highway to Valour* (1941) – rank among the most sensitive of imaginative recreations of Newfoundland life. Her later book, *The Caribou Hut* (1949), is an account of the efforts of the St John's War Association to provide 'entertainment and comfort' to servicemen who visited Newfoundland during World War II.

The central character in *Highway to Valour* is Mageila Michelet, of an outport called 'Feather-the-Nest.' Mageila is described as 'the seventh daughter of a seventh daughter, with healing in her hands and infinite silence on her lips.' Her closest companion in the village is Mrs Slater, an old, solitary widow 'with a bent back, sunless flesh, and gnarled wind-bitten hands.' The setting of the following scene is the south coast of Newfoundland in 1929, a few minutes before the great tidal wave strikes. Mageila is on her way to the house of a neighbour, Mrs Butler, to cure Bertie Butler's toothache.

BETWEEN SEA AND settlement she walked slowly, feeling the soundlessness of snow underfoot. 'First snow is delicate,' she thought, 'soft as a chick, white as a duck on a pond, different altogether from the dense piling-up of drifts.'

* Margaret Duley *Highway to Valour* (New York: The Macmillan Company 1941). Reprinted by permission of Ms Margot Duley Morrow and Mrs Florence Duley

There were so few people around that she walked alone, coldly bathed in the dwindling glare of the western sky. Marvelling again at the stillness, she savoured the relaxation of a Newfoundlander perpetually tightened from the torment of wind. Now she felt herself walking softly like an Indian, moccasin-clad, easy in body, unblown and unpuckered. Occasionally she paused, knowing she was seeing stark beauty bathed in red. A streak of sunset on snow made her think of blood on white fleece. Her narrow world had brought her close to the slaying-knife, the axe, and the barbed hook striking at the fruit of the sea. Blood, blood, she thought unhappily, visualizing the beauty of the slain lamb and the proud strut of the rooster laid low on the block; but she bade herself look at them, firmly knowing such things must be. Something whispered to her to turn round and see her father's store-houses high up on the hill, only a hundred yards or so below Mrs Slater's highest house. Poor Mrs Slater, she thought, with a deep gush of pity for the old woman who was her self-chosen friend. Then she wondered how she dared pity anyone so profoundly self-contained as Mrs Slater. But the well-being of her youth sighed for the hump on a back, the drag of feet, and the stiffness of hands. Would her father give Mrs Slater a box of groceries for Christmas?

Christmas, she questioned with ice-cold wonder. Now the dying red and dulling white suggested a bright season pushed out of place by the thing beyond perception. Even while she told herself time did not stand still, she felt Christmas would not come. She searched the sky, wide-eyed with wonder. 'Is it that I expect my own death?' she ventured to ask, but the thought chilled her, as the drop of the sun was chilling the world. She crept to the edge of the road and stood in the shadow of a dark point of land. From the horizon inward the sea held a sullen glaze, breaking in froth at the shore-line. She visualized it in other gigantic moods. It was a monster, a sword, a knife, a big blurred being with slobbering lips. It was too big for people, she knew, letting it grow considerably darker before she threw off her chilly trance. With a shiver she straightened and began to climb a rocky path to a house some distance above sea-level.

She saw square outlines, pointed logs stacked up for winter, and a kitchen door wide open in welcome, and she knew she had taken a long time to come a little distance. Lamplight made a yellow square on the first delicate snow. She wished for decision to advance and get on with what she had to do, but she felt useless as driftwood turned about on the sea. She had an instinct to retreat and let Bertie Butler cry himself to sleep. His toothache seemed a mere nothing in face of things at large in the air. Once more she implored the sky with words softly articulate on her lips, 'God, what do I know? How can I cure pain when I am full of it myself?'

But though the sky held nothing but the growth of the moon, she remembered it would be round above a round world; and she seemed to hear old Mrs Slater saying, 'God is in Heaven and thou upon earth: therefore let thy words be few.' Question and entreaty eased out of her, leaving her able to advance. If the world fell around her ears she could do nothing but her job. She even invited the thought of death, daring to think it would be deep and rich as the sea and earth that enclosed it. 'It will be round,' she thought. 'Only dying will be pointed and sharp: the wrench of the tree when it leaves its root, the snap of the flower from the plant.' With no more hesitation she advanced, letting louder feet announce her presence. Almost at once she was welcomed by a thin-faced woman with a sunken mouth, spare shoulders, and a body stout below the waist. The very sight of her made Mageila feel how ordinariness could lessen big incomprehensible moods.

'Mrs Butler, I'm so sorry –'

'Oh, Miss Mageila, dear, 'tis of no consequence. Bertie has been at it that long now.'

Smiling widely, Mrs Butler revealed false teeth like curves of pearl buttons.

'Come in now, Miss, and take a chair.'

Mageila knew prosperity was relative. Her family would be considered poverty-stricken according to some standards of living, but to this they represented wealth. The kitchen was scrubbed and warm with the perilous comfort of a hand-to-mouth existence. There was a wood-stove, a pile of kindling, a box of twigs, a table covered with white oil-cloth, wooden chairs, three-cornered shelves cluttered with household utensils, and a wide settle on which lay a bundled-up baby pawing the air with fat curled hands. On a chair beside it sat Bertie Butler, a six-year-old boy with eyes made small from weeping. From the circle of a black stocking tied round his head, his face peered out peaked and shadowed with childish grief.

'Poor Bertie,' said Mageila, advancing to the settle and sitting down at the baby's bundled feet.

With her head on one side Mrs Butler stood by, smiling with warm-hearted motherhood but with nothing to say in front of a force beyond herself. As if ready to proffer return thanks, her eyes wandered from the kettle to a brown tea-pot on the three-cornered shelf.

Mageila slipped off her gloves, loosened her coat, and sat still – letting the little boy get used to her before she spoke a word. When silence was comfortably warm she smiled at the baby, patting it with a long hand.

'It's a happy baby, Bertie. What's its name?'

'Valda,' he whispered at once.

'Valda?' said Mageila, making the name sound deeper and richer.

Leaning towards the boy, she untied the black stocking while she talked to him with infinite comfort. 'I don't think we need the stocking, Bertie. You're warm and cosy by the stove. Is the pain there?' she asked, touching the child's tear-stained cheek.

A small soiled hand indicated another spot. 'There,' he quavered.

'There,' said Mageila, going round the pain with quiet circular motions. 'Bertie, you're tired and sleepy. Look at me before you go to sleep.'

From under swollen lids Bertie looked up, letting his eyes trance as if they were too weary for further motion.

Mageila held them, lost for a long moment to everything but the child. 'Bertie,' she said, with the natural command she had always known, 'you haven't got the toothache any more. It's quite gone, and you're going to sleep. Remember, you're going to sleep.'

'Y-yes,' quavered the child.

As if the cure was accomplished Mrs Butler leaned over the stove, peering inside the kettle. 'You'll have a cup of tea, Miss, for your trouble.'

But for a minute Mageila had no thought for the mother. She sat stroking the child's cheek until he nodded on the edge of exhaustion. 'You can close your eyes, Bertie,' she said.

The swollen lids drooped, willing and anxious to fall, and the body wilted against the back of the chair. Like comfortable response at the right moment, Mageila stood up and helped him to his feet.

'Lie here, Bertie, at the baby's feet. There's room on this big sofa. Now if we had something to cover you...'

Bertie lay in a tired crook, relaxed like a child darkly comfortable at the bottom of a pit.

'Here, Miss,' said the mother, taking a winter coat from a hook on the wall, but out of respect she refrained from covering her own child. When Bertie was tucked up, she stood looking down with a smile round her sunken mouth.

'The like of that now, and he hasn't had a wink these two nights.'

'He'll sleep now,' said Mageila, sitting down quietly in Bertie's stiff chair.

'Yes, Miss, that he will, and God bless you for what you've got. 'Tis hard to see them suffer,' said Mrs Butler, walking cheerfully towards her tea-pot. She knew her son had been charmed into a painless sleep. Mageila knew it too. Service like this was part of her, like her own arms and legs. It was born in her; had grown with her when she had not known about it and elders had called her from play, unmindful of the grime on her childish hands.

'You'll take a cup of tea for your trouble, Miss.'

'Thank you,' she agreed, knowing she must stay when her instinct was to go.

Now that her task was accomplished she was invaded again. Her possession had barely departed long enough to let her cure Bertie Butler. As the thing came back she knew she could not expel it. She was reminded of those who had been possessed of devils, and what was incomprehensible before was credible now. If the invasion spread beyond her she would begin to run, and perhaps rush to the edge of the cliff and leap over. By the strongest effort of will she sat leashed. To go without breaking bread would be a wound to Mrs Butler's pride, but as the kitchen door darkened she started like a creature prepared for the worst. It was only Mr Butler, a short square man in blue overalls and a cap behind a coxcomb of curls. His smile was a bit of warmth in a bleak face and encompassed his domain.

'Miss Mageila,' he said, touching the brim of his cap.

'Mr Butler,' she murmured courteously.

'How is the toothache?' he asked, stepping inside the kitchen.

'Look of 'un, sleepin' sound? Ain't it wunnerful now?' said Mrs Butler, falling into excited dialect at the sight of her own man. 'Come in, Jabe, and see 'un. He's lovely now.'

Mr Butler entered the kitchen, bringing in a breath of cold air blended with sea, earth, stable, and hay. With the unity of simplicity he stood beside his wife and looked down at his son. Then the baby opened its mouth in a big square, emiting a wail.

'Well,' said Mr Butler, as if the impossible had happened, ' 'tain't like Valda now to cry at the sight of her fadder.'

But the baby wailed on, making her mother touch her breast as if she possessed its peace. Uncertainly she placed the tea-pot on the table, but her husband directed her otherwise.

'Make the tea, woman. It's the storm in the air that ails her. 'Tis wunnerful strange for the time of year. Wunnerful uneasy like.'

'I'll hold the baby,' said Mageila with dry lips, stooping to conceal uneasiness in herself.

Thankfully she lifted the fat bundle, glad of warmth and something to mind but herself. Gratified at the promotion of her child, Mrs Butler warmed her tea-pot from the kettle as Mageila bent her head and inhaled warm earthy flesh. Mrs Butler was swishing water round the sides of the tea-pot when her head jerked like a spring.

'What's that?' she asked, wild-eyed. 'Jabe!' she screamed, and the wide fling of her arms sent an arc of boiling water in the air.

'Watch out, woman,' he ordered, grabbing her arm; but Mrs Butler's screams went pointing into the air. 'It's thunder! Hold your tongue,' yelled her husband.

'Thunder,' sobbed Mrs Butler. 'Thunder is over not unner!'

'It has come,' thought Mageila. Without warning, with nothing before but her own difference, she felt the house tremble, saw the china rain off the three-cornered shelves, watched a sugar-bowl empty itself on the floor, and knew beyond doubt that the rocks trembled and called out in a long rumbling voice. Without being told she knew what it was.

'It's an earthquake,' she said, clutching the crying child.

But Mr Butler was a seaman and he would not believe. 'That don't happen here. 'Tis from the sea,' he yelled. 'Hold on to the child.'

'Yes,' she said, making herself hold without desperation.

Now that the thing was here, her possession retreated – leaving her with a sense of responsibility towards something smaller than herself. She made a soothing sound, bracing herself against the wall. But there was no support from shivering wood; so she stood forward with feet apart, while deeply inside she experienced the trapped agony of humanity in the face of natural forces. If she seized the baby and ran, where could she go over rocking earth? Then she remembered hearing that earthquakes were supposed to be worse inside houses, so she measured the length to the door. But another rain of crockery hit Mrs Butler, collapsing her with arms outspread like a wall-crucifixion. Then, as if the wall stung her, she scuttled away in the middle of the floor.

'Jabe,' she screeched, 'the walls are fair liftin'!'

'Hold your tongue,' commanded her husband, jerking her to her feet. 'That's no way to take on. Let the boy sleep.'

Beyond personal concern, Mr Butler raised his head as he heard the plaintive distress of animals enclosed in a stable. At once he made a step to the door, but his wife burdened his arm with human claims.

'No, don't go now,' she implored with shrill supplication.

'Shushhh,' crooned Mageila, as much to the mother as to the child.

Then the rocking and the rumbling ceased as abruptly as it had begun, bringing such relief to Mrs Butler that she collapsed on a chair and extended her arms across the table in limp reaction. Momentarily dazed, Mr Butler stood inert as Mageila sat down with a small thud. The baby stopped crying and there was a fathom-deep fall into silence as they fearfully savoured survival, with strained ears waiting for more. When suspension went on, they dared open their mouths and speak.

'Mr Butler, take the baby,' said Mageila, standing up. 'I must go at once. My father –'

'No, no, don't leave me, Miss; don't leave me,' moaned Mrs Butler, beginning to sob from some hard core; and when the sound reached her lips they jibbered, loosening her teeth.

Unheeding, refusing the baby, Mr Butler took a step to the door. 'T'beasts,' he muttered implacably.

Mrs Butler moved her head on the table as if she would wound herself. 'Don't go, don't go; somebody stay with me,' she sobbed.

Still holding the baby, Mageila saw the wrecked kitchen with its broken china, spilled sugar, and pools of water on the floor. 'I must go,' she said, with the will to service sternly leashed for her own.

Mr Butler took another step forward, reducing his wife to harder sobs. The baby whimpered unhappily, but its mother would not heed. Seeing the rising hysteria, Mageila knew she would be detained if she did not do something at once. Without pity she gave the baby a hard nip, making it roar louder than its mother.

'Mrs Butler,' she said sternly, 'take your baby. It needs you.'

Instinct stronger than hysteria made the woman sit up and extend a limp arm, which kept growing more and more vital until clutching increased the baby's cries.

'Shushhh,' she jibbered, rocking the baby, herself, and her own misery. Outer sight returned and she moaned for lesser things. 'M' china, m' cups and saucers. M' lovely tea-set. Oh...'

But as her child cried louder she pulled up her sweater with automatic maternity, and when contact was established both slumped and went silent, as if they had found a measure of healing.

Seeing the baby drawing from a source needing replenishment in itself, Mageila spoke as quickly as her slow speech would permit.

'I'll look across. If it's all right I'll sweep the kitchen and make the tea.'

'There, Mother,' said Mr Butler. 'Now just bide a while until she comes.'

With Mr Butler, Mageila went outside to look down at Feather-the-Nest. Overhead the mood made a pale disc in a sky like frozen smoke. Its light revealed the world in solid outlines, suggesting that the earthquake had been nothing but a dream of human instability. Only the sea spoke of disquiet, rolling turbulently as if it had sucked the earthquake.

'Quare,' said Mr Butler grimly. 'Mighty fast it's come up.'

Peering anxiously, Mageila stepped to the edge of shelving rock – unmindful of the sea aspiring to the height of the house. The settlement stood intact and the moon made the houses look like cardboard boxes built by children in a desolate place. Feather-Cake predominated, as if a larger child had built with a fanciful hand. As every window gleamed with light, she knew they reported excitement.

'Nothin' wrong but the way they take on,' said Mr Butler.

Then Mageila knew her ears were receiving the shrill echoes of many human voices talking of new experiences. They would all shout together and there would be no terror like unto every special terror. Even her sisters would be like that, she thought, shivering in their beds with the clothes drawn up under their chins. But not her mother. She had enough courage and authority to rebuke the very earth for its foolishness. At once she would order her daughters to be quiet and sit up and have a nice cup of tea and feel better. In her effort to do something practical she would sweep the maid aside and boil the kettle herself. Her father would leave her in charge, go out, and look for his youngest daughter. As if she could see him walking towards her, Mageila was conscious of his surge of anxiety.

'I'm all right, Papa,' she said, deeply articulate.

Over her shoulder she saw Mr Butler on his way to the stable and one moment more she appraised the sea, hearing it sighing and singing in a different way. 'Is this all?' she asked herself slowly. 'Was the earthquake all that I felt?' At once she was filled with an urgency to run down the rocky path and desert Mrs Butler. But it was not in her to act like that, so she turned resolutely to render the assistance that would free her. Inside the kitchen she found nothing had stirred but the rise and fall of breath; so she worked with the sound of the sea in her ears, gathering up china, replacing objects on shelves, mopping up water, and straightening the listed kettle.

'You shouldn't do that, Miss,' muttered Mrs Butler, looking uneasily at the open door. 'The sea is wunnerful loud.'

'Yes,' said Mageila, 'the wind must be coming up.'

'No, 'tis not wind,' said the woman. 'M' ears know the sound of that.'

'Just sit still,' said Mageila soothingly, 'and I'll make you a cup of tea.'

'Kind you are, Miss,' muttered the woman, sitting on the edge of her chair like leashed maternity; but her lips and her eyes would not still for her child. 'Think of that now,' she mused uneasily. 'An earthquake; that's what it was.'

Mageila saw that she was reliving it, assembling it, and that when she could recapture it she would present it for shrill conversation. As if working to be gone before that time, she coaxed the fire with houghs and kindling; and when the kettle boiled again she made a pot of tea.

But Mrs Butler had lost interest in replenishment. ' 'Tain't over,' she said, lifting a taut strained face.

'There,' said Mageila, firmly reaching for her coat and scarf. 'Drink your tea.'

'What is it? What is it?' moaned Mrs Butler, and Mageila was reminded of second-meeting: rocking, rocking and singing of being washed in the blood, while the sea went on outside straining to reach the church.

'Just the sea, just the sea,' she said, but she turned her back so that Mrs Butler would not notice her dread.

She knew it was the sea and something else. Now nothing could hold her. All the Butlers could die at her feet and she would still walk away to her own. If there was more, she must be with them when it came.

But Bertie Butler sat up like a small resurrection, with anxious deathlike eyes.

'Miss, what's that?' he asked fearfully.

Unconsciously delaying herself, Mageila put a firm hand on his shoulder. 'Just the sea, Bertie.'

' 'Tis loud, Miss,' said the boy, imploring explanation with his eyes.

'But we don't know all of the sea, Bertie,' she explained. 'We never come to the end of the sea.'

There was a wild roar and a pound as waves broke on the shelving rock.

'But it knows the end of us,' muttered Mrs Butler with a hint of panic.

'I'm going,' said Mageila without looking back. 'Bertie, stay with your mother like a good boy.'

'Yes, Miss,' said Bertie, dumbly obedient.

It was on and over so quickly that she could never recapture the split second of infinite living. As she ran with down-bent head to challenge obstruction she collided with Mr Butler, charging with a loud 'Lord Jesus!' on his lips.

'Inside,' he roared, as if his frail dwelling could protect them.

Dumb from collision, she swerved but stood cloven to the rocks by what she saw. There was nothing in front of her but a wall of advancing water, and the awful clarity of her mind photographed the infinite grandeur of peril. The sea was upright, glossily taut and curved at the top like a reaping-hook. It was coming to take her, and she could not move; but even as she waited for the strike, she saw the wave break at her feet and spit in her face.

Then it churned and boiled and receded, meeting another wave and propelling it back on the shore.

'Inside,' roared Mr Butler, and she landed on the kitchen floor from the urgency of Mr Butler's hip.

Then the sea struck as noisily as a cannon, lifting the house with savage buoyancy and sweeping it inland until it toppled on higher rock. There was a sense of sucking round the house, of water sweeping in, of sea-strength being mustered for a higher life on its bosom. When it swept the house outward, they were in a boat that was not a boat and on a bottom that let in much water. Its icy feel round her body made Mageila leap with a wild sense of self-preservation. With the same mental clarity she saw Mrs Butler's open mouth, witless eyes, bare breasts, and arms relinquishing her child. On its way to the floor Mageila snatched the baby, then held it high on her chest. She saw Mr Butler seize Bertie with one hand and give a dislocating jerk to his wife's arm with the other.

'We'll ground agin, Miss. I've got the two of them. Can you leap for it?'

'Yes,' she said, feeling a rain of objects falling round her head and hearing hot wood-ashes sizzling in the water.

They grounded and the floor felt ripped by rock. Mageila saw Mr Butler leap, dragging a grotesque woman and a limp obedient boy. But he went, seeming to fall into a foaming cauldron.

'Now, Miss,' he called in a loud encouraging voice.

'I'm coming.'

Self-preservation took her beyond herself, making the baby a featherweight in her arms. She felt the step underfoot, the cold air on her face; she saw the seethe of water, but she knew there was land. She went out high and wide and strong as an eagle. She felt the wild soar of herself and the strange primal exaltation of danger. She felt winged and beaked to help herself in the air. She remembered a dream of flying when she did not fall. But she did, terribly, shatteringly, crashing on rock, tearing her flesh, lacerating her knees as she made a last spurt to climb as high as she could. Then a spur of rock winded her and she lay gasping with breath that had to run out. She slumped face forward; but cold snow cleared her mind, permitting the effort of pushing the baby aside so that she would not lie on it. Then as if it was too defenceless she covered it with an arm, while all around her sea-sounds mingled with shrill human cries.

However, she was indifferent to every pain but her own. The sea was a dagger in her chest, assaulting her breath and leaving her icily cold. The chill in herself was unbearable, beyond the iciness of any polar winter. It was running up her legs, entering her body, and when it reached her chest she must die. Her heart was a bird fluttering in darkness, and she fell fathoms deep into unconsciousness she could not fight.

'WHITE BREAD AND CANNED FOOD' (1947)*

Patrick Dalzel Job, an Englishman with a hankering to see the new world and an ambition to build a schooner to replace the one he had lost in Norway during the Nazi occupation, came to Newfoundland in 1947. He was accompanied by his Norwegian wife Bet and his young son Iain. Job, who had only a moderate income, had been assured before leaving Britain that 'Newfoundland abounded with ship-building timber, and that a yard on the east coast of the Colony ... would perhaps build my boat for about the price which I could pay.'

EARLY ON A bright morning in late summer we dropped down – my young wife and the baby and I – over woods and lakes, and more woods and more lakes, to a broad, sandy airfield, where we left the rather empty luxury of the American 'Constellation' for the more hospitable comfort of Gander's deceptively modern airport buildings.

The excellence of the food which we ate in the great hall was gratifying, but the cost was startling, and when the baby was satisfied we moved on without delay, to the railway station. A dollar, the taxi cost, for those few hundred yards. 'Um,' we said, 'airport prices – it will be different in the country.'

The station certainly had no resemblance to the airport. There were a few grimy shack-buildings, including a small waiting-room floored with cigarette ends and tobacco-juice, but there was nothing else. No express before night, the station-agent said; but there might

* Patrick Dalzel Job, pseud. *The Settlers* (London: Constable 1957) 12-15. Reprinted by permission of Constable & Co Ltd

be a 'way-freight' during the day – oh, about ten o'clock, perhaps. Could we travel in that? Of course.

Bet sallied out to find a shop, and came back looking rather alarmed. The prices were very high and there did not seem to be any fresh provisions. We hoped that this was not a bad omen.

People were appearing now in ones and twos, inquiring for news of the way-freight before tackling the agent. We asked about fresh food – especially milk for our baby. Why no, they said, it was difficult to get 'cow's milk' in the outports; people liked canned milk better. Well, there was TB and that. Yes, they could get their cows tested, but then you never knew, someone might be unlucky and be told to kill a cow – it wasn't worth it. Fresh butter? You could get it from the city, but nobody did – it cost upwards of a dollar a pound. 'Green label' (Newfoundland margarine) was better.

We felt our illusions slipping away; but there was some compensation in the charming accent and the helpful friendliness of the people. The speech was not much like either Canadian or American; for the outport Newfoundlanders, after generations of isolation, still retain something of the words, tone and idiom of the first Irish and West-of England settlers, mixed with the accent and idiom of a new world and of a new way of living. Their trace of accent is, however, the only remaining link with the land of their ancestors, which is now much more remote in distance and sentiment than is that prosperous neighbour, the United States.

The men's clothes, of course, were those of the American working man, and new to us, with their gaudy colours and varied assortment of headgear set at rakish angles. Almost the first thing we noticed was that all the shirts – mostly of some fabulous tartan – were either very new and clean, or old and very dirty; and we found later that this typifies much of the Newfoundlander's way of living. He buys a tartan shirt every six months or so, wears it until it is dirty and torn, and then gets a new one; and he treats his shoes, his house, his boat and his gun in the same way. Three hundred years of insecurity have left him almost incapable of planning ahead, and he lives from day to day.

The conversation in the waiting-room had a foreign sound. The women spoke quietly for the most part, but the men's voices were the words coming violently between clenched teeth as they chewed and spat. The Newfoundlander's bitter mode of speech, and his repeated use (even with his women-folk) of words that are unprintable by any standard, are misleading at first; centuries of exploitation and graft, which began with the English 'fishing admirals,' have given him much hardihood but have sapped his initiative and his ability to resist injustice.

By ten o'clock some thirty or forty people were crowded into the waiting-room, but nobody knew what was happening to the expected train. Another hour passed before someone said that there was definite news; we were advised to buy our tickets, and I took our few bags to be checked by the clerk. The clerk refused my modest tip – 'You'll need every cent you've got in this damn' country,' he said.

Iain was now sticky with gifts of lollipops. It was very hot and very dusty. Every ten minutes or so some urchin would shout 'Here she comes,' and the waiting people would crowd on to the railway to stare expectantly at the level, dusty western horizon before retiring again to the one bench around the waiting-room.

In the early afternoon a hoarse and distant whistle announced the solemn approach of a long-chimneyed locomotive, complete with bell and cow-catcher and drawing some thirty trucks, with one small coach at the rear end. The crowd from the waiting-room went off in a body along the lines, but the train ignored them disdainfully and clanged through the station to reverse with a crash 100 yards beyond. The intending passengers, who had followed hopefully in pursuit, scattered, and then trotted westwards again until the coach came to a stop on a side-line some distance outside the station.

We were the last people to get on board, but someone called 'This way, my dear,' to Bet, and we found that the two best seats had been kept for us. Two passengers went off for a bottle of water from the station-agent, to wash down the infant's lollipops, and eventually a whole seat was cleared as a cot.

The windows had double glass and double shutters, fitted with a variety of makeshift catches. People set about trying to get some air into the coach, and in a few minutes everybody was well smeared with soot. After about an hour's wait we had moved about a foot in small jerks, but there was then a crash of colliding box-cars, and we set off at a good twenty miles an hour. Two minutes later we were down to walking pace, until a second kick took us to a group of new wooden houses in the bush.

The train stopped at lumber-camps, at solitary huts and in empty glades. After one long halt, we climbed down from the coach into the sunlit bush, and walked all round the train. We counted thirty-seven trucks and our one little coach, but there was no engine, no engine-driver and no brakeman.

In the few stations the whole local population lined the railway, to talk with the passengers as we bumped slowly past yellow-painted wooden sheds and piled-up timber-waggons. If we stopped, things were enlivened by dungareed urchins, who peered through the smoky windows to comment shrilly and blasphemously on the passengers, or who galloped through the coach, in at one door and out of the other, in uproarious follow-my-leader.

During the first five hours of our rail journey we had been apparently on level ground, or climbing very slowly, and the train had moved decorously when it moved at all; but later we began to sway downhill at terrifying speeds, through forest-land and burned areas and along the shores of the many lakes of all shapes and sizes, which the Newfoundlanders modestly call 'ponds.'

Once we stopped to pick blueberries; at least, the train came to a halt for no other apparent reason, and the coach emptied immediately while passengers of all ages scattered into the sunshine, grabbing handfuls of the wild fruit or cutting whole branches to be plucked at leisure in the train. Iain received contributions from all sides, and he slept contentedly for the rest of the day, so far as the way-freight's explosive method of progress allowed.

It was nearing midnight when the train crawled to a stop among the many lights of a considerable settlement. ... Half an hour later we were being plied with hot food at the lodgings which the superintendent [of the shipyard] had found for us outside the settlement; and, indeed, this red-painted wooden house, set on the grassy shore of the southern inlet, became nearly a family home for us. We did not live there after the first few weeks, but we were always welcomed by 'Grandma' and 'Grandpa' as though we were a favourite elder son and daughter rather than strangers from another land; and our year-old boy became the object of even more love and kindness than the old couple showered on their own much-spoilt grandchildren. ... The kindness of 'Grandpa' and 'Grandma'; the warm autumn sun; the blueberries in the woods; the calm water of the inlet; and the short green grass where Iain accepted the homage of a crowd of little girls every day after school – all this made life very peaceful and pleasant for us.

The rest of the settlement was not so encouraging. Between 'Grandpa's' and the yard, disorderly, straggling groups of wooden shacks stretched for two miles; the houses were mostly dirty, and all were surrounded by rubbish, by heaps of rusty tins, by tumble-down out-houses and by all the odorous evidence of non-existent sanitation. The immediate vicinity of the yard was even more depressing, with ugly, soot-stained buildings, and shops where the prices were so high that our budget would obviously need complete revision if we were ever to hope for a new boat.

We had expected that conditions would be perhaps like those in Norway, where it is possible to live extremely cheaply in the coast villages if one is satisfied with plain but honest food. Fish, we thought, would be plentiful and cheap, as would also be dairy produce. Already at Gander we had learned the truth about dairy produce, and we now found that there was very little fresh fish to be had, while wholesome flour and oatmeal were unobtainable locally. Unlike Norway, it is considered a sign of social inferiority to eat fresh fish in Newfoundland, so there is little or no demand for it except at the actual fishing ports; and the only flour used is bleached white – I have heard it said that all flour supplied to Newfoundland is of the whitest and finest kind made in North America.

The favourite diet of the Newfoundlander of 1947 was white bread and canned food of one kind or another; and a family's social standing could be judged by the size of the heap of empty tins beside the house. This, together with the lack of wholemeals and of sea-fish, meant that the cost of living was very high, especially in the outports.

HARD CASH (1950)*

Arthur Reginald Scammell was born at Change Islands on 12 February 1913. He was educated at St Margaret's School, Change Islands, and at Memorial University College, McGill University, and

* Arthur Scammell *My Newfoundland* (Montreal: Harvest House 1966) 30-4. Reprinted by permission of the author

the University of Vermont. He taught in Newfoundland schools for more than six years and afterwards in Montreal. He is best known as the composer of the ballad 'The Squid Jiggin' Ground.' He was a frequent contributor to and associate editor of the *Atlantic Guardian,* which was founded in 1945, and he also published extensively in *The Newfoundland Quarterly.* He published *Songs of a Newfoundlander* in 1940, *Mirrored Moments* in 1945, and *My Newfoundland,* a collection of his stories, poems, and songs in 1966. In November 1973, an album of his songs and poems entitled 'My Newfoundland,' sung and recited by the author, was released under The 'Audat' label.

'WE PAID FOR IT in hard cash.' Such a statement could only be heard on rare occasions and about certain individuals in Newfoundland outports twenty-five or thirty years ago. 'Nowadays, every second youngster you meet can jingle silver or peel off the odd greenback to the never-failing amazement of the old-time storekeeper. But in my boyhood days in Newfoundland it was almost impossible for a small boy to get his hands on any hard cash.

The small needs of my brothers and myself were taken care of by our parents via 'the account' at the village store. We were clothed, fed and sent to school without our hardly becoming aware of any medium of exchange except the cod that father caught and that we helped to 'make.' Our school books too, were bought at the store – scribblers, exercise books, pencils, slates, a *Royal Reader* and a copybook. Everything went on father's account. As we got old enough to work on the 'room' at ten or twelve cents an hour, 'yaffling fish' we got a huge kick out of taking up the value of our earnings in those little personal necessities which meant to us gracious living. But that was later.

I remember the ritual of mother laying out our pennies for Sunday school collection on the dresser – big substantial pennies which gave a feeling of wealth out of all proportion to their face value. This penny could be lost by getting tangled in your handkerchief, or by being used as a bookmark to find the page of the hymn you had to learn. If this happened, and you found yourself penniless when it was time to get out your cent, there were two dire consequences. You lost face with the class when the teacher asked for your collection and marked it down in the class register book, and worst of all, your brothers or sisters might report it at home. You would then become for a day or two a family disgrace – a blood relation who didn't have sense enough to use hard cash in the way it was meant to be used.

I do not want to give the impression that we were unusually poor. We had plenty of plain food to eat and enough to wear, but actual money was scarce in almost every household. There was a bit of silver for church collection on Sundays, 'small money' we called it which was a good name because those five-cent pieces were no bigger than herring scales. Sometimes we scraped together a bit of change for the odd peppermint knob and there were a few extra cents around the house Christmas time. But everything else went on the account.

It caused quite a stir, I remember, among the small fry when we heard that a certain merchant was offering the grand sum of two cents each for horsestingers' wings. We knew them as 'hosstingers' and I understand the modern name is dragonflies. Years later I found out the wings were used for cleaning the delicate insides of watches. At the time, however, we didn't enquire into the consumer angle of this new industry, nor did we bother to find out from any government department if the hosstinger season was open or if our insect resources could stand indiscriminate and prolonged hunting of this species. Here was a chance to get some hard cash and we got it. Our social values altered. We became lower-lower, lower-middle or upper-upper in the social scale, depending upon how many of the precious wings we had collected in our 'SEA-DOG' match boxes. In one week the few remaining hosstingers on Change Islands were setting new speed records, and the price had dropped to one cent. In two weeks you couldn't find one within a mile of the place, and we were considering hiring Hyde's big motor boat to go to Fogo, six miles away, for a load. Then the inevitable happened. The glutted hosstinger wing market collapsed, and I, with the rest of the hunters, was right back where I was before – just a penny above a beggar.

We used to knit trap linnet during the winter to pay for our school fees. School fees could not be put on the account and the schoolmaster wouldn't accept fish, tomcods or rounders. He turned up his nose at cod tongues and sounds, dried caplin and slated herring. He even shook his head at bake-apple jam, squash-berry jelly and 'meshberries.' He had to have the hard cash.

So father would bring home bales of cotton twine to be knit into trap linnet or netting for the trap fishermen. For this linnet they would pay cash – twenty cents a fathom. Don't ask me where *they* got the cash. Perhaps *they* sold hosstingers' wings too. Anyway father would say, 'Now boys, every spare minute you get this winter, you've got to help me knit this twine. Get busy and fill needles.' We got busy and fathom by fathom the linnet would grow in spite of galled fingers, aching backs and the black looks of three young boys whose ears were cocked to the laughing shouts of luckier youngsters playing 'cat' out on the frozen cove after supper – youngsters who could find the money for school fees in some less painful fashion or whose fathers were not so education-conscious as ours.

Every day when we came home to dinner there would so many needles of twine each, set aside in separate piles for us to knit before we went back to school. If we had something for dinner that I liked, say roasted bullbirds, or fish and potatoes with pork scruncheons, I'd ignore the needles till my stomach juices started churning. If we had, say pea soup or boiled rice (with or without figs), I'd knit a couple of needles to try and work up an appetite for it.

We used to learn Hygienè then. Not health, Hygiene. Hygiene was something you learned chapter by chapter and had very little bearing on daily habits. So father thought too, for when we pointed out to him that the book said we should rest after eating, he pointed out to us that unless we emptied our quota of needles every day, we wouldn't get the chance of learning Hygiene or anything else. So we knit the twine and went on learning by heart more and more about Hygiene. We took courage though from the last sentence on a certain page of the book containing the rules of health. The last sentence was 'Are we downhearted? NO!' I don't know why the author put that in, but it certainly did me more good than all the ten or twelve health rules that preceded it.

Then came the great Christmas of our lives. I must say this for my parents. No matter how poor the voyage or how low the price of fish we always had our stockings full on Christmas morning – via the account of course. This Christmas we each got the usual toys, candies, apples, oranges, nuts etc., and then, right up in the toe of our homespun stockings a crisp, new dollar bill. Here was wealth! Here was affluence! We had evolved through the copper age, the silver age, and here we were at one smack, in the dollar era! We unravelled our stockings trying to find more, but that was all there was. I kept mine for weeks in my little money-purse (we never called them purses), and every time I was tempted to slip back into the silver age something stopped me.

Came a Sunday evening when there was a special missionary service and a special missionary collection. It had been blowing hard from the South'erd that day, and from where we lived we couldn't hear the church bell very well. So it happened that when we did hear it we had to leave for church in a hurry, and as I had been out on the bridge listening, I missed the giving-out-collection ritual. I didn't think about it until the hymn after the sermon – the collection hymn – was given out. I was just going to give mother a nudge in the ribs asking her to shell out, when I thought of my dollar bill. I had it with me, money-purse and all. It gave me a curious sense of power, detachment. Here was a financial crisis. The minister's sermon had been eloquent, the plight of the heathen heart-rending. I could help. But if I was going to spend my first and last dollar in any cause however deserving, I wanted something in return. I wanted glory. I wanted attention. How could I get this better than by putting my dollar bill in the collection plate?

I joined the singing at the second line of 'From Greenland's Icy Mountains,' watching for the sidesman to come down the aisle of the church. Now he was at the pew in front of us, occupied by the merchant who bought hosstingers' wings. He put in a fifty-cent piece and my lip curled. The plate came to father. As head of the family he sat on the outside nearest the aisle. His voice rang half a tone louder as his quarter hit the half-dollar. My two brothers parted reluctantly with their paltry nickles. Mother's dime followed and my moment came, just as the congregation was singing:

Till like a sea of glory
It spreads from pole to pole.

Casually, nonchalantly, I opened my hand and my dollar bill spread like a banner, covering all the silver from view. Father's jaw dropped. The dignified sidesman who had been singing lustily, missed half a line and nearly dropped the plate. My two brothers involuntarily started to make a grab for the greenback, then paused with open mouths from which no sound issued. Mother's alto was hopelessly disorganized. Close proximity to moneyed people always made her nervous. But from my end of the pew came high exultant notes, from one who had tasted all the sweets of philanthropy, and from whom the prospect of tomorrow's ruin could not rob the ecstasy of today.

MEMORIES OF DIDDER HILL (1951)*

Ron Pollett (1900-55) was born in New Harbor, Trinity Bay. He taught school for three years and then worked at Grand Falls. In the company of hundreds of other Newfoundlanders he emigrated in the early 1920s to the United States, where he worked in New York as a printer. He was one of the most prolific and popular contributors to the *Atlantic Guardian,* his writing being dominated by the theme of émigré experience. Thirty-two of the stories he contributed to this journal were published in 1956 in the volume entitled *The Ocean at My Door.*

AS I WRITE this composition I'm looking out the window I always look out of when I'm writing. It's three stories up and affords a view of the sky directly over Coney Island. Off to the right, the part I can't see, is the sky over the harbor entrance to New York.

I'm living in Brooklyn – anyway, I'm residing in Brooklyn, and the time is January.

I have a much better aspect than thousands of others in Brooklyn. But it's still not the rosy picture I cut out for myself when I scrubbed the squidsquirt from my neck and quit my outport home to seek a fortune.

I left Trinity Bay and came to the States the circuitous way; three years as an outport school teacher, three more in Grand Falls adding long columns of figures in the newsprint mill, and two in Montreal smudging my hands with printers' ink. So when I finally landed on Didder Hill in Prospect Park, Brooklyn, the herring scales were already rubbed off my boots and I knew a light bulb when I saw one.

* Ron Pollett *The Ocean at my Door* (St John's: Guardian Ltd [1955]). Reprinted by permission of *The Atlantic Advocate* and Ron Pollett, Jr

What happened to me after that is not too important. But I'll probably get around to shooting off about it one of these days.

This was in the mid-20s when Newfoundlanders flocked into New York by the *Nerissa, Sylvia,* and *Rosalind* boatload, joining uncles and cousins who already had created a Little Newfoundland in South Brooklyn. On Sunday afternoons all the newcomers and most of the old hoisted sail and set course for the nearby park through the 9th Street entrance. They all converged on Didder Hill where they were almost certain to meet someone one time or another from down the home Bay. The place was the next best thing to the jigging ground.

This mound is little more than a grassy knob, a sort of blackberry knap underneath the spreading shade trees a quarter mile along the flagstone path from the entrance. The park itself is an enormous stretch – 526 acres of meadows, man-made ponds, and wild woods enough to get lost in, right in the heart of the city. It's quite a pretty spot, green with wide pasture of trimmed turf grass fringed by tall leaf trees. Yet the outporters, many raw from bald headlands and the heaving sea, gamboled not on the greensward but instead sat sweating salt water in the sultry heat under the boughs on Didder Hill.

How the mound came by that odd name is interesting history. The story is, it was so christened by a big-eared cop with a twinkling eye who overheard a group of baymen chewing the rag while sprawled on the knob one hot afternoon when the sun could roast a caplin on the brick walk. 'Now did'er, boy? Ya don't say, now did 'er?' They were doubtless discussing the sailing prowess of some schooner they'd known on the Labrador the summer before or maybe only the straw hats with which they fanned their melting brows. But, 'Did 'er, boy? Now, did 'er?'

A lonesome lad in the cruel city, I wouldn't miss Didder Hill on a bet. Here, I could get the taste and smell of home. Other outporters must have felt the same way, because the knap grew blacker and blacker with blue-serge suits and hook-up bluchers as fresh brownberry faces were added every summer. According as one group skimmed off their wool peaker caps and donned quiffs or straws, another batch heaved up to the hill with spray-salt in their neck wrinkles. This kept up all through the 20s.

Among us bunch of young Newfers then making our mark on the face of New York was a fair sprinkling of home girls. The distaff contingent likewise was sweetened regularly with arrivals on every boat. They brought natural complexions, contours firm and trim, a swinging gait from active outdoor life, and normally glinting hair, but soon took to the high heels and the mincing tread and the make-up of their already citified forerunners. These were the housemaids who gained a fine reputation in New York as smart and efficient workers so that later arrivals needed only mention the word 'Newfoundland' to be hired on the spot. Those of the home girls with sufficient education to start a nursing career usually entered that profession, and likewise won renown – as 'Canadian' nurses than which there are none better.

Hundreds of these girls married their own kind and have reared a generation who always can locate Newfoundland on the map – which, I believe, is more than can be said of ninety per cent of school graduates in Brooklyn.

If the immigration pace of the 1920s had continued, there'd be cobwebs across half the lanes in Newfoundland today. All you needed then to undertake the big adventure were the bare fare and a health certificate. But the financial depression of the 30s brought quota and other restrictions which pushed the door practically shut and it's never been opened more than a peep ever since. So with the unending spools of red tape and the reams of fly-paper tangling the heels of would-be immigrants from the outports today, Didder Hill has become a lonesome place indeed.

And the loss is New York's – or Boston's or that of any place else in the States where the villagers might come and settle and work. The hardy breed of strong men who were born to work with their hands could contribute much to heavy construction and similar he-man occupations that newcomers from many other countries, as well as city-breds themselves, either shun or are not physically equipped to handle.

At least ninety per cent of the home folk who entered on the big wave following the first World War pitched in at the building trades, notably iron construction work, and helped erect such new-world monuments as the Empire State Building and the George Washington Bridge. Trades like carpentry, ship building and repair, and longshore work came easy to men whose fathers built their own homes and boats and who themselves wielded hammers, saws, and adzes from their toddling days. And they too, like the housemaids and nurses, gained recognition as experts and conscientious workmen.

Meantime, Toronto and Montreal and other cities and provinces of the north mainland, to which entrance is easy since Newfoundland became part of Canada a couple of years back, gather in those of the sturdy outlanders who sprout wings. Strong backs, stout hearts, willing hands, and a burning determination to make good are the prize package the mainland is reaping. And what more could any country ask?

As for the home colony in South Brooklyn, it can hardly be called that any more. Most of the settlers moved off as soon as their families fledged and after the prosperity of overtime wages in the war years of the 40s – away to better and newer housing and roomier streets than in this old part of the city; away out on Long Island into homes of their own like they had in the outports or into modern apartments in the near suburbs. The section is now giving berth to the recent influx of Caribbean races into the city – and the sparrows in the boughs on Didder Hill hear a new kind of lingo which, by the way, could flabbergast them no more than the idiomatic aberrations of the salty 20s.

So today it's like a trip to the graveyard to visit the intersection of 9th Street and Fifth Avenue, the night-time 'village square' which once was fat with outporters and pumpy with handshakes. Only an odd die-hard, complete with barrel belly, eyeglasses, and a forlorn look, remains to stanchion up the brick buildings or warm the stone ramps with his tired bottom. But he hasn't forgotten the genuine 'How's ya boy?' as he inquires where you live now...

Some of us do toy with the idea of spending our second childhood in the same place we enjoyed our first. In the city we've usually never owned any property except a few sticks of furniture under someone else's roof, and the thought of lolling in your own luxurious bungalow in a beauty spot overlooking the shimmering sea seems a pretty good dream. Too, the idea of never, never again having to buck the city hordes on the buses and railways and drag your aching feet over the hard pavements, but instead just be free as the wind to pass your time fishing or sitting on the verandah watching lazy clouds change color in the sunset – that sort of picture does look inviting, to say the least. But it all might be the same kind of mirage you saw in the magazine ad in the first place, back in your youth when you set out to see and conquer the world.

Because, of course you can't really go home again. Your ties are now in Brooklyn where your children were born and where they always will be. Too, the long winters and late springs of the outports seep into aging bones molded to a more salubrious climate, and the moan, screech, and roar of sea gales over cold craggy headlands can grow dreary when you have nothing to do but sit and listen while looking out the window at the snow. Besides, your parents have passed, of course, and so have most of your uncles and aunts and others who made up the life you used to know. Then there's the problem of getting used to 'home' cooking again after the infinite variety of edibles in New York.

But there's absolutely no reason why the exile facing retirement, and fairly well heeled as he should be after a lifetime of striving, can't build himself a comfortable nook in the homeland and spend at least the fine-weather season there having fun as a change from twiddling his thumbs in the city. Those of us from the Avalon, for one section, ought to make out pretty well on the network of motor roads where visitors may drop in regularly for tea and a chat, bringing the kind of happy companionship we seldom could have in the city. Along with that, there'd be boats and fishhooks – and pension cheques in the mail.

Anyway, it's an idea. This replanting would of course have firmer roots than when we merely hopped in on a short visit to the home grounds, as many have done through the years, and got fidgety after the novelty wore off; now there'd be no urgent business pulling us back to the city – nothing but the armchair waiting in Brooklyn and almost anything is better than that.

And back in your birthplace, with no big rent to pay and with everybody bidding you the time o' day, you might even learn to stroke your whiskers in contentment like the old geezers who never left home at all.

A motor route across Newfoundland would help us bring in our pots and pans. Indeed, we may need such a highway long before we can come back as greybeard summer residents. They're digging bomb shelters in New York.

'THIS UNQUIET SEABOARD' (1958)*

Farley Mowat was born in Belleville, Ontario, in 1921 and attended the University of Toronto, his career there being interrupted by service in the armed forces. His writing has been largely concerned with the impact of modern technology on traditional societies, and he has had a keen interest in Newfoundland history and life for a long time. In addition to the book from which the following extract is taken, he has published a number of other works which have, either in whole or in part, Newfoundland as their setting: *The Serpent's Coil* (1961), *The Black Joke* (1962), *Westviking* (1965), (with John de Visser) *This Rock Within the Sea: A Heritage Lost* (1968), *The Boat Who Wouldn't Float* (1969), and *A Whale for the Killing* (1972). He has also written extensively about Newfoundland in magazines and periodicals.

THE NORTH ATLANTIC is a hungry ocean, hungry for men and ships, and it knows how to satisfy its appetites. From September through to June a sequence of almost perpetual gales march eastward down the great ditch of the St Lawrence valley and out to the waiting sea. They are abetted by the hurricanes which spawn in the Caribbean and which drive north-eastward up the coasts as far as Labrador. Only in summer are there periods of relative calm on the eastern approaches to the continent, and even in summer, fierce storms are common.

Gales, and the high seas that accompany them are, of course, the weapons of all oceans; but this unquiet seaboard has two special weapons of its own.

First of all it has the ice – continental masses of it that come sweeping down with the Greenland current to form a great, amoeba-like bulge extending from the coasts of Nova Scotia eastward as much as a thousand miles, and southward five hundred miles from Flemish Cap. The bulge swells and shrinks and throws out new

* From *The Grey Seas Under* (Boston: Little, Brown & Co 1958) 18-20. Reprinted by permission of Little, Brown and Company (Canada) Ltd. From *The Grey Seas Under* by Farley Mowat, by permission of Little, Brown and Company in association with Atlantic Monthly Press

pseudopods from mouth to mouth, but there is no season of the year when it or its accompanying icebergs withdrew completely from the shipping lanes.

The second weapon is in many ways the most formidable of all. It is the fog. There is no fog anywhere to compare with the palpable grey shroud which lies almost perpetually across the northern sea approaches, and which often flows far over the land itself. There are not a score of days during any given year when between Labrador and the Gulf of Maine the fog vanishes completely. Even in the rare fine days of summer it remains in wait, a dozen or so miles offshore, ready at any moment to roll in and obliterate the world. It has presence, continuity, and a vitality that verges on the animate. In conjunction with its ready ally, the rock-girt coasts, it is a great killer of men and ships.

The coasts themselves are brutally hard. Newfoundland, Labrador, Nova Scotia, and the Gulf shores appear to have been created for the special purpose of destroying vessels. They are of malignant grey rock that has flung its fragments into the sea with an insane abandon until, in many places, these form an impenetrable *chevaux-de-frise* to which the Newfoundland seamen, out of a perilous familiarity, have given the prophetic name of 'sunkers.'

The coasts are of tremendous length. Newfoundland alone exposes nearly six thousand miles of rock to the breaking seas. Everywhere the shores are indented with false harbors that offer hope to storm-driven ships and which then repulse them with a multitude of reefs. The names upon those coasts betray their nature. Cape aux Morts, Cape Diable, Rocks of Massacre, Dead Sailor's Rock, Bay of Despair, Malignant Cove, Baie Mauvais, Misery Point, Mistaken Point, False Hope, Confusion Bay, Salvage Point, and a plethora of Wreck Bays, Points and Islands.

Yet by the very nature of their animosity towards seafaring men these coasts have brought out of themselves the matter of their own defeat. Men in these parts have always had to take their living from the sea, or starve; and those who survived the merciless winnowing became a race apart. There are no finer seamen in the world. The best of them come from the outports of Newfoundland and Nova Scotia, and from the islands of Cape Breton and the Magdalens. The best of them are men to ponder over, for they can hold their own no matter how the seas and the fog and ice and rocks may strive against them.

And yet it is also true that these men do not properly belong in our times, for they follow an outmoded creed with undeviating certainty. They believe that man must not attempt to overmaster the primordial and elemental forces and break them to his hand. They believe that he who would survive must learn to be a part of wind and water, rock and soil, nor ever stand in braggarts' opposition to these things.

'Ah, me son,' as one old Newfoundland skipper phrases it, 'we don't be *takin'* nothing from the sea. We has to sneak up on what we wants, and wiggle it away.'

A LULLABY TOO ROUGH (1963)*

Paul West was born in 1930 in Eckington, Derbyshire, and studied at the University of Birmingham, Lincoln College, Oxford, and Columbia University. From 1954 to 1957 he was in the Royal Air Force, serving on the staff of the Officer Cadet Training Unit and lecturing on English language and international affairs. From 1957 to 1962 he taught English at Montreal University. An extremely versatile and prolific writer, he has published poems, essays, novels, and critical works. His book *I, Said the Sparrow* (1963) gives an account of his early life in England. Among his many scholarly articles is a critical comment on E.J. Pratt's poetry entitled 'E.J. Pratt's Four-ton Gulliver,' which appeared in *Canadian Literature* in 1964.

I STILL FIND my first impression the overpowering one: of fog or knocking sea, but the essentially cheating and clandestine view from an aeroplane; a view of Newfoundland's tenacity. First came Stephenville and Gander; desolate arenas important with uniforms; sloughs of seeming despond prinked round with conifers; the type of the deservedly isolated place. Then St John's, gaudily painted shanty-town on the slate two hundred feet below the swaying North Star aircraft. The town, as I first saw it, seemed nothing of the Oldest City in North America. It clutched and clung like the snails in

* From Paul West 'A Lullaby too Rough: Impressions of Newfoundland' *Tamarack Review* (Summer 1963). Reprinted by permission of the author

Homer, like the bits torn from the hands of Odysseus. Perhaps the mist might dissolve it or the sea gnaw it down; but from the air, beleaguered and threatened as it looked, it could also be seen cultivating a sullen aplomb. From the air it looks precarious; from the sea, as you sneak in through the Narrows, as sheer a pair of nautical jaws as one could wish for a landfall, the effect is altogether different: still the shanty town with much rust and much gesticulating new paint, but also the settled centre of a kind of commerce. Silver oil-tanks glitter in whatever sun there is; the harbour has the slack gape of a transatlantic Cardiff or Merseyside in miniature. But, for modern man, it is surely more provoking to fly over the city and province, tracing the outline of civilization; in fact one almost feels that the actual outlines of this civilization can be deciphered only from the air, like the plans of ancient cities.

After brawling Toronto, where sinisterly energetic young men and even more sinisterly relaxed older men warned me about dung-carts in the streets, the lack of running water and the constant threat of insurrection, I expected some kind of violent Arcadia. Tycoons would cower at the first sight of a short blade. Eminent visitors would dash across the tarmac to their TCA plane, vainly fending off ordure bombs from the local pom-poms, hopefully dropping leaflets about sanitation in the delusion that such a scheme might catch on. I expected large dogs and gumbooted madmen everywhere. What I found seemed, on first impression, like nothing so much as a community of Irish mystics cut adrift on the Atlantic, talking an arcane incomprehensible language and tending to make no vowel sounds at all. Thus, I soon found I had landed in *Nfln,* as it was pronounced.

I was fortunate in my arrival because the rain was pouring. So from the first I could catch a sight of the genius of the place, this place that has icebergs in June. Flying over the province, I had noticed hundreds of little lakes; these are *ponds.* It all looked Finnish, perfunctory, and sparse. Miles and miles of timber hemmed in smallish areas of shaggy-looking rock. Settlements seemed few, roads fewer. And yet St. John's has its Torbay airport, rich in its name with associations of Cornwall and now brought up to date. When I landed, I found the old terminal: something rather like the anteroom to a scruffy palace of varieties; all chaos, confusion, and crowd. I was slow to realize that I had landed on an island and that islands have their own way of running airports, no matter whose sign is erected. Thus, none of that dismal ritual of the baggage checks.

You have, or had (for the twentieth century changes all once it arrives thoroughly) to sprint outside and rescue your bags from the scrum; then fight your way into one of those light-blue Bugden 'limousines' which work on some kind of Turkish principle: get as many in as you can. As for red-caps, porters, guidance, signposting, information, there was none of this. Very quickly it seemed to be pioneer land: bustle, jostle, no time to talk. I now realize that all the haste was a combination of two things: first, the Newfoundlander anxious to put on a show for the visitors – for nothing suits the Newfoundlander less than speed; and a certain atavistic urge to get away from the airport and its modern monsters as soon as possible...

Not all is idyll. Not all is repellent either. At the side of a pond a girl in red windproof is swabbing down the family truck: this new machine startles anyone who dismisses most of the twentieth century once he leaves the main centres. I myself have to think in terms of pictures: outdoor privies like enlarged telephone kiosks; two hens mincing carefully along a narrow plank; half-a-dozen swarthy labourers repairing a wharf in the most leisurely of ways but with modern drills; fishing boats at anchor, rocking in a thin sun, each a little wheelhouse that reminds me of a conning-tower; chatty shopping in the general store; root cellars below frost level; barns with neat stalls for the animals; the whole family out battering at the potato-patch; white, scrubbed-looking churches; Orange Lodges with the district number painted boldly on the front; myriad children, some of them Eskimo-dark and egregious – most of them are very quiet at first and will not have a word for weeks; an older generation, all the girls in headscarves, promenading in the evening along the potholed roads; the shape of a split cod, its rough feel, the salt biting into its tissue; ancient iron stoves whorled and fluted into an extreme of decorativeness; the sound of clapboard being nailed – and this by the children who are helping to build a new house about twenty yards from the one in which they are now living; barking dogs who call everyone to the door because a stranger, or a strange thing, is passing through the village; May snow collected and bottled as a lotion for sore eyes; the stinky liquefied jellyfish used as a cure for rheumatism; bleeding stanched by cobwebs; coughing stopped by kerosene and molasses; stabbing at fish with a pitchfork when the water is clear; men who bend iron bars in the kitchen fire and repair impossible breaks with magical dispatch; men who will take the porch off one house and fit it onto another house – without leaving it 'squishy' (lop-sided); men who crouch over the sides of small boats, dropping their jiggers among the cod; a cold, callous wind that discovers every part of you; love-affairs recorded in red paint on the grey rocks; an unfailing courtesy when you ask directions; grinning faces three abreast behind the windscreen of a truck driven with delirious indolence; salt-encrusted fishing suit and boots; horses dragging capelin from the beach for fertilizing the vegetable patches; boatmen seining for capelin as the fish pour into shallow water to spawn; capelin who miss the nets; capelin dead in furrows in the land, decaying to make a good potato; children shouting as the water is torn by any frantic fish – capelin or pothead whale; wool caps, shoulder bags, shining hooks; sandwiches 'excursion biscuit' which you take fishing, and all kinds of jam or jelly; squid-baited hooks dangling inches above the sea-bottom, the dead eyes of live cod – yellow stones in sheathed brown meat, fish stew, diced pork, 'bilin' the kittle,' roasting capelin threaded on a wire; wooden anchors, with boulders caged in by stout battens; a fire made in the boat by shaving a lump of birch onto an iron plate rammed across a fish bin; fish stew cooking while the boat rocks; fish stew eaten with birchwood forks; seas both civil and loppy; fish being tossed from the boat up to the stage on a cliff-top; the single-tined forks used in this – 'pews'; men in caps and baggy sweaters holding three-foot fish by the jaws, and smoking their pipes while they do it; one woman, at a table, splitting open the fish and cutting round the heads; another woman hauling out the entrails and snapping the heads off; a scattering of severed spines round your feet; degutted fish in wheelless barrows; the triangular shape of cod stored away in salt with an archivist's precision; fish on flakes of branches and boards, in the right amount of sun and wind, slowly 'making'; slime, caked salt, tannic tea; small icebergs floating by, little noticed; fires made from fir and spruce 'blasty boughs' which crack in the flames; cliffs conquered by wooden platforms; fish-flakes, for drying cod, which look like funeral pyres awaiting the corpse; quintals of fish – 112 pounds; cod-cullers in the merchants' store-rooms, assessing complexion, texture and weight; going out to turn the fish on the flake; racing out to cover them from rain; men bent double who seem to be thatching rudimentary houses with dried cod; cod in austere barrels all ready for export; quick-freezing plants for halibut and other fillets; good luck if you see the moon over your left shoulder; also in horse-shoes, two black crows, clothes inside-out, finding a pin or a white button, a rooster sounding off on your doorstep, bees blundering into the room; bad luck through coiling a rope against the sun, buying a brook in May, red-haired women, black cats, solitary crows, whistling while floating on water; death augured by banshees and broken clocks striking the hour; death heralded by a glaring cat who looks you in the eyes; taboos about stepping over a child and the terrible power of a widow's curse; trapped dead hares on sale in the streets; little carts drawn by horses at a brisk pace; genuine weather-prophets who have to know when it will be safe to spread fish for drying; high gulls heralding storms; hoar frost in autumn foretelling rain and south-winds; goats returning, far hills looking close, dreaming of horses, sharp-horned moons, soot falling, dogs sleeping all day, lively spiders, playful cats, mackerel skies and mares' tails – all telling of bad weather to come...

The island is full of noises: majestic, dying, vulgar, fatuous, phantom, reassuring, lunatic, unique. I have not heard them all. Some of them will prevail over the others; some of them should, but they will not; some of them should not, and they will. In ten years' time a good many creases will have been ironed out, many of the ancientry wronged and gone, and King Fish will be unthroned. It is a matter of pitting hope against the foretaste. On this island, which stratifies its history, neither Prospero nor prosperity will rule entirely. I am grateful for having been able to look in on its ancient nonage and its impossibly lively fortitude.

THE ISLAND OF AUKS (1965)*

Franklin Russell was born in New Zealand in 1922 and arrived in Canada in 1954. His writing has been largely concerned with nature, and he has travelled extensively in Newfoundland. In 1961 he published *Watchers of the Pond* and in 1964 *Argen the Gull.* In the following extract he describes his visit to the Funk Islands.

* Franklin Russell *The Secret Islands* (New York: Simon & Shuster 1965). Reprinted from *The Secret Islands* by permission of W.W. Norton & Company, Inc. Copyright © 1965 by Franklin Russell. Reprinted by permission of Collins-Knowlton-Wing, Inc. and by permission of the Canadian Publishers, McClelland & Stewart Limited, Toronto.

ARTHUR STURGE was caught in an immortal moment, straining back on his oar as he moved the heavy dory toward Funk Island. This was the last lunge of the journey; the long-liner heaved behind us; Uncle Jacob had bellowed his final exhortation of good luck.

I saw the island close up as I glanced over Sturge's shoulder, and I knew I was duplicating the experience of a thousand men before me. From the boat it seemed incredible that such a stream of humanity – explorers, Indians, sealers, whalers, codfishermen – had ever reached this lonely place. Yet the island, and its auks, had drawn them as it was drawing me.

The island was a blank wall of rock, thirty feet high, suave and bland, and topped by a thin, fast-moving frieze of murres who, presumably, were anxiously watching our boat. I have read about a moment of truth, even written about it, but not until I was in this dory, in this place, did I really understand what it meant. It was the final throw of the dice. Would we be able to land?

'Hard to say. Them waves is risin' high....'

I looked toward the island and saw the water pitching, silent and ominous, up the blank rock. I had come this far, but now I could think only of being capsized – dashed against the rocks or maimed under the boat's keel. I had already talked to a dozen men who had traveled thousands of miles only to be turned back at this point.

I sat in the back of the dory, carried forward by the momentum of a determination long sustained. In a moment, the boat was rising and falling against the rock face on six-foot waves.

'Get up front,' Arthur Sturge said.

He eased the boat toward the rock. Willie hunched in the bows. At the peak of a wave, he jumped, grabbed at the rock face, and clung. I could see that the rock was gouged with handholds into which my fingers must fit as I jumped.

'Arl roight!' Arthur shouted.

Willie now had his back to the rocks; he was facing me so that he might try to seize me if I fell. The boat rose and wobbled at its peak; I jumped, hit the rocks, and felt my fingers slip into the grooves. As I clung there, I realized the grooves were man-made. Of course. Other men had met the same problem. Of course they had done something about it. These grooves into which my fingers fitted so neatly might have been cut in Drake's time, or before, when the

Beothuk Indians came to plunder the island; or had they been cut by Eskimos, a thousand years before Christ?

Muscles knotted, and I strained upward. The problems of landing on Funk Island have remained unchanged. Rockets to the moon and the splitting of the atom mean nothing when it comes to landing on Funk Island. The equation for success is constant: an open boat with a skillful oarsman and a man willing to jump.

Willie had disappeared over the top of the rock while I was still absorbed in finding hand- and foot-holds in rock slippery with algae and bird excrement. I mounted the crest of the rock and Funk Island spread out, an explosion of sight, sound, and smell. I saw, but I did not see; I saw dark masses of murres in the distance; I saw curtains of buzzing kittiwakes interposing themselves like thousands of pretty white butterflies; I saw rolling hummocks of bare rock. But it was the sound that came to me first. We walked forward over intransigent, bare granite, and the sound swelled like thunder. A literate biologist has described it as 'a rushing of waters,' but that description does not satisfy poet or artist. It is orchestral, if a million players can be imagined: rich, sensuous, hypnotic.

When we came to the edge of the first great concourse of birds, perhaps two hundred thousand of them staining the rock densely black and white, the orchestral analogy became even more vivid because I could hear, among those thousands of voices, rippling spasms of pathos and melancholy – Brahmsian. The adult birds cried ehr-ehr-ehr, crescendo, diminuendo, gushes of emotion. The cries of the flying birds – and there were thousands in the air – swelled and faded in haunting harmony as they passed low overhead. Buried in this amalgam of voices were the piping screams of the young murres, sounds so piercing they hurt the ear.

We moved around the periphery of the murres. With every step, I was conscious of new expansions in the scope of sound. A sibilant undertone to the massive main theme was faintly discernible, the sound of innumerable wings beating: flacka-flacka-flacka-flacka. Wings struck each other – clack, clack, clack – as birds, flying in thick layers, collided in mid-air. Then another buried sound, a sub-melody, a counterpoint: gaggla-gaggla-gaggla. The gannets were hidden somewhere among the murre hordes. Other sounds were reduced to minutiae in the uproar: the thin cries of herring gulls, the rasping moans of kittiwakes hovering high overhead.

I had been on the island an hour and only now was I really registering the sound of it.

Next, overwhelmingly, came real vision. The murres were massed so thickly they obscured the ground. The birds stood shoulder to shoulder, eyeball to eyeball. In places, they were so densely packed that if one bird stretched or flapped her wings, she sent a sympathetic spasm rippling away from her on all sides.

All life was in constant, riotous motion. Murre heads wavered and darted; wings beat; birds landed clumsily among the upraised heads of their comrades; birds took off and thrashed passageways through the birds ahead of them, knocking them down. Chicks ran from adult to adult; eggs rolled across bare rock, displaced by kicking feet.

The murres heeded me, yet they did not. I approached them and a rising roar of protest sounded, a concentration of the general uproar, which seemed not directed at me at all but at the outrage of intrusion. I walked away from them and the roar died instantly.

The sun was well up, a brilliant star in an azure sky, and I walked to the quiet shore, away from the main masses of murres. Willie had disappeared into a gully. Perhaps I needed time to assimilate. But there was no time. The multiple dimensions of the sight came pouring in. The air streamed with birds coming at me. I threw up my hands, shouted at them, but the shout was lost, ineffectual, not causing a single bird to swerve or otherwise acknowledge me.

At least a hundred thousand birds were aloft at once. They circled the island endlessly, like fighter bombers making strafing runs on a target, flying the full length of the island, then turning out to sea and sweeping back offshore to begin another run. They came on relentlessly and the sky danced with them.

This was not, I realized, the hostile reaction of individual birds who saw their nests threatened. Instead, the murres were a tribe of animals resisting a threat to their island. Individually, they intimidated nothing. Collectively, they emanated power and strength. I looked into a thousand cold eyes and felt chill, impersonal hostility in the air.

I climbed to the top of a ridge and looked down the length of the island, looked into the masses of birds hurtling toward me, looked down to the grounded hordes, a living, writhing backbone of murres, murres, murres. Then, after the visual shock came the olfactory impact.

The smell of Funk Island is the smell of death. It is probably the source of the island's name, which in various languages means 'to steam,' 'to create a great stench,' 'to smoke'; it may also mean 'fear.' The island certainly smells ghastly. No battlefield could ever concentrate such a coalition of dead and dying.

A change of wind brought the smell to us, choking, sickening. As I walked down a slope and out of the force of the wind, the air clotted with the smell. In a hollow at the bottom of the slope, it had collected in such concentration that I gagged and my throat constricted. The fishermen *knew* the smell was poisonous. Uncle Jacob Sturge had told me how one fisherman who tried to run through the concentration of birds was nearly gassed unconscious.

The smell of Funk Island comes from a combination of corruption. There are no scavengers, except bacteria, so dead bodies lie where they have fallen. The debris of a million creatures has nowhere to go. Eggs by the scores of thousands lie everywhere, so that I could not see which were being brooded, which were rotten. In one small gully, unwanted or untended eggs had been kicked together in a one hundred foot driftline by the constantly moving feet of the birds.

The smell of the island came in diminishing waves as the sea breeze died and the heat rose from the rocks. A ripple of explosions fled away among a nearby concentration of birds. I listened; the sound was manlike. It reminded me of a popgun I had used when I was a boy. From a nearby hill packed with murres, another flurry of explosions, then single shots haphazardly firing all around me. If the smell of the island needed an exemplifying sound, this was it. The explosions were the sound of rotten eggs bursting in the growing heat.

I walked, while the smell gathered in my nostrils and took on various identities. It was the thin, sour smell of bird excrement: acidic, astringent, more than a hundred tons of it splashed on the island every day. Underlying that smell was the stench of the rotting fish which lay everywhere after being vomited up by the parent murres but not eaten by the nestlings. The smell was of putrescence, of oil, of fish, and of an indescribable other thing: the stench of a million creatures packed together in a small place.

I walked halfway down the length of the island, a distance of perhaps five hundred feet, but my progress was slow because of the difficulty I had in assimilating everything I saw.

In my mind were scraps of history. I was thinking, for instance, of how Newfoundland's ancient Indians, the Beothuks, camped in a gulch when they were on bird- and egg-hunting expeditions; of how, until recently, the gulch was an archaeological repository of old knives, spoons, belaying pins, and broken pots, testifying to more than two hundred years of exploitation of the island by hunters of meat, oil, eggs, and feathers.

Willie appeared on a far ridge. He was standing at the edge of Indian Gulch. I walked toward him along the rim of a concourse of murres. A feeble spring flowed into the gulch and created a small pond, which was also fed by the sea during heavy swells. Sea water belched up into it through a narrow crack in the rock. Into this pond poured a ceaseless flow of excrement, coughed-up fish, bodies, rotten eggs, and live nestlings. By mid-summer, the water was mucid, pea-green, fermenting, almost bubbling with corruption.

The murres were not distressed by this putrid mess; as Willie walked along the top of the gulch, hundreds of them dropped down to the water and floated. Suddenly, the pond was roiled into green foam as a group of birds took off. Their departure triggered another flight, which because murres fly poorly, was a failure. The birds crashed on top of each other or piled into heaps along the steep banks. This drew a sympathetic flight from murres perched precariously on the cliffs and a cloud of birds took off. Their departure sent eggs and nestlings spilling off the cliffs into the water.

But on Funk Island, nothing matters. Death is nothing. Life is nothing. Chaos is order. Order is a mystery. Time is meaningless. The deep-throated roar of the colony cries out to a heedless sky. The human observer, cowed by its primitive energy, by its suggestion of the unnameable, stumbles on blindly.

As I walked, I examined my growing sense of reality and sought a guidepost to what it all meant. I had thought (an hour before? two hours? it was nearer to four hours) that a sweep of Brahmsian rhetoric could describe the island. Already, the image was obsolete. Now, I felt a mechanistic sense, Prokofievian, an imperative monotone, the sound of Mars. The struggling, homuncular forms piled together in such utter, inhuman chaos denied any ordered view of the universe.

I had to wonder whether a poet had preceded me to the island; or did the island have a counterpart elsewhere? De la Mare's disgust at the massacre?

And silence fell: the rushing sun
  Stood still in paths of heat,
Gazing in waves of horror on
  The dead about my feet.

It was nearly noon, and sun flames reached for the island and scorched it. I was enervated, but I was also recovering normal sensibility, which brought me *details* of the life of the murre colony. Everywhere I looked now, young murres looked back. In places, they were packed thirty and forty together among the adults. There is only one word to describe them and it is not in any dictionary. They are murrelings: tiny, rotund, dusky balls of fluff with the most piercing voices ever given a young bird. Their piping screams must be essential for them to assert themselves above the roar of the adults. How else could they identify themselves to their parents? Yet, bafflement grew as I watched them. One murreling in that featureless mass of birds was infinitely smaller than one needle in a stack of hay. How contact is kept with the parent birds remains a mystery of biology.

Warmed by the scope of destruction in the colony, I was not surprised to find that the murrelings were expendable. Life moves to and from the colony at high speed. A murreling fell from a rock, bounced into an evil puddle, and was trampled by a throng of adults. Hearing screams from a rock I disengaged a murreling jammed in a crevice, looked down, saw a mass of fluffy bodies wedged deeper in the crevice. Murrelings fell from cliffs into the sea, rose and floated in foam, screaming. Murrelings lay dead among pustular eggs; they lay in heaps and windrows in olivaceous puddles.

I knew from murre literature that the murrelings often became shocked by prolonged rain and died by the thousands. That, in the context of this island, was not surprising. An *individual* death was shocking. Willie had walked back up the other side of the island and we met at the edge of a group of murres. Willie groaned.

'I don't feel well,' he said, rolling his eyes in mock nausea.

As he spoke, I looked over his shoulder in horror. In the middle of the murre mass, standing on slightly higher ground, was a group of gannets. These birds, though inferior in number, occupied the best territory. Though dominant, they seemed to have an amicable relationship with the murres. In places, murres and gannets were mixed together; murrelings gathered around gannets as though they were murres.

A gannet on a nest had reached down casually for one of these nearby murrelings, and as I watched, up-ended it and swallowed the struggling youngster. It was not the sight of such casual destruction that was shocking it was the sound of the murreling dying.

It screamed when it was seized by the gannet's beak, which was bigger than the murreling's entire body. It screamed as it was hoisted into the air. Horrifyingly, it screamed loudest as it was being swallowed. The gannet, though a big, powerful bird, had to swallow hard to get the murreling down. Its neck writhed and its beak gaped and all the time the awful screams of the murreling came up out of the gannet's throat. The cries became fainter and fainter.

'Horrible,' Willie said. 'Oi never gets used to it.'

The roar of the birds became a lamentation, a collusion of agony and sorrow. The flying creatures seemed to be in streaming retreat. Why *that* murreling and not any of the others still around at the feet of the gannet? If gannets really relished murre flesh, surely they would quickly wipe out all the murrelings near them. But they do not.

It was now afternoon and the sun plashed white and pitiless light on rock. For some time, I had been aware of a growing disorientation. I took a picture to the east, seventy thousand birds; to the west, one hundred thousand; in the air, twenty thousand. The noise, the smell, the screams, the corpses, the green puddles, pushed bonily into my chest. I fumbled with film but could not decide how to reload the camera or, indeed, remember what setting to use, or how to release the shutter.

'Oi t'ink oi'll go and sit behind dat rock,' Willie said. 'Oi goes funny in de head after a while here.'

Uncle Jacob had mentioned that the island could drive a man mad. I was being sickened by the pressure of it. Once, in Australia, I watched men systematically kill several hundred thousand rabbits they had penned against a fence. The steady thocking of cudgels hammering rabbit skulls continued hour after hour, eventually dulling the eye and diminishing the hearing. On Funk Island, my observing sense was losing its ability to see and to record.

I sought release in reverie and walked, half-conscious of what I was doing, toward an incongruous green field that lay alone in the middle of the island. Its bareness suggested another place of personal memory, and an association of ideas. My ancestors were Scottish and fought the English at Culloden. When I went to Culloden, two hundred years after the battle, I was overwhelmed by those long, sinister mounds of mass burial of the clans.

This Funk Island field was also a midden of slain creatures. It was a great natural-history site, as significant to an ornithologist as Ashurbanipal's palace would be to an archaeologist. Here, generations of flightless great auks had flocked to breed after eight months of oceanic wandering. Their occupancy built up soil. Here, also, they were slain throughout the eighteenth century until they became extinct, probably early in the nineteenth.

A puffin bolted out of the ground ahead and flipped a bone from her burrow entrance as she left. I knelt and clawed a handful of bones out of the burrow. I saw other burrows, bones spilling out of them as though they were entrances to a disorderly catacomb.

This was not fantasy. These were great-auk bones, still oozing out of the earth nearly a hundred and fifty years after the last bird had gone. The bones permeated the ground under my feet; puffins dug among them and kicked them aside to find graveyard sanctuary. Life in the midst of death.

All at once, walking across bare rock, the murres well distant, I felt a release. Willie was not in sight; the longliner was off fishing somewhere. The granite underfoot changed texture, became a desert I had walked, then a heath, a moor I had tramped, and eventually, all the bare and empty places of earth I had ever known. I felt the presence of friends and heard their voices. But something was wrong. Some were still friends but others had closed, deceitful faces. Inhibition and self-deception fell away; flushes of hate and love passed as the faces moved back and forth. Forgotten incidents came to mind. What was happening?

Uncle Jacob's voice: 'A man could go mad on the Funks.'

This was enough. I turned toward the shore, to the *Doris and Lydia,* which had appeared from nowhere. Willie leaped eagerly from his place of refuge behind a rock. The roar of the murres receded. I imagined the island empty during much of the long year, naked as a statue against the silent hiss of mist coming out of the Labrador Current, or the thunder of an Atlantic gale piling thirty-foot waves up the sides of the island.

'She be a sight to see in the winter,' Uncle Benny had said.

The seasons of millennia switched back and forth. The island suffocated in the original gases of earth: argon, radon, krypton, xenon, neon. The island disappeared in yellow fog, and water slid down its sides. The island was a corpse, dead a million years, its surface liquefied, with rot running into its granite intestines. The island festered, and rivulets of pus coursed down its sides. The island was death. The island was life.

Only in retrospect could the island become real. Later, I was to return to the island and actually live on it in order to turn my disbelief into lasting memory. Willie moved parallel to me, jumping from rock to rock and displacing a fluttering canopy of kittiwakes. He was a different man now as he met me at the landing site, beaming and lighthearted.

'So dat's de Funks, eh?' he said, and he was proud that I had seen it.

In the boat below us, Arthur and Cyril smiled. Arthur was relaxed now, in contrast to his silent, absorbed intensity when he was trying to get me to the island, and on it. Both men, and Willie, poised at the top of the cliff, were caught for a moment by the camera, like toreros who have survived a bloody afternoon and will hear the bugles again tomorrow.

With a final look over my shoulder at the silently fleeing birds, I slid down the cliff to the boat and Funk Island became a part of the history of my life.

TOMORROW WILL BE SUNDAY (1966)*

Harold Horwood was born in St John's and attended Prince of Wales College. He was an associate of J.R. Smallwood in the campaign to unite Newfoundland with Canada. In 1949 he became the first member ever to sit in the House of Assembly for Labrador. He did not contest the 1951 election and afterwards worked for the St John's *Evening Telegram,* for which he wrote a current affairs column 'Political Notebook.' A keen student of natural history, he has written extensively in the *Evening Telegram* and elsewhere on environmental problems. From 1946 to 1948 he published *Protocol,* a literary review, with his brother Charles. In 1967 he published *The*

* Harold Horwood *Tomorrow will be Sunday* (Garden City, NY: Doubleday & Co 1966). Reprinted by permission of the author and Doubleday & Company, Inc.

Foxes of Beachy Cove, a work which reflected his love of nature, and in 1969 *Newfoundland,* a descriptive work in a series on the Canadian provinces. His second novel *The White Eskimo* appeared in 1972.

The extract below is the final chapter of Horwood's first novel, *Tomorrow will be Sunday.* It describes the thoughts and actions of Eli Pallisher, the central character of the book, on the eve of his departure from Caplin Bight, his outport home.

IT WAS THE low tide of August in the dark of the moon – spring low, when the sea sank far down from its accustomed bourn into the caves and hollows of the shore, and a terrible pre-dawn stillness hung over Caplin Bight as Eli made his way along the rocks of the Point to the tiny inlet known as Mooring Cove, a more cleft in the cliff, a gunshot from the sunkers, lashed by the surf of the ocean sea.

But now there was no surf, only the soundless breath of the Atlantic, swelling from afar, rhythmically, a slow pulse beat, so silent that he could hear the gushing of the mill brook a quarter of a mile away, and the creaking of the great wheel that turned day and night throughout the summer – a sound that would haunt his sleep forevermore – mingled with the sputtering of small boat engines muffled in fog and the dry groaning of manila rigging as the mighty ghosts of his childhood ships sailed and rustled behind the world.

Tonight, for yet a small space, he belonged to his village. With the coming of day he would board the coastal boat and sail out through the sunkers to a world he had so far glimpsed only in passing.

The small sounds of the night came out around him – the faint scratching of crabs on the sea-smoothed stones, numberless crabs pursuing their small designs all around him in the darkness, hunting and killing and eating in the dense forest of the rockweed that hung, damp and lifeless, above the black water, then moving on to hunt and eat anew – the all-but-silent breaching of the surface-feeding fish, making small swirls in the inklike sea, gulping down thousands of the new-hatched larvae that floated outward from the rocks on the slack water at the tail of the ebb tide.

Eli found a comfortable perch on the slick basalt and sat there for a long time, meditating upon the eternity that stretched backward through his years in Caplin Bight toward the infinitely far-off miracle of his birth, and the vague promise of the road that stretched before him, through other times and places, toward some other eternity, equally remote.

He could feel, rather than hear, the ceaseless rustle of the small shore life around him – countless snails creeping over the damp stone, grazing on the green scum of algae, like tiny sheep on a pasture – rock spiders that scurried about, trapping the minute sand fleas in the crevices – rough-shelled whelks advancing remorselessly, armed with diabolical weapons that could pierce the hardest shell, seeking what they might devour.

And the sea, rising and falling in a rhythm long established before the first living creature crawled out upon its shore, ordering and directing it all, mother and teacher of life upon the planet – the sea: he could feel it now, subtly, in his blood – the stir, the change, the renewal: without sight of its waters, without sound of its surge, he knew that the tide had turned.

And then, so gradually that its beginnings could not be seen, out of the northeast came the pre-dawn twilight. Diffused at first, without direction, it picked out the contours of the rocks, revealed the shape of the tiny island that lay in the middle of the inlet, and disclosed the rocking motion of silent waters, far down below the tidal pools, where the laminaria kelps – the oldest living things on earth – lay limp along the sea.

The broad band of the rock-clinging barnacles and limpets now stood out whitely around the shore – a fathom-wide chalk mark, stretching away forever between the line of the tides, uniting Caplin Bight to the lands of the north and the south, curving around headland and cove along the thousands of miles of shore line of this mighty ocean-bound island. The lower pools in the hollows of the great flat rocks were full of sponges in a vast variety of fanciful shapes, but all without color in this pre-dawn light, as though color had been drained out of the earth by the long ordeal of the night. In those pools, too, the false corrals grew, like tiny rock gardens with fanciful plants among the pale blossoms of the sea anemones.

So gently at first that it could not be noticed, the tide began to flow. The bed of huge brown mussels, which was exposed on the seaward side of the island, now had trickles of water surging through its lower channels, filling for a moment, then emptying again into the sea. And as the surge rose up, advancing and retreating, the mussels opened one by one, spreading their wide valves to the life-giving water, awaiting the larvae and the small sea insects and the granules of photo-plankton that would be brought to them by the rising of the tide.

The northeast sky now had a glowing arc, shading through green and pearl to crimson, with its outer edges lost in the darkness between the stars. And Eli sat, watching the world renew itself from the vast resources of the universe, the rhythm of the tides tying the moon in its orbit to the lowliest limpet upon the rock, the anchored forests of kelp and the tiny floating algae drinking once again their brimming cup of light from the unimaginable depths of space.

The tide was flowing now with urgency, pressing up into the rock pools, entering the caves where the crabs had retreated before the burgeoning dawn, sounding there, with a hollow rhythm, its sad, nostalgic moaning, like the voice of a shell held, empty, to the ear of a listening child.

Far off, behind him, there was a faint cough or two, strangled and tentative – then the subdued chug-chug-chugging of a one-cylinder engine, as the first trap boat circled among the mooring collars of the harbor and slipped between the sunkers into the open bay. The boat put the first gulls, sleeping upon the water or upon the offshore rocks, to flight, and spoke apologetically to the otherwise silent world, never asserting its dominance, but seeking permission, hesitantly, to intrude upon the privacy of nature. Three generations of fishermen had made its voice as much a part of the sea as the mewing of the gulls above it.

One of the big birds came now, banking around the headland on swishing wings – a greater black-backed gull, called by the fishermen a saddle-back – as large as a goose, planing confidently into this small, deserted cove, which was its own special preserve, where it came each dawn with the first light of day to kill and eat the crabs that were tardy in seeking shelter from the apocalypse of the morning.

Catching sight of Eli sitting motionless upon the rocks, the big bird braked in mid-air, hovered for a second, flapping, hoping that it might not have seen aright, then wheeled above him, screaming imprecations, and, catching the light updraft of air from the face of the cliff, rose effortlessly and swept down in a long, graceful arc above the open sea.

The coming of the gull roused Eli out of his meditation. The world and the sea were now washed in blue-green light, and the tide was in full flood, surging up the ranked bastions of the rocks. Within spitting distance, it almost seemed, the trap boats were passing, the fishermen huddled over their tillers, seemingly oblivious to his presence. Soon, he knew, the light would turn to red, and then to gold, and the day would be upon him.

He rose and stretched his muscles, cramped from long sitting in the cool night. He slipped lithely out of his clothes, then stepped down between the rocks into the sea, that rose, chilling, past his groin, and received him, as he slid underneath its limpid surface, with a sort of final cold caress – a baptism of ice. He sank in a long, gliding curve, which imitated the flight of the gull, searching the bottom where monstrous shapes of blue and green and soft brown rose toward him – a vague world where exact form had vanished, and masses and colors were grouped like the patterns of an abstract painting.

His long glide brought him to the rocks on the far side of the inlet, and he clambered out, dripping, the sharp roughness of the tiny barnacles giving perfect purchase for his hands and feet, and he sat, shivering a little, with the sweet taste of the sea in his mouth and the keen smell of the kelp beds rising all around him.

Then he dived from the rock, making a long, straight arrow of his body, and cleft the water cleanly, and swam to the edge of the little island, where he lay face down in the shallows, letting the faint breathing of the water pulse up and down along his sides and trickle across the hollow of his back. He could feel the bands and bulbs of the laminaria slithering under his naked body, and he rolled in them gently, sampling their taste and finding them good – and while the light brightened he lay with the laminaria, man and alga, the alpha and omega of creation.

Then he swam back to the shore and rose from the sea, primordial and renewed. The sky was now blazing with light, and the full flood of the tide had swept up over the land until it had buried most of the zone of life that nestles between the marks of the spring tides along the shore. So rapidly was the water rising that it had reached almost to the place where Eli had dropped his clothes on the coarse black stone.

He picked them up, making a bundle, and climbed over the smooth rocks, through the opalescent light of dawn. And as he climbed, the sun climbed with him, until it stood upon the horizon, blazing like an open hearth, its level rays striking him. So he stretched tall upon the cliff top, washed clean, empty of all feeling except this feeling of cleanness, dipped in the night of the ocean and washed in the blood of the sun.

He faced the sea for a moment and looked down at his cold body, like marble stained red by the raw day. Then, whole and content, he began to cross the dew-wet stones toward the white pillars of the sleeping house that rose above him like an eagle perched upon a crag against the sky.

UNCLE MOSE BEGINS HIS CHRONICLES (1966)*

Edward Russell was born at Coley's point, Conception Bay, in 1904 and attended Bishop Feild College and Memorial University College. He taught school from 1920 to 1935 and was afterwards a magistrate and a director of co-operatives. From 1949 to 1951 he was minister of natural resources in the Newfoundland government. He subsequently returned to the teaching profession, first at the high school and later at the university level. He has published extensively in both newspapers and magazines. His play 'The Holdin' Ground,' first heard on the Canadian Broadcasting Corporation in 1955, quickly established itself as a Newfoundland favourite, and was published in 1972. The 'Chronicles of Uncle Mose,' which he produced over many years for radio, drew heavily on his rich experience of Newfoundland outport life. He published memoirs in the St John's *Evening Telegram* in October and November 1966.

I SUPPOSE BEFORE I begin telling you about the people who live in Pigeon Inlet, I ought to tell you something about the place itself. Well, there's not much to tell. Even though you've never seen it, you must have seen dozens of places just like it. We're all fishermen here and apart from our gardens and Levi Bartle's saw-mill, there's nothing except fish and sometimes not too much of that. We've got as good a harbour as you'd care to see, deep water, good holding ground – and if anybody ever wants to build a fish plant, we've got

* Edward Russell 'The Chronicles of Uncle Mose' *New Newfoundland Quarterly* (November 1966). Reprinted by permission of the author

the perfect place for it – right up the harbour at the mouth of Bartle's Brook.

We're right in the middle of a stretch of coast about forty or fifty miles long – with five or six smaller places spread out along the shore on each side of us. The people from these places might possibly move in to Pigeon Inlet if ever we get one of those fish plants we hear so much about these days. True, there's not much room along the water-front for many more new families, but some fellows were here a few years ago from the Department of Agriculture (fine fellows they were too) and they did what they called a soil survey.

They said there's hundreds of acres of good soil about a mile in on the back. It'd need lime and fertilizer but if we had a road to it and people were so minded they could live in there and walk out every day to catch fish – or to work in the fish plant – if we had a fish plant.

I'm going to say a lot about fish plants later on so I'll change the subject now except to say just one thing.

I told you there were five or six small places stretched out along the shore on both sides of us. I forgot to add that one of these places is a goodish-sized place almost as big as Pigeon Inlet. The name of that place is Hartley's Harbour. It's about six miles from here and the Hartley's Harbour people think there's no place like theirs. I bet, that if ever a fish plant comes to this shore, *they'll* want it in Hartley's Harbour. They think they're the capital of the shore. They've already got the District Nurse stationed there, which they should never have had only through skullduggery. Remind me to tell you the story sometime. Anyway, they're going to be unreasonable enough to want the fish plant, but you watch out. They won't get it. We will. That is – if one comes.

Now to get back to the people of Pigeon Inlet and I'm going to start off by telling you about the Executive of our Fishermen's Local. We were one of the first places to start a Local after the big meeting in St John's some years ago. We figured, like I suppose most fishermen did, that a Local couldn't do any harm and it might do a lot of good. Only a few joined to start with, but there are more and more coming in all the time. I'll tell you the reason why another time – but I first must tell you about our Executive.

Skipper Joe Irwin is our president and Bill Prior is vice-president. I'm the secretary and Sam Bartle is treasurer. Grampa Walcott is our honorary president. We had to give Grampa some kind of a title or he'd break his heart. I'll tell you about him first.

Grampa Walcott is the oldest man in Pigeon Inlet. He's 82 years young. Anyhow he's smart as a cricket and wants to be into everything. He's only a handful and you'd think the wind'd blow him away, but no matter how stormy the night, he can get to a lodge meeting or a Local meeting as well as any of us. He went fishing when he was seven or eight years old and hasn't had a summer ashore since – that's 75 summers fishin'.

Of course he doesn't do much fishing now. Just handlining in shoal water. But he always supervises the drawing of our salmon net berths every spring in April. We always give him Number One berth – that's the one right at the mouth of the Inlet – the one easiest to get to – and he always fires the gun at 12 o'clock every May the tenth when the rest of us claim our berths. He's quite a character.

He couldn't read or write until ten years ago when the adult education teacher was here. We always used to say he expected to live to 90, but since he learned to read he says he's going to reach the 100 mark. He says he's got more to live for now.

It was Grampa who gave us a real smart idea the very first time we had our Local Executive meeting. He said to the other four of us: 'Boys,' he said, 'Executive members ought to do something special for the Local. Let's form a sort of club – the five of us. A sort of study club, or discussion club, or listening group. Whatever happens between Local meetings, things like radio speeches about the fishery, or statements by the Government, or Board of Trade meetings – or the doings of NAFEL [Newfoundland Associated Fish Exporters Ltd] – or things like that, we ought to get together and talk them over among ourselves. Then at the next Local meeting we'd be able to explain it to the others – so that we'd all have a good idea about what's going on.'

We thought Grampa's idea was a good one and the five of us here have been meeting together off and on ever since and we're going to keep it up – because there's going to be a lot of things worth studying and discussing in the next few months and years. We believe it would be a good idea for every local to do the same thing. Anyhow, it has done us a lot of good. We believe that Pigeon Inlet Local is as wide awake as any in the Island – and our delegate, whoever he happens to be – will always be able to give a good account of himself.

Now I'm going to tell you about the other four of us on the Executive – Bill Prior, Sam Bartle and Skipper Joe Irwin.

There's not much to tell about Sam Bartle. He's in his thirties – the youngest of the five of us. He's able to turn his hand to almost anything and could give up the fishery tomorrow if he wanted to. But he doesn't want to – unless he's got to. In fact he worked in St John's winter before last and could have got a steady all year round job – but he turned it down and came back to Pigeon Inlet to continue fishin' in the spring. The way Sam explained it was that he couldn't get a place for his family to live. He could get two or three rooms in a flat up over a laundry or a restaurant or some such place, but he wants room enough for his young growing children to kick around in – and he couldn't find that in St John's for love nor money. So he came back to his fine big house and his fishing. Besides, fishing is in his blood and he doesn't intend to give it up unless he's going to be starved out of it. What he wants someone to tell him – someone, government or business or federation or someone – is 'Is he going to be starved out of it?' If he is, the quicker they tell him, the better.

Bill Prior is about the same, only a few years older, and a bit more tied down to the fishery. Bill is the ablest man on the shore. There's a cross-beam overhead in Levi Bartle's fish store where you're allowed to write your name in lead pencil, provided you've got a 56-pound weight hooked onto your finger while you're doing it. There are only three names on that beam and Bill's name is the highest of the lot.

As for me, Mose Mitchell, I'm not really a Pigeon Inletter at all. I'm from the Sou' West Coast. Went Bank fishin' when I was sixteen and got a belly-full after thirty-four years of it – 20 years out of Grand Bank and 14 out of Lunenburg. I had neither chick nor child. So I hauled up my killick and came to St John's. Couldn't stand the dust and smoke and noise and used to get heart sick whenever I looked out the Narrows. Then one day I met this fellow Joe Irwin. He was short-handed, carrying a load of freight North to Pigeon Inlet, so I shipped with him and came here and I've been here ever since. Not married yet, but there's still time. Only in the prime of life yet. Guess I'll end my days here – especially if we get that fish plant.

Now let me tell you about our President, Skipper Joe Irwin, the man who brought me here three and a half years ago. Joe is about my age – fifty – well, never mind the odd figures – the prime of life – like I said. He's as good a man as ever water wet.

His schooner is the only one in the place. She's lying up all the year except when he takes a load of dry fish or lumber to St John's each fall and brings back a load of supplies. He used to go Labrador fishing in her till he had to give it up. It got so that the more fish he'd catch, the more money he'd lose. Like he said in our Executive meeting one night: 'Boys,' he said, 'I was like a mouse trying to chew his way through a twelve inch partition. The harder I'd gnaw, the further I'd go in the hole.' Another time when he was taking out his last load of Labrador fish and a round tripper from the Kyle asked him what made it so thin and squat-looking, Skipper Joe nearly lost his temper. He said: 'Ma'am, if you'd been in the hold of my schooner for the past two months with twelve hundred quintals of fish on top of you, you'd be thin and squat lookin', too.'

Anyway, he's finished with the Labrador fishery and he's settled down to shore fishin' like the rest of us.

Now that you know a bit about me, Skipper Joe, Grampa Walcott, Sam Bartle and Bill Prior, you'll be able to get a better idea of the things we talk over in our executive meetings – our study groups. You'll know why we read all the papers and listen to all the radio news – hungry for anything about the fishery. It doesn't matter as much about me. I'm single and between ourselves I've got a few dollars. It doesn't matter much about Grampa Walcott. He only fishes for the good of his health and if he never saw another cod's tail, he and Grandma would be all right with their old age pension. But what about Sam Bartle and Bill Prior with their families? What about all the others like them in Pigeon Inlet? What about Skipper Joe Irwin, with a fine seventy-ton schooner and no use to put her to? Oh, I tell you we're interested in it all – trying to understand all we can about long lining, Danish seining, fish plants, drying plants, fishermen's insurance and all the rest of it. Above all, we're interested in the one big question: 'What's wrong with a place like Pigeon Inlet if people can't make a decent living here?' We've got a few ideas on that question already and I'll tell you about some of them in the next issue.

BEOTHUCK INDIAN SKELETON IN GLASS CASE (1968)*

Alfred Purdy was born in 1918 near Wooler, Ontario, and attended Albert College, Belleville. He is the author of several volumes of poetry: *The Enchanged Echo* (1944), *Pressed on Sand* (1955), *Emu, Remember!* (1957), *The Crafte So Longe to Lerne* (1959), *Poems for All the Annettes* (1962, 1968), *The Blur in Between* (1963), *The Cariboo Horses* (1965), for which he received the Governor General's Award, *North of Summer* (1967), *Love in a Burning Building* (1970), *Selected Poems* (1972), and *Sex and Death* (1973).

BEOTHUCK INDIAN SKELETON IN GLASS CASE

(St John's Museum, Nfld)
Six feet three inches
a man of 40
and not made for crawling on
his belly surely
the sight of this walking sunset
must have amazed white pygmies
from fog-bound fishing villages
of Joe Batt's Arm and Famish Gut
before they tracked him down

He's the same height I am
which makes me speculate
he'd have the same bother
with low doorways and car seats
and keep bumping his head on things
never stand face to face with a girl and have to lie down with her
to be properly friends
But that's as far as it goes
my death is some way off yet
and enemies blend with the landscape
I gawk at the gawking tourists
over this last symbol

* A.W. Purdy, *Wild Grape Wine* (Toronto: McClelland & Stewart Ltd 1968). Reprinted by permission of McClelland & Stewart Ltd, The Canadian Publishers, Toronto

of his extinct nation
consider the great auks and plants
of the remote carboniferous
and man-apes hitch-hiking towards a camera
I ought to feel sadness here
but can't
only a slight amazement
at the gawking tourists
that these specimens survived
and the man in the glass case didn't

WHAT DO THE YOUNG PEOPLE DREAM OF?*

Eugène Cloutier was born in 1921 in Sherbrooke and was educated at Laval and the Sorbonne. He has written two dialogue novels, *Les témoins* (1953) and *Les inutiles* (1956). In 1962 he published a play 'Le dernier beatnik' in *Ecrits du Canada français* XIV. The book from which the following extract is taken is an abridgement and translation (by Joyce Marshall) of a manuscript from which *Le Canada sans passeport* (1967) was also taken. Cloutier published *Journées japonaises* in 1969 and *En Tunisie* in 1970.

WHAT DO THE young people dream of? I went from one little fishing port to another [on the Avalon Peninsula]. Of course I do not intend to describe each one in turn, though I am very much tempted to do so, for the surroundings change before your eyes and the cove you are about to discover is entirely different from the one you have just left. The villages are also different, and the populations – sometimes Scottish, sometimes Irish, sometimes English – are never the same. I shall simply evoke a few memories that seem to me to cast some light upon one of the most engaging and most romantic provinces in Canada.

On the way to Pouch Cove I picked up a young man who was walking in the rain. His truck had broken down a few miles back and

* Eugène Cloutier *No Passport: A Discovery of Canada* (Toronto: Oxford University Press 1968). Reprinted by permission of Oxford University Press, Canadian Branch

I don't know how far he had travelled on foot in search of a gas station – and without success. While I busied myself with his problem, he talked to me freely about the existence of the young people of Newfoundland. He was about twenty-five. He had served two years in the army, in various parts of Canada, chiefly in British Columbia. Why? By choice, because he had wanted to travel a little. For a time he had fancied making it his career. And then his father needed him to help in his general store. He came back, found his old friends, including a girl who had now grown up and wisely waited for him to specify certain plans for the future. When I asked him if he believed he would remain in Newfoundland all his life, he said 'Yes' with a sigh and after a dreamy silence.

It is true that his truck had broken down. When he continued on his way shortly afterwards he was able to smile again and of his own accord showed me a photograph of his fiancée. One does not really believe in a marriage in those parts until after the young couple have left the church on their wedding morning. Many young men spend two or three seasons fishing and set out for elsewhere with their nest egg. More and more of them do it. For this reason the government is endeavouring by every means possible to create new jobs each year. As for the successors to the old fishermen, it is no doubt possible, and even probable, that they will be found, but I don't believe in it. Television and films, which are present wherever electricity goes, have put the young men in touch with a universe that is fascinating and so much easier. Their dreams are quite similar to those of all the adolescents of the world: in short, big cars, money, life.

A lad of fifteen explained all this to me beside a black rock, where his father and two brothers were struggling to raise the baskets of cod to the vertical with the help of an arrangement of cables.

He concluded with a smile that took on an indescribably pathetic quality here, at just this moment, 'I'm studying. I'm not ever going to do that work. I'm going to go away.'

ICELAND POPPIES (1968)*

Paul O'Neill was born in St John's in 1928. He lived during his boyhood in Bay de Verde, Conception Bay, and St John's, and attended St Bonaventure's College. He studied theatre in England and attended Georgetown University, Washington, DC, where he met the American poet Daniel Berrigan. He has travelled widely and is by profession a broadcaster. His poetry, which had for long had considerable local acclaim, was collected into *Spindrift and Morning Light* in 1968.

ICELAND POPPIES

Love of the love of
my long dead love
you do not know me
yet from this wistful loneliness
that is surrendered time
I cry about my love for you
when to my kitchen door you bring
the August splendor of
Iceland poppies planted in the spring.

I am another one who roamed
in meadows of warm earth,
a gentle wind, a mist of rain,
and plucked from summer roots
those stems of sculptured blooms
you now place in the
antique vases of my aging rooms
which I arranged with
bursts of that same petaled art
to brighten up a grief of shadows
in the heart.

Blood image of my line
you are anxiety of needs come right

* Paul O'Neill, *Spindrift and Morning Light* (St John's: Valhala Press 1968). Reprinted by permission of the author

because in long and long ago,
with blindness of an ancestor, I feared
you might not cherish
in some hollow of your youth
the lustre, pewter, rose glass
and old willow plates of blue
which in this burning out of sparks
our name passed down to you.

But what was fear
has disappeared in knowing you are one
who sees the muted glory of a flower
in the afternoon and
brings its splash of wonder
from the plunder of lamenting winds
to droop in loveliness
where I spread blossoms
years from yesterday,
I will not worry that the heritage
might come to harm
when you walk in with
clusters of the Iceland poppy
on each arm.

SELECTED SECONDARY MATERIAL ON ASPECTS OF NEWFOUNDLAND LITERATURE

Atlantic Guardian II 9 (September 1946) [note on Ron Pollett]

Axford, P. 'Ballads of Newfoundland Give Clues to Its Life' *Saturday Night* LXIV (1949)

- 'Saga of Newfoundland' *Canadian Forum* XXVII (1947)

Baxter, James Phinnex *A Memoir of Jacques Cartier* (New York: Dodd, Mead 1906)

Beattie, Munro 'E.J. Pratt' in *Literary History of Canada* ed. Carl F. Klinck (Toronto: University of Toronto Press 1965)

Birney, Earle 'E.J. Pratt and his Critics' in *Masks of Poetry* ed. A.J.M. Smith (Toronto: McClelland & Stewart Ltd 1962)

Black, W.A. 'The Labrador Floater Codfishery' *Annals of the Association of American Geographers* L (1960)

Brown, E.K. *On Canadian Poetry* (Toronto: The Ryerson Press 1943)

Buitenhuis, Peter 'Introduction' to his edition of Pratt's *Selected Poems* (Toronto: Macmillan 1968)

C., J.A. 'The Passing of the Founder' *The Newfoundland Quarterly* (December 1944) [a tribute to John J. Evans, founder of *The Newfoundland Quarterly*]

Casey, George 'Traditions and Neighbourhoods: The Folklife of a Newfoundland Fishing Outport' (unpublished MA thesis, Memorial University 1971)

Casey, G.J., N.V. Rosenberg, & W.W. Wareham 'Repertoire Categorization and Performer-Audience Relationships: Some Newfoundland Folksong Examples' *Journal of the Society for Ethnomusicology* XVI (September 1972)

Cogswell, Fred 'E.J. Pratt's Literary Reputation' *Canadian Literature* (Winter 1964)

- 'Way of the Sea, a Symbolic Epic' *Dalhousie Review* XXXV (1956)

Coish, Alec G. 'The Narrative Poetry of E.J. Pratt' *The Newfoundland Teacher's Association Journal* (December 1963)

Daniel J. Carroll,' *The Newfoundland Quarterly* (December 1907)

Davey, Frank 'E.J. Pratt: Apostle of Corporate Man' *Canadian Literature* (Winter 1970)

Desbarats, Peter 'Introduction' to *What They Used to Tell About: Indian Legends from Labrador* (Toronto: McClelland & Stewart Ltd 1969)

Devereux, E.J. 'Early Printing in Newfoundland' *Dalhousie Review* XLIII (1963)

- 'The Beothuck Indians in Newfoundland in Fact and Fiction' *Dalhousie Review* L (1970-1)

Devine, P.K. *Devine's Folk Lore of Newfoundland* (St John's 1937)

Doyle, Gerald S. 'Let's Sing Our Folk Songs in Our Schools' *The Newfoundland Teacher's Association Journal* (January 1956)

Dudek, Louis 'Poet of the Machine Age' *Tamarack Review* (1958) [on Pratt's poetry]

Duley, Margaret 'Glimpses into Local Literature' *Atlantic Guardian* (July 1956)

Dunbabin, Thomas 'The First Newfoundland Novel' *Dalhousie Review* XL (1960-1) [an article on Lowell's *New Priest in Conception Bay*]

England, G.A. 'Newfoundland Dialect Items' *Dialect Notes* V (1925)

Fay, C.R. 'New light on George Cartwright' *Dalhousie Review* XXXIV (1954-5)

Frye, Northrop 'Editor's Introduction' to Pratt's *Collected Poems* (Toronto: Macmillan 1958)

- 'Letters in Canada: Poetry' *University of Toronto Quarterly* XXII (1953)

- *Silence in the Sea* (St John's: Memorial University 1968) [an appreciation of Pratt's poetry]

- 'The Narrative Tradition in English-Canadian Poetry' in *Canadian Anthology* ed. Carl Klinck & Reginald Watters (Toronto: Gage 1966)

Frye, Northrop & Roy Daniells 'Ned Pratt: Two Recollections' *Canadian Literature* (Summer 1964)

Galloway, David 'Robert Hayman (1575-1629): Some Materials for the Life of a Colonial Governor and First "Canadian" Author' *William and Mary Quarterly* XXIV (1967)

Gibbs, Robert J. 'The Living Contour: The Whale Symbol in Melville and Pratt' *Canadian Literature* (Spring 1969)

Gosse, Philip *An Apple a Day* (London: Cassel & Co 1948)

Graustein, Jeanette E. 'Collegians in Labrador and Greenland, 1860' *Explorers Journal* XLVII (1970)

Greenleaf, E.B. 'Introduction' to *Ballads and Sea Songs of Newfoundland* (Cambridge, Mass.: Harvard University Press 1933)

- 'Newfoundland Words' *American Speech* VI (1931)

Grenfell, Wilfred T. 'An Appreciation' [of Norman Duncan] in Norman Duncan *Harbour Tales Down North* (New York: Fleming H. Revell Co 1918)

- *Labrador: The Country and the People* (New York: Macmillan 1909) [contains accounts of Cartwright, Wallace, and Hubbard]
Halpert, Herbert 'Folklore and Newfoundland' *Papers of the Bibliographical Society of Canada* VIII (1969)
Halpert, Herbert & G.M. Story *Christmas Mumming in Newfoundland* (Toronto: University of Toronto Press 1969)
Halpert, Herbert & Neil V. Rosenberg 'Folklore Work at Memorial University' *Canadian Forum* LIII (March 1974)
Hamilton, William B. 'Society and Schools in Newfoundland' in J. Donald Wilson, Robert M. Stamp, & Louis-Philippe Audet *Canadian Education: A History* (Scarborough, Ont.: Prentice-Hall 1970)
Harrington, Michael 'Lone Eagle of God' *Atlantic Guardian* (September 1950) [an appreciation of the poet L.G. Fitzgerald, author of *Lone Eagles of God* (1949)]
- 'My Twelve Years in the "Barrel" ' *Atlantic Guardian* (November-December 1956)
- 'Newfoundland Bookshelf' *Atlantic Guardian* (September 1951)
- 'The Trailblazer' *Atlantic Advocate* (September 1965) [an article on Cormack]
Hathaway, E.J. 'Who's Who in Canadian Literature: Norman Duncan' *Canadian Bookman* VIII (1926)
Hewson, John 'The Sagamore Memberton' *The Newfoundland Quarterly* (June 1970) [on J.P. Howley's interest in the Beothucks]
Horwood, Harold 'E.J. Pratt and William Blake: An Analysis' *Dalhousie Review* XXXIX (1959-60)
- 'Newfoundland Literature has Vigor, Character' *Saturday Night* LXIV (1949)
- 'Number Ten Reports' *Northern Review* IV (1950-1)
- 'Poetry in Newfoundland' *Northern Review* III (1950)
Hunter, A.C. 'A French Visitor of 100 Years Ago' *The Newfoundland Quarterly* (Fall 1968) [an article on Count Arthur Jean de Gobineau, a nineteenth-century traveller in Newfoundland]
Ingstad, Helge *Westward to Vinland* (Toronto: Macmillan 1969)
Innis, Mary Q. 'Philip Henry Gosse in Canada' *Dalhousie Review* XVIII (1937)
Johnson, Charles H. 'The Literature of Newfoundland' *The Newfoundland Quarterly* (April 1934)

Jones, Douglas G. *Butterfly on Rock: A Study of Themes and Images in Canadian Literature* (Toronto: University of Toronto Press 1970)

Karpeles, Maud 'Introduction' to *Folk Songs from Newfoundland* (Hamden, Conn.: Archon Books 1970)

Kerr, J. Lennox *Wilfred Grenfell: His Life and Work* (New York: Dodd, Mead 1959) [the most important biography to date]

King, C.A. 'The Mind of E.J. Pratt' *Canadian Forum* XXXVI (1956)

Kirwin, William 'Lines, Coves and Squares in Newfoundland Names' *American Speech* XL (1965)

Klinck, Carl F., ed. *Literary History of Canada* (Toronto: University of Toronto Press 1965; rev. 1970)

L., J.J. 'Sixty Years in the Printing Business' *The Newfoundland Quarterly* (April 1935) [a tribute to John J. Evans, founder of *The Newfoundland Quarterly*]

'Larboard Watch,' pseud. 'From the Crow's Nest' *The Newfoundland Quarterly* (Fall 1960; Winter 1960; Spring 1961; Summer 1961; Fall 1961; Winter 1961-2; Spring 1962; Summer 1962; Winter 1964) [articles on Jukes, James Cook, Bonnycastle, S.T. Davis, Hubbard, R.B. McCrea, Cartwright, Beckles Willson, Charles Pedley, J.G. Rogers, Whitbourne, and others]

Leach, MacEdward 'Introduction' to *Folk Ballads & Songs of the Lower Labrador Coast* (Ottawa: The National Museum of Canada, Bulletin No 201 1965)

Livesay, Dorothy 'The Polished Lens: Poetic techniques of Pratt and Klein' *Canadian Literature* (Summer 1965)

Logan, J.D. & D.G. French *Highways of Canadian Literature* (Toronto: McClelland & Stewart Ltd 1924) [brief note on Duncan]

MacDonald, Robert Gear 'Some Poets of Newfoundland and Their Work' *The Newfoundland Quarterly* (April & July 1938)

McGrath, M. Helen 'The Bard from Newfoundland: The Story of Dr E.J. Pratt' *Atlantic Advocate* (November 1958)

MacKay, L.A. 'The Poetry of E.J. Pratt' *Canadian Forum* XXIV (1944)

MacKinnon, M.H.M. 'Parnassus in Newfoundland' *Dalhousie Review* XXXII (1952-3) [an article on Hayman's *Quodlibets*]

– 'The Man and the Teacher' *Tamarack Review* (1958) [a comment on Pratt]

Morris, Don 'The Bait Skiff Tragedy of 1852' *The Daily News Magazine* (18 June 1970) [the historical background to Grace's 'Petty Harbour Bait Skiff']

Mott, L.F. 'Items From Newfoundland' *Dialect Notes* v *(1926)*

Murphy, James *The Old Sealing Days* (St John's: Newfoundland Archives 1971) [a reprint of a series of articles with pertinent biographical information, first published in 1916 in the St John's *Evening Herald* by one of the most prolific collectors of Newfoundland lore]

Murphy, Michael P. 'The Balladeers of Newfoundland' *Atlantic Guardian* (September-October 1956)

Neary, Peter ' "Wabana You're a Corker': Two Ballads with Some Notes Towards an Understanding of the Social History of Bell Island and Conception Bay,' paper read to Canadian Historical Association, annual meeting, Kingston (June 1973)

- *The Political Economy of Newfoundland 1929-1972* (Toronto: Copp Clark 1973)

- 'Peter Neary Interviews David French: Of Many-Coloured Glass' *Canadian Forum* LIII (March 1974)

- Review of Farley Mowat and David Blackwood, *Wake of the Great Sealers* in *Newfoundland Quarterly* LXX 3 (January 1974)

'Newfoundlandia' [editorial] *The Newfoundland Quarterly* (December 1957)

Niven, F. 'To Remember Norman Duncan' *Saturday Night* LVII (1942)

O'Flaherty, Patrick 'Introduction' to *The New Priest in Conception Bay* (Toronto: McClelland & Stewart Ltd 1974)

- 'Newfoundland Writing, 1949-74: A Comment' *Canadian Forum* LIII (March 1974)

O'Reilley, Rev. J. 'A National Literature and What It is Not' *The Newfoundland Quarterly* (March 1909)

Orkin, M.M. 'Newfoundland English' ch. 4 of *Speaking Canadian English* (Toronto: General Publishing Co 1970)

Pacey, Desmond, ed. *A Book of Canadian Short Stories* (Toronto: The Ryerson Press 1947) [brief comment on Duncan]

- *Creative Writing in Canada* (Toronto: The Ryerson Press 1952) [brief treatment of Duncan, extensive comment on Pratt]

- 'E.J. Pratt' in his *Ten Canadian Poets* (Toronto: The Ryerson Press 1958)

Patterson, Rev. George 'Notes on the Folklore and Dialect of the People of Newfoundland' *Journal of American Folklore* IX (1896)

- 'Notes on the Dialect of the People of Newfoundland' *Transactions of the Nova Scotian Institute of Natural Science* IX (1896)

Peacock, Kenneth 'Introduction' to vol. I of *Songs of the Newfoundland Outports* 3 vols (National Museum of Canada 1965)

- 'The Native Songs of Newfoundland' *National Museum of Canada Bulletin* No 190 (1960)

Pitt, David G., ed. *E.J. Pratt* (Toronto: The Ryerson Press 1969) [a selection of critical writings on Pratt]

- 'Introduction' to his selection of Pratt's poems, *Here the Tides Flow* (Toronto: Macmillan 1962)

Poole, C.F. 'For Love of Men's Souls: The Beginnings of Education in Newfoundland' *Dalhousie Review* L (1970-1)

Pratt, Mildred Claire *The Silent Ancestors: The Forebears of E.J. Pratt* (Toronto: McClelland & Stewart Ltd 1971)

Pritchard, Allan 'From These Uncouth Shores: Seventeenth-Century Literature of Newfoundland' *Canadian Literature* (Autumn 1962) [principally on Hayman's *Quodlibets*]

Prowse, D.W. 'Books on Newfoundland' *The Newfoundland Quarterly* (June 1904)

Rashley, R.E. *Poetry in Canada: The First Three Steps* (Toronto: The Ryerson Press 1958) [contains an appreciation of Pratt's poetry]

'Robert Gear MacDonald's Book of Poems' *The Newfoundland Quarterly* (March 1909) [a review of *From the Isle of Avalon* (1908)]

Rowe, Frederick W. *The Development of Education in Newfoundland* (Toronto: The Ryerson Press 1969)

Seary, E.R. *Place Names of the Avalon Peninsula of the Island of Newfoundland* (Toronto: University of Toronto Press 1971)

- 'Regional Humanism' *The Newfoundland Quarterly* (November 1966)

- 'The Anatomy of Newfoundland Place Names' *Names, Journal of the American Name Society* VI (1958)

Seary, E.R., G.M. Story, & W. Kirwin *The Avalon Peninsula of Newfoundland: An Ethno-Linguistic Study* (Ottawa: The National Museum of Canada, Bulletin No 219 1968)

Sharman, Vincent 'Illusion and an Atonement: E.J. Pratt and Christianity' *Canadian Literature* (Winter 1964)

Smallwood, J.R. *The Book of Newfoundland* vols I, II (St John's: Newfoundland Book Publishers, Ltd 1937); vols III, IV (St John's: Newfoundland Book Publishers 1967) [among items of interest are: T.D. Carew 'Journalism in Newfoundland' (vol. I); P.K. Devine 'Newfoundland Folk-Lore' (vol. I); Frederick R. Emerson 'Newfoundland Folk Music' (vol. I); T.H. O'Neill & R.A. Young 'Old-time theatricals in St John's' (vol. II); C.H. Johnson 'Songs and Sagas of Newfoundland' (vol. II); Helge Ingstad 'The Norse Discovery of Newfoundland' (vol. III); E.R. Seary 'The Place-Names of Newfoundland' (vol. III); J.R. Thoms 'Cormack's Great Walk Across Newfoundland' (vol. III); G.M. Story 'The Dialects of Newfoundland' (vol. III); Arthur R. Scammell 'Outport Memories' (vol. IV); Rae Perlin 'Art in Newfoundland' (vol.IV); Sylvia Wigh 'Recent Developments in the Theatre' (vol. IV); C.R. Granger, ed. 'Recent Newfoundland Poetry' (vol. IV)]

Smith, A.J.M. *Some Poems of E.J. Pratt: Aspects of Imagery and Theme* (St John's: Memorial University 1969)

- 'The Poet' *Tamarack Review* (1958) [on Pratt's poetry]

Smith, G.C.M. 'Edward Sharpham and Robert Hayman' *Notes and Queries* 10th series x (1908)

- 'Robert Hayman and the Plantation of Newfoundland' *English Historical Review* XXXIII (1918)

Sparkes, Stanley 'Newfoundlandia in the Classroom' *The Newfoundland Teacher's Association Journal* (November 1970)

Stevenson, Lionel *Appraisals of Canadian Literature* (Toronto: Macmillan 1926) [brief appreciation of Duncan]

Stevenson, O.J. 'The Boy Eternal' in his *A People's Best* (Toronto: Musson 1927) [a comment on Duncan]

Story, G.M. *A Newfoundland Dialect Dictionary: A Survey of the Problems* [pamp.] (Humanities Association of Canada 1956)

'Bacon and the Fisheries of Newfoundland: A Bibliographical Ghost' *The Newfoundland Quarterly* (November 1966)

- 'Dialect and the Standard Language' *The Newfoundland Teacher's Association Journal* (December 1957)

- 'Judge Prowse (1834-1914)' *The Newfoundland Quarterly* (Spring 1971)

- 'Newfoundland Dialect' in A.B. Perlin, ed. *The Story of Newfoundland* (St John's: privately printed 1959)
- 'Newfoundland Dialect: An Historical View' *The Canadian Geographical Journal* (April 1965)
- 'Newfoundland English Usage' in *Encyclopedia Canadiana* VII
- 'Notes from a Berry Patch' *Proceedings of the Royal Society of Canada* X (1972)
- 'Research in the Language and Place-Names of Newfoundland' *Journal of the Canadian Linguistic Association* III (1957)
- 'The Newfoundlander Who is Canada's Greatest Poet' *The Newfoundland Record* (September-October 1962)
- 'The St John's Balladeers' *The English Quarterly* IV (1971)

Story, G.M., W. Kirwin, & J.D.A. Widdowson 'Collecting for *The Dictionary of Newfoundland English*' *Annals of the New York Academy of Sciences* CLII (1972)

Sutherland, John *The Poetry of E.J. Pratt* (Toronto: The Ryerson Press 1956)

Szwed, John F. 'A Newfoundland Song-Maker and Community of Song' in *Folksongs and Their Makers*, intro. Ray B. Browne (Bowling Green, Ohio: Bowling Green University Press 1970) [an account of a contemporary Newfoundland folk-singer]

'The Late Archbishop Howley' *The Newfoundland Quarterly* (December 1914) [Archbishop Michael Francis Howley published a volume of poetry entitled *Poems and other Verses* (1903)]

Thomas, Aaron *The Newfoundland Journal of Aaron Thomas*, ed. J.M. Murray (Toronto: Longmans 1968)

Tomkinson, Grace 'Shakespeare in Newfoundland' *Dalhousie Review* XX (1940-1)

Townsend, Charles W., ed. *Captain Cartwright and His Labrador Journal* (London: Williams & Norgate 1911)

Wareham, Wilfred 'Social Change and Musical Tradition: The Role of Singing in the Life of a Newfoundland Traditional Singer' (unpublished and restricted MA thesis, Memorial University 1971)

Watt, Frank W. 'Edwin John Pratt' *University of Toronto Quarterly* XXIX (1959)

Wells, Henry W. & Carl F. Klinck *Edwin J. Pratt: The Man and His Poetry* (Toronto: The Ryerson Press 1956)

West, Paul 'E.J. Pratt's Four-Ton Gulliver' *Canadian Literature* (Winter 1964)

Wheeler, E.P. *List of Labrador Eskimo Place Names* (Ottawa: National Museum of Canada Bulletin, No 131 1953)

Whiteway, Louise 'The Athenaeum Movement: St John's Athenaeum (1861-1898)' *Dalhousie Review* L (1970-1)

Widdowson, J.D.A. 'The Dialect of Fortune Harbour' *Folia Linguistica* II (1972)

Wigh, Sylvia 'Theatre in Newfoundland' *Atlantic Advocate* XLVII (1958)

Williamson, R.A. *The Cabot Voyages and Bristol Discovery Under Henry* VII (Cambridge: University Press 1962)

Wilson, Milton *E.J. Pratt* (Toronto: McClelland & Stewart Ltd 1969)

– 'Pratt's Comedy' *Journal of Canadian Studies* III (1968)

The Social History of Canada

General Editor: MICHAEL BLISS

1 The Wretched of Canada: letters to R.B. Bennett 1930-1935
Edited and introduced by
L.M. GRAYSON AND MICHAEL BLISS

2 Canada and the Canadian Question
GOLDWIN SMITH
Introduction, Carl Berger

3 My Neighbor
J.S. WOODSWORTH
Introduction, Richard Allen

4 The Bunkhouse Man
E.W. BRADWIN
Introduction, Jean Burnet

5 In Times like These
NELLIE MCCLUNG
Introduction, Veronica Strong-Boag

6 The City below the Hill
H.B. AMES
Introduction, P.F.W. Rutherford

7 Strangers within Our Gates
J.S. WOODSWORTH
Introduction, Marilyn Barber

8 The Rapids
ALAN SULLIVAN
Introduction, Michael Bliss

9 Philosophy of Railroads and Other Essays
T.C. KEEFER
Introduction, H.V. Nelles

10 The Americanization of Canada 1907
SAMUEL E. MOFFETT
Introduction, Allan Smith

11 Rural Life in Canada: its trend and tasks
JOHN MACDOUGALL
Introduction, R. Craig Brown

12 The New Christianity
SALEM BLAND
Introduction, Richard Allen

13 Canada Investigates Industrialism: the Royal Commission on the Relations of Labor and Capital
Edited and introduced by
GREG KEALEY

14 Industry and Humanity
WILLIAM LYON MACKENZIE KING
Introduction, David Jay Bercuson

15 The Social Criticism of Stephen Leacock: the unsolved riddle of social justice and other essays
STEPHEN LEACOCK
Edited and introduced by Alan Bowker

16 A Dutch Homesteader on the Prairies: the letters of Willem De Gelder
WILLEM DE GELDER
Translated and introduced by H. Ganzevoort

17 The Tragedy of Quebec: the expulsion of its Protestant farmers
Robert Sellar
Introduction, Robert Hill

18 The Woman Suffrage Movement in Canada
CATHERINE L. CLEVERDON
Introduction, Ramsay Cook

19 The Queen v Louis Riel
Introduction, Desmond Morton

20 The Writing on the Wall
HILDA GLYNN-WARD
Introduction, Patricia E. Roy

21 By Great Waters: a Newfoundland and Labrador anthology
Edited and introduced by PETER NEARY and PATRICK O'FLAHERTY

University of Toronto Press

www.ingramcontent.com/pod-product-compliance
Lightning Source LLC
Chambersburg PA
CBHW020716130726
47899CB00012B/1901

* 9 7 8 0 8 0 2 0 6 2 3 3 8 *